CHINESE MULTINATIONALS

Foreword by Liu Chuanzhi

CHINESE MULTINATIONALS

Editor

Jean-Paul Larçon

HEC Paris

NEW JERSEY · LONDON · SINGAPORE · BEIJING · SHANGHAI · HONG KONG · TAIPEI · CHENNAI

Published by

World Scientific Publishing Co. Pte. Ltd.

5 Toh Tuck Link, Singapore 596224

USA office: 27 Warren Street, Suite 401-402, Hackensack, NJ 07601

UK office: 57 Shelton Street, Covent Garden, London WC2H 9HE

British Library Cataloguing-in-Publication Data
A catalogue record for this book is available from the British Library.

CHINESE MULTINATIONALS

ISBN-13 978-981-283-500-0
ISBN-10 981-283-500-8
ISBN-13 978-981-283-559-8 (pbk)
ISBN-10 981-283-559-8 (pbk)

Typeset by Stallion Press
Email: enquiries@stallionpress.com

Printed in Singapore.

 **TSINGHUA SCHOOL OF ECONOMICS AND MANAGEMENT**

As one of the first economics and management schools in China, Tsinghua SEM is among the premier schools in China and in Asia. The School was established in 1984. Professor Zhu Rongji, Founding Dean, later became the fifth Premier of the People's Republic of China.

Since 1984, Tsinghua SEM has thrived along with the reform, opening-up, and development of the Chinese economy. Today it continues to strive for building a world-class school of economics and management. The School benefits from the synergy of bringing two academic disciplines, economics and management, into one institution. Tsinghua SEM is committed to the excellence of both research and teaching for the purpose of advancing knowledge and educating future leaders.

HEC PARIS

Founded in 1881, HEC School of Management, Paris (HEC Paris) is among the top European schools of business. It has built its reputation through the highly selective French "Grande Ecole" system, attracting individuals with both high academic potential and entrepreneurial spirit.

Located in the heart of the Paris business community, the School has earned international reputation through a portfolio of advanced management programs such as the Master of Science, the MBA, and EMBAs. This is further solidified by HEC's strong international presence founded on its network of alliances with leading institutions and companies.

HEC's strategy is characterized by two major orientations: a strong emphasis on research and publication, and close links with the international business community.

FOREWORD

Liu Chuanzhi

President and CEO of Legend Holdings Ltd

Chinese Multinationals, which is the product of a cooperation between HEC Paris and the School of Economics and Management of Tsinghua University, discusses the internationalization strategies of Chinese enterprises. In my opinion, this book goes to press at an opportune time and therefore bears great significance. As I did in the chapters analyzing Lenovo's acquisition of IBM's PC business, I would like to share my thoughts and experience of this phenomenon.

I will begin by explaining the significance of this acquisition. The current business environment demands that Chinese enterprises go to the global market. A large number of Chinese companies will choose to "go global" for development. In the process of "going outward", they are bound to be confronted with various kinds of problems and difficulties that they have never experienced in China. This juncture calls for companies to take the lead and spearhead the movement beyond China's borders. If breakthroughs are achieved, these pioneering companies will serve as examples; subsequent Chinese companies will be able to avoid similar pitfalls and gain confidence in this endeavor.

This is what I see of prime significance in Lenovo's acquisition of IBM's PC unit. Acquisition and the subsequent integration of the two companies is a classic problem studied in textbooks of any business school. While Lenovo represents a company operating in a developing country, IBM is considered an iconic company featuring American-style capitalism. In this sense, Lenovo's merger with IBM's PC business can be viewed as a relatively weaker company's buy out of a stronger one, which is considered the most difficult type of acquisition. Lenovo's experience can therefore provide management academics, both at home and abroad, with a vivid case of overseas acquisition.

The risks associated with the acquisition are threefold. The first two risks are whether the brand of the new entity can be recognized by international customers, and whether key employees in the acquired company are willing to stay. These are typical issues generated when a relatively weaker company acquires a stronger company. However, the third risk, that of blending the different company cultures, is common in all cases of acquisition. It seems that up to now, the first two risks have been properly handled. But whether the acquisition will experience success depends on how well the new Lenovo can integrate the two cultures. While top-notch companies in China and America — especially when they are in the same industry — are quite close in terms of core values, differences in thinking and behavior between Chinese and American people are numerous. For example, I conscientiously grant some concessions during negotiations with my business partners because I always opt for long-term cooperation and benefits and at the same time want to express my sincerity and respect for the other party. But international companies, generally speaking, will not show any appreciation and may have the feeling that I don't know what I'm giving up. Another example of cultural difference is that while in the West employees tend to be very direct when talking about compensation with their bosses, their Chinese counterparts would be much more indirect and subtle in the hope that their effort and value will be recognized and they will be rewarded with better pay accordingly. However, should Chinese employees approach this more aggressively, their employers, not being used to such behaviour, will most probably not tolerate.

As a representative of Legend Holdings — the controlling shareholder of Lenovo Group Limited — I hope, first and foremost, that the whole value of this alliance will be greater than the sum of its parts. The new Lenovo is expected to improve in turnover rate and profit ratio and thus create higher return for the shareholders. This should be considered the basic requirement for an acquisition. Yet, this alone will not suffice. We aspire for further strategic pursuits in that we want to see Chinese people controlling or taking positions in the core management team. Of course, the most important results are higher profits and a greater return for shareholders. My strategic concern will be gradually accomplished during the post-M&A integration, because a sense of when to advance and retreat, or whether we should be flexible or rigid, is an art. While a lack of preparation spells failure, more haste may produce fewer results. The key lies in the capabilities of the Chinese managers and the attitude of their American colleagues.

PREFACE

Zhao Chunjun

Emeritus Dean of Tsinghua School of Economics and Management
Vice Chairman of China Academy of Management

Since launching reform and opening up the country, China has experienced sustained rapid economic development, and many Chinese enterprises have gradually begun to increase the pace of their internationalization. "Going overseas," so as to seize greater market share, more resources, and richer and advanced management experiences, has become a common undertaking of many Chinese enterprises. Thanks to China's access to the World Trade Organization (WTO) in 2001, the internationalization process of Chinese enterprises though still in its initial stage, has developed with great dynamism and diversity. This is yet another "long march" for the growth of Chinese entrepreneurs and China's economic development. There are both successful experiences as well as bitter lessons. *Chinese Multinationals*, a book jointly written by professors of HEC Paris, professors of the Tsinghua SEM, and other Chinese scholars, offers a snapshot of this process.

Economic globalization is an irreversible process. The year-on-year increase of the total global trade volume, foreign direct investments (FDI) international flows of financial capital, social, political, cultural, scientific and technological exchange and integration, all serve as the best proof of the growing trend of globalization.

China has only opened up to the rest of the world for less than 30 years. Undoubtedly, a Chinese company will find making a leap to a transnational enterprise arduous and formidable. There are far-reaching challenges to investing in an unfamiliar market and establishing a presence. At the strategic level, it has an impact on growth alternatives, international marketing, technological transfer and competition, intellectual property rights, potential strategic partnerships, access to the international capital market, M&A etc. At the same time, the impact of social, cultural and political factors on the corporate strategy and policies have to be dealt with actively by senior management. At the operational level, almost all traditional management functions and processes need to change in order to adapt to the requirements of internationalization especially. This is true organizational structural adjustments and cross-cultural management — topics of great novelty for many Chinese corporate leaders. Though we cannot say yet that China's multinational enterprises have already acquired a complete set of experiences or success models, the diverse cases of Chinese enterprises at different stages of internationalization presented in this book offer a rich appraisal to help the reader to acquire a better understanding of the current phase of internationalization of some major Chinese enterprises.

We acknowledge the pioneering work undertaken by the Chinese and French authors of this book. We also extend our gratitude to Professor J-P Larçon of HEC for his hardwork and endurance in conceptualizing, organizing, editing and publishing this book. His enthusiasm and persistence are laudable. I hope that scholars of both countries will continue this endeavor and further their collaboration significantly in researching into the internationalization of Chinese enterprises.

CONTENTS

ACKNOWLEDGMENT

This book is the fruit of a longstanding cooperation between HEC School of Management, Paris (HEC Paris) and Tsinghua SEM (Beijing). The two institutions have, in particular, developed joint research programs and faculty exchange in the area of business strategy.

There is abundant literature on the strategies of foreign multinationals in China, but much less information on the strategy of emerging Chinese multinationals. That is why the two schools have joined forces to systematically study the internationalization process of a series of leading mainland China companies operating in a variety of economic sectors.

The HEC Paris–Tsinghua SEM Research Project on Chinese Multinationals is an initiative of Professor Zhao Chunjun, Vice Chairman of the Academic Committee and Member of the University Council of Tsinghua University and former Dean of Tsinghua SEM Professor Chen Guoqing, Executive Associate Dean of Tsinghua SEM, and Professor Jean-Paul Larçon of HEC Paris.

The project has been supported by Professor Qian Yingyi, Dean of Tsinghua SEM and Professor Bernard Ramanantsoa, Dean of HEC Paris.

It has received the support of the Chamber of Commerce and Industry of Paris (CCIP), the Embassy of the People's Republic of China in the Republic of France, the French Embassy in China, and the National Natural Science Foundation of China (NSFC).

AXA CEO Henri de Castries gave a strong personal impulsion to the project through the "AXA Initiative", a framework established in 2006 to promote research cooperation between HEC Paris and Tsinghua SEM.

The project has mobilized 15 experts from Beijing and Paris-based research centers:

— HEC Paris Strategy Department,
— Tsinghua SEM Strategy and Marketing Departments,
— the Enterprise Research Institute, Development Research Center (DRC) of the State Council,
— the Institute of World Economics & Politics of the Chinese Academy of Social Sciences (CASS).

We would like especially to thank Mr. Chen Xiaohong, Director of the Enterprise Research Institute (ERI), Development Research Center (DRC) of the State Council and Mr. Yu Yongding, Director of the Institute of World Economics & Politics (IWEP) of the Chinese Academy of Social Sciences (CASS).

Field work was coordinated in China by Professor Wang Yihua (Tsinghua SEM) and in Europe by Mrs Geneviève Barré (HEC Paris).

The response to this research project from the corporate world has been exceptionally positive.

We would especially like to thank the CEOs of leading corporations who willingly shared their knowledge:

Bank of China, Baosteel Group, Beijing Jeep, Bird, BOE Technology Group, China National Offshore Oil Corporation, China National Petroleum Corporation, China WorldBest Group, Haier Group, Hisense Group, Holley Group, Huawei Technologies, Jincheng Group, Lenovo Group, China Non-ferrous Metal Industry's Foreign Engineering & Construction Co., Nuctech Company, Shanghai Electric, Shougang Group, TCL Corporation, Tsingtao Brewery Group, Wahaha Group, Wanxiang Group, Youngor.

Among personalities, corporate leaders, top executives and company representatives who have dedicated a lot of their time to the interview and data collection process, we would like to thank especially:

Phan Nhay, General Manager Paris Branch (Bank of China),
Wu Dongying, Director Strategy & Planning Dept. and Feng Aihua, Senior Manager, International Business Development Department (Baosteel),
Che Luxin, Manager, Strategy & Information and Xie Wei Manager (Beijing Jeep Corporation, Ltd),
Zhu Zhaojiang, General Manager, International Department; Shangguan Yanyun, General Manager Planning Dept, Liu Fangming; General Manager, Bird Sagem and Gérard Cautin, Deputy General Manager (Bird),
Zhou Xiwen, President, Haier University (Haier Corp.) and Patrick Bailly, Marketing Director, Europe (Haier Group),
Shiong Frank, Manager, Marketing Dept. (Hisense),
Song Yixin, VP; Li Lilian, VP Europe, Xu Linda, Huawai University VP; Wen Patrick, President France (Huawei Technologies),
Anne-Pierre Guignard, Marketing Director (Lenovo France),
Sun Xiaoming, General Manager International Marketing and Wang Chuanxin, Marketing Manager (Nuctech Cy Ltd),
Yuan Bing, Vice General Manager, TCL Multimedia, Deng Rui, Strategic Planning Dept Chen Weiyan, Senior Analyst (TCL Group),
Yang Huajiang, President, Assistant Marketing Dept (Tsingtao Brewery Co.),
Jiao Changyong, Assistant General Manager and Shan Qining, Foreign Liaison Office (Wahaha Group),

Shen Zhijun, Development Dept General Manager, and Wang Yang, HRM Manager (Wanxiang Group),
Jack Sun, General Manager (Youngor).

Special thanks to Dr Lu Guanqiu, founder and Chairman of Wanxiang Group, for the time and attention he dedicated to our work.

Jean-Paul Larçon
HEC Paris

ABOUT THE AUTHORS

Geneviève Barré

Geneviève Barré is specialized in China's industrial, research, and education policy. For 20 years she contributed to economic cooperation projects between Europe and China. She worked on China's Special Economic Zones at the Organisation for Economic Co-operation and Development (Oborne, Publications Development Centre, OECD, Paris,1986) and is a coauthor of reports on Foreign Investment in China and on China's Innovation Climate (OECD, Paris, 2000).

Chen Guoqing

Professor Chen Guoqing, the Executive Associate Dean of Tsinghua University's School of Economics and Management, is China's National Chang-Jiang Scholars Professor of Management Science and Engineering, and EMC^2 Chair Professor of Information Systems. He serves as associate/area editor and member of the editorial board for several international journals. His teaching and research interests include IT Management and e-Business, Business Intelligence and Management Decisions, Soft Computing and Data Modeling.

François Duhamel

François Duhamel is a professor of International Business at the Universidad de Las Américas in Puebla (Mexico), where he teaches courses on International Supply Chain Management, Business in Asia, and Strategic Management. His research focuses on global outsourcing and the strategic organization of multinationals from emerging countries. With Bertrand Quélin he co-published, "Bringing Together Strategic Outsourcing and Corporate Strategy: Outsourcing Motives and Risks", *European Management Journal*, 2003.

Pierre Dussauge

Pierre Dussauge is a professor of Strategic Management at HEC Paris. He was a visiting professor of Corporate Strategy at the Ross Business School of the University of Michigan in Ann Arbor from 1991 to 2003 and at other leading international institutions such as Insead, the ISB (Hyderabad), and Tsinghua SEM (Beijing). He is the author or coauthor of several books in the field of strategic management and strategic alliances such as *Cooperative Strategy*, J. Wiley & Sons, 1999.

Hu Zuohao

Hu Zuohao, Ph.D, Kyoto University, is an associate professor at the Department of Marketing of Tsinghua School of Economics and Management and the Executive Associate Director of China Business Research Center. His research interests are Marketing Strategy, International Marketing, Channel Management, Consumer Behaviour and Brand Strategy. He is the coauthor of *Marketing Innovation of Japanese's Household Electronic Appliance Companies*, Tsinghua University Press, 2002.

Jin Zhanming

Zhanming Jin is a professor at the Department of Business Strategy and Policy of Tsinghua School of Economics and Management. His research interests are the strategy of multinationals, M&A and alliances, the strategy of small high-tech companies in the IT industry, and the impact of e-business on the structure of competition. He published several books and articles such as *Strategic Management*, 2nd edition, Tsinghua University Press, 2004.

Kang Rongping

Kang Ronging is a senior research fellow at the Institute of World Economics & Politics (IWEP), Chinese Academy of Social Sciences (CASS). He specializes in multinational corporations. He is the chief editor of the yearbook of the World Chinese Entrepreneurs, a standing member of China International Economic Relationship Society, and an executive member of China PECC Business Forum. He is the author or coauthor of several books, including *The Growth of Chinese Transnational Corporations*, National Defense University Press, 2001.

Jean-Paul Larçon

Jean-Paul Larçon is a professor of International Strategy at HEC Paris. His research interests are emerging markets and international management. He was a visiting professor at CEIBS (Shanghai), ESADE (Spain), NHH (Norway), St Petersburg State University (Russia), and Warsaw University of Technology (Poland). He is the author or coauthor of several books and articles in the field of international strategy, entrepreneurship in economies in transition, and strategy in emerging markets.

Li Donghong

Li Donghong is an assistant professor of Strategy at the School of Economics and Management, Tsinghua University. He was a visiting scholar at HEC Paris. He teaches Strategic Management and Strategic Alliances. His special fields of research interest are Strategy and Organizational Change for Firm's Sustained Growth, Resource-based View, and Strategic Alliances involved in China's companies.

Li Zhaoxi

Li Zhaoxi is a senior research fellow and the deputy director of the Enterprise Research Institute (ERI) of the Development Research Center of the State Council (DRC). His work and publications are focused on enterprise growth and competition, state-owned enterprises reform, corporate governance, sino-foreign joint ventures, and SMEs. He is a coauthor of *Corporate Reforms and Adjustments in Korea and China under Structural Changes and Economic Dynamism*, Korea Development Institute, 2007.

Wang Gao

Wang Gao, PhD, Yale University, is an associate professor and deputy chair of the Marketing Department at Tsinghua SEM, as well as an associate director of China Retail Research Center of Tsinghua University. His research areas focus on marketing models and quantitative methods, consumer purchase behavior, brand equity, customer equity, customer value analysis, sales promotion, segmentation and positioning, and customer satisfaction.

Wang Yihua

Wang Yihua is a professor of Strategy at Tsinghua School of Economics and Management. She specializes in corporate strategy, organization, and cross-cultural management. She is the author or coauthor of many books and articles such as "Individual Perception, Bargaining Behavior, and Negotiation Outcomes", *International Journal of Cross Cultural Management*, 2002.

Research Associates

DING Huaming, HU Ling, LÜ Ping, SONG Zhicheng and, WANG Yiping

Other Contributions

The book has benefited from translation services of Eric Sautedé and copyediting by Sean Donovan and Karen Lemasson, HEC Paris.

ABOUT THE EDITOR

Professor Jean-Paul Larçon is HEC Paris' expert on multinationals of emerging markets. He directed the 2005–2008 research project on Chinese Multinationals developed by HEC Paris and Tsinghua University's School of Economics and Management. His experience in the strategy of large Chinese companies is based on years of contact with corporate leaders, joint international projects, field research, and top management executive education programs in China, as well as cooperation with government agencies and leading Chinese business schools.

INTRODUCTION AND ORGANIZATION OF THE BOOK

Prof. Chen Guoqing, Tsinghua School of Economics and Management
Prof. Jean-Paul Larçon, HEC Paris

The objective of this book is to document the different facets of the internationalization process of emerging Chinese multinationals during the 30-year period of rapid economic development and implementation of the reform and opening up policy.

It is a view from the inside, based on Chinese governmental and corporate sources of information and in-depth interviews and information from some 20 companies at different stages of their international development, with different ownership structures, and covering different economic sectors. Thus the substance of the information presented in the book comes from the field.

The list of companies most frequently quoted in the book is in Annex 1. The list of the major international investments of selected Chinese companies can be found in Annex 2.

Deng Xiaoping's new "open door" policy was announced in December 1978, opening the door for foreign companies to invest in China and bring technology, financing, and know-how in exchange for market entry. Coupled with economic and institutional reforms, this policy led to the blooming of China's economy and sustained economic growth at a very high level for 30 years.

China's average economic growth was 12.4 percent from 1991 to 2000, and 8.8 percent from 2001 to 2005, the period which constitutes China's 10th Five-Year Plan. China became the fourth largest world economic power and a leading export nation.

In 2001 China joined the World Trade Organisation, an extension of the reform and opening up policy, which challenged Chinese companies' competitiveness, and provided new opportunities for growth in international markets.

China's objective for the 11th Plan (2006–2010) is an economic growth of 7.5 percent, the increase of personal consumption, especially in the rural areas, and building a "harmonious socialist society". The policy of an open-door to international trade and direct investment is not only continued but also enhanced.

While opening the door to foreigners, China has started little by little to invest abroad in order to have access to natural resources, new markets, capital, technology, and knowledge. This move has been carefully controlled and at the same time encouraged by the Chinese government. China has adopted a "go global" strategy to boost investment overseas.

Thus, the two facets of China's "open door" policy complement each other. On the one hand foreigners are encouraged to invest in the country. On the other hand, Chinese companies are encouraged to grow internationally, develop exports, and practice all forms of outward foreign direct investment and cooperation.

This book is about the emergence of international champions among Chinese companies which have the ambition and the capacity to compete at the global level. These companies rapidly increase their activities, sales, assets, or number of employees abroad. Some of them are already mature multinationals with a high percentage of activities abroad in a variety of countries. Others are emerging multinationals in the early stages of development.

Many of these international champions are also national leaders. Through consolidation in the domestic market, China has developed a series of very large companies.

Twenty-two very large Chinese enterprises with strong international presence or high international potential are listed in the *Fortune* 500 Global List 2007:

— three oil and gas companies: Sinopec, China National Petroleum Company (CNPC) and China National Offshore Oil Co (CNOOC),
— a trading, oil and chemical group: Sinochem,
— a steel giant: Baosteel Group,
— two electricity companies: State Grid Corporation of China and China Southern Power Grid,
— two telecom companies: China Mobile Communications and China Telecommunications,
— the two largest car companies: China FAW Group and Shanghai Automotive,
— engineering and construction companies: China Railway Engineering, China Railway Construction, and China State Construction Engineering Corporation,
— the largest food importer, exporter and manufacturer: Cofco International Co.,
— a diversified group producing and trading metals, minerals and electrical products: China Minmetals,
— the second-largest group of shipping companies worldwide: China Ocean Shipping (Group) Company (COSCO).

— five financial institutions: Industrial & Commercial Bank of China (ICBC), China Life Insurance, Bank of China, China Construction Bank, Agricultural Bank of China.

All these very large companies are under state control at the holding level and have subsidiaries listed on Chinese or international stock exchanges. They are at different stages of their internationalization process.

The two largest companies are in the oil and gas business: Sinopec (revenues 2006 US$132 billion) and China National Petroleum (revenues 2006 US$111 billion), ranking respectively No. 17 and No. 24 among the world largest companies, and Nos. 7 and 8 respectively in the petroleum refining industry. They are very seeking very actively resources outside China.

Most banks and financial institutions are still at an initial stage of their internationalization process, having started major initiatives in 2006–2007.

ICBC's public offering in 2006, which was the world's largest ever initial public offering, was a landmark for the transformation of a state-owned commercial bank into a public company.

In 2007, the Chinese government created the China Investment Corporation (CIC), one of the largest state-controlled sovereign wealth funds, to handle US$200 billion of the country's forex reserves. Among the first investments made in 2007 was an investment of US$3 billion for a 9.9 percent interest in New York-based private equity firm Blackstone Group LP and a US$5 billion stake in investment bank Morgan Stanley.

In 2007, China Development Bank (CDB), one of the country's three policy lender involved in the financing of large domestic projects such as the Three Gorges Dam or Shanghai Pudong Airport, participated along with Temasek, the investment company of the government of Singapore, and Barclays in an attempt to buy ABN AMRO.

In the steel industry, which is still in a phase of consolidation within China, Shanghai Baosteel is entering into the internationalization process after restructuring its domestic activities. It is a latecomer but the consolidation of the industry at a global level in 2006–2007 with, for example, the Mittal-Arcelor deal, might oblige it to increase rapidly its international presence.

On the other hand, a number of Chinese companies already have a very strong international presence and a high degree of internationalization.

In 2004, a mainland state-owned enterprise, the China International Trust and Investment Company (CITIC), already ranked number 5 among the top 100 non-financial transnational corporations from developing countries, with foreign assets of US$14.5 billion representing 17 percent of its total assets.

China Ocean Shipping (Group) Company followed, ranking No. 8, with foreign assets of 60 percent (UNCTAD 2006).

The other mainland China companies in the top 100 were China State Construction Engineering Corporation, the two oil companies CNPC and CNOOC, Sinochem, TCL Corp. (electric and electronic equipment), China Minmetals, Cofco International, and BOE Technology Group (display technology).

China's Cofco International ranked 84 among the top 100 transnationals (TNCs) from developing countries, but number one among China's mainland companies in terms of degree of internationalization with a *transnationality index* — the average ratio of foreign assets, sales, and employment to total activity — of 86.6 percent.

The growth of many Chinese multinationals is characterized by multiple learning dimensions such as innovation, strategy, alliances, culture, and technology management. One important element in the internationalization process, which is worth mentioning but will not be discussed in further detail due to the limitation of our scope, is information technology (IT), which often served as an enabler for re-engineering business processes and seizing competitive advantages. In recent years we have witnessed a variety of cases including COSCO, Lenovo, Sinopec and many other companies discussed in the book where IT became more and more pervasive in their businesses, from strategic to operational levels, involving investment, marketing, knowledge transfer, and value chain re-structuring.

The book is organized in the following manner:

— Chapter 1 puts into perspective the three dimensions of corporate strategies of Chinese multinationals: integration strategies, diversification strategies, and globalization.
— Chapters 2 and 3 present the policy framework and orientations of China's outward Foreign Direct Investment
— Chapter 4 describes the internationalization process, first moves, and goals of Chinese corporations
— Chapters 5 to 8 look at the different facets of the international development of Chinese companies: corporate strategy, international marketing, technology strategy, innovation and knowledge transfer, corporate culture and organization.
— Chapter 9 focuses on the relationship between Chinese multinationals' moves and the reorganization of the value chain at a global level.
— Chapter 10 is devoted to the role of joint ventures and alliances in the management of Chinese multinationals.

The financial sector, which is still at the earliest stages of the internationalization process, is not presented in the book and more importance is given to non-governmental and private companies than to traditional SOEs, even if large state-controlled enterprises dominated China's international investment scene in the past.

Chapter 1

CORPORATE STRATEGIES OF CHINESE MULTINATIONALS

Jin Zhanming

Tsinghua School of Economics and Management

1. Strategic Management in Chinese Enterprises

China has always considered the quality of management at the company level as a key factor of China's competitiveness.

This was made very explicit in the Development Report of China's International Competitiveness in 2001: "The international competitiveness of a nation depends, to a large extent, on the competitiveness of its national enterprises at the microeconomic level. In other words, without competitive enterprises, national competitiveness would be built on quick-sand and any sound macroeconomic policy would be nothing more than engaging in idle theorizing" (Renmin University, 2001).

Management and especially corporate strategy are the key drivers of Chinese companies' and China's competitiveness.

With the rapid progress of globalization, local competition has become global and global competition has become local. The implication is that Chinese enterprises will be facing ever greater challenges, locally and globally. In such circumstances, Chinese enterprises have had to elaborate new strategies in line with the economic globalization trend.

Multinational Companies (MNCs) are seen as key actors of economic globalization, which is why MNCs are a key instrument of China's economic global ambitions.

Multinationals have played a key role in the twentieth century and their influence will grow further in the future as a major force of resource allocation

1

worldwide. Multinational enterprises have access to technology, physical assets and human capital, management, and markets. The opening-up of China has been accompanied by the internationalization of its domestic enterprises and the Chinese government is supporting this development and nurturing China's emerging multinationals.

This chapter describes these strategies based on HEC–Tsinghua SEM Research Project on Chinese Multinationals (2005–2008) and in-depth investigation and interviews with top management of leading mainland corporations.

1.1. *Strategy and the Chinese Economy*

The word "strategy" in China refers traditionally to the conduct of warfare. Business strategy is a relatively young discipline in the country which has been influenced by contributions of western scholars such as Chester Barnard's *Functions of the Executive* or Igor Ansoff's *Corporate Strategy*.

Corporate strategy provides overall direction, policies, and plans for the company as a whole to achieve long-term growth and stability in a changing environment. Strategic management traditionally includes three levels: corporate strategy, business strategies and functional strategies. This chapter deals mainly with the strategies of Chinese emerging MNCs at the corporate level.

Yang Rongping and Ke Yinbin (2004) have identified three stages of strategic development of Chinese enterprises linked to the transformation of their economic environment.

— *The 1980s.* In this period, the dominant economic system was the planned economy and the strategies of Chinese SOEs were generally specialized in production for a specific industry.
— *The 1990s.* In this period, China embarked on the transformation from a planned economy towards a market economy. Chinese enterprises made a major change in their corporate strategies: diversification became the leading strategy in the 1990s.
— *Since 2000.* The market economy has become the dominant economic system in China. The corporate strategies in China started to diverge: diversification remained the dominant pattern even if some companies started reducing their number or core businesses and if a few companies developed successful focused strategies.

1.2. *Corporate Strategy in Chinese Enterprises*

Chinese enterprises are in a complex and unique situation that influences their strategy in a very specific way. They have to adapt their strategy to a new environment and improve their capabilities before participating effectively in global economic integration.

However, strategic management of these enterprises is lagging behind other countries:

— there was no need for strategy in earlier times. Companies did not have the decision-making power during the previous regime of a planned economy. They could only implement the production and sales targets objectives defined by the state. They were managed as giant production lines.
— property rights remain ambiguous. Companies have more decision-making power, but in many cases corporate leaders are still nominated by the government. Another problem is that the careers of these leaders are not tied to the performance of the enterprises. Naturally, they tend to ignore changes in the business environment and long-term growth issues.
— strategy can be confused with planning. Some business leaders have a long-term view and commitment, but they can also be rather ambivalent towards corporate strategy. They still equate strategy to the rigid long-term plans elaborated by the state, even if the environment or the policies are changing. They have difficulty recognizing the need for flexible strategies and providing meaningful guidance for decision-making in an ever changing environment.
— strategy differs from day-to-day management. Chinese enterprises started to embrace a market economy not so long ago, and there is a temptation for business leaders to spend too much time in micromanagement and neglect strategic decision-making at the top.

The three growth avenues open to Chinese enterprises are closely interrelated and cannot be separated: integration, diversification, and globalization (Figure 1.1). When diversification and integration strategies cross the international boundary, they become part of the globalization strategy. Sometimes integration strategies

Figure 1.1: Corporate strategies: integration, diversification, and globalization.

and diversification strategies are combined. For the sake of analysis, however, the three strategies will be discussed separately here.

The authors have chosen the qualitative research approach to study the new strategies of Chinese enterprises. This is done to provide Chinese and international readers with a viewpoint that is both realistic and straightforward so that they can appreciate the specificity of strategies followed by Chinese enterprises. Of course, one or two examples of success or failure cannot represent the overall mode of strategy employed by Chinese enterprises.

Cases have been chosen based on two considerations. First, the authors focused on companies that accepted in-depth interviews and discussions on strategic issues. Second, a rather high number of non state-owned enterprises were chosen because they experienced less influence from the state. These private enterprises are investing more overseas in recent years and several of them have entered international markets. Some are structuring themselves as multinational enterprises, expanding their sales network and reorganizing their production capacity on a global basis. These companies represent a leading economic force in China and a new image of the country. Their strategies will of course have a decisive impact on the future development of enterprises in China.

2. Integration Strategies in Chinese Enterprises

The level of concentration is quite low in most sectors of Chinese industry. For instance, the total production of over 200 auto manufacturers is lower than that of General Electric. Even the production of the largest iron and steel company, Shanghai Baosteel Group, accounts for only 10 percent of the total production of iron and steel in China. This is far less competitive than other multinationals (Li Rong, 2004). Therefore it is imperative for Chinese enterprises to carry out integration strategies in order to create economies of scale, enlarge the scope of their activities, and achieve a better control of key elements of the value chain. This leads to strategies of both vertical and horizontal integration.

In recent years Chinese companies have favored M&A over organic growth in order to move and grow more rapidly, especially on the international scene.

2.1. *The Logic of Integration*

In the early 1980s, the prevailing trend was specialization, with several large scale enterprises having monopolies in such sectors as iron and steel, chemicals, telecommunications, railways, and aviation.

For example, the Report on the Development of China's Petroleum and Chemical Industry notes the following: "2003–2004 illustrates well a policy based on integration. The major move of reorganization of the industry in 1998 was to break the monopoly into two large enterprises: Sinopec (China Petroleum & Chemical Corporation) and CNPC (China National Petroleum Corporation), with different geographic responsibilities in China and which integrated upstream and downstream" (Lu Wei, 2004).

In 2004, the rise in oil price increased the production costs and reduced the profits of many refineries. Jilin petrochemical company — one of the nine petro-chemical units of CNPC — integrated further refining and chemical activities and became very profitable.

In that case the integration strategy was closely related to the past monopoly framework and tradition. However, with the increasing maturity of the domestic market, more and more enterprises and sectors have also followed integration strategies to achieve growth.

This will be illustrated by two cases: Shanghai Baosteel and Tsingtao Beer.

2.2. Cases of Integration: Shanghai Baosteel and Tsingtao Beer

Case 1: Horizontal and Vertical Integration of Shangai Baosteel

Baosteel's objective is "to transform itself in a highly competitive integrated company in order to be publicly listed on an international capital market" announced Xie Qihua, the Chairwoman of Shanghai Baosteel, in 2003 (Annex 2 A1).The strategy was defined as the consolidation of Baosteel's presence in the steel industry and moderate diversification in steel-related industries (Baosteel, 2003).

At the beginning of August 2004, is was rumored that Baosteel was planning an acquisition and was going to pay dividends of RMB3.5 per share or make a free share allotment. On August 12th Baosteel publicized its plan to transfer quality assets to its listed subsidiary Baoshan Iron & Steel Co. Ltd. in order to integrate further its production, purchasing, and sales activities.

In 1998, when the Baosteel Group Corporation was created as the government-controlled holding company for the new group, the assets of the group were limited to those of Baoshan Iron & Steel Co., Ltd. (Baosteel Co.). The strategy since 1998 had been to enlarge the scale and scope of activities in three major dimensions: building production capacity in the iron and steel business, vertical integration along the value chain, and acquisitions in related industries.

To build capacity, Baosteel made a series of acquisitions, including Yisteel's steel smelting and rolling line which is the biggest in China in terms of production capacity and has state-of-the-art technology. Baosteel also bought Wusteel's newly installed special steel production line, Ningbo Baoxin Stainless Steel Co.

(the world's biggest steel cold rolling line), and Shanghai Meishan Iron & Steel Co. (a production base for top grade construction sheet and electric steel).

Baosteel also integrated vertically. Downwardly, the company developed a sales and distribution network throughout China and in 10 foreign countries. Upwardly, Baosteel has 10 overseas subsidiaries controlling key mineral resources in Australia and Brazil. The development of the Majishan ore terminal in the port of Zhoushan was also a strategic investment made to secure a stable and economical source of iron ore.

Investments in steel-related industries mainly consisted of Baoxin Software which specializes in information technology and automation services, and Baosteel Chemical which specializes in coal chemistry using by-products from steel manufacturing.

Through these investments, Baosteel was completing its integration process and strengthening its competitiveness in its core iron and steel business. Following the same principle, it developed also strong partnerships up and down the value chain. Upwardly, the company cultivated partnerships with the suppliers of minerals, coal, and shipping services to insure the long-term stability of supplies and efficient logistics. Downwardly, Baosteel partnered with key industrial clients in the car and electronic appliance industry to develop its sales.

These long-term strategic partnerships with suppliers and clients helped Baosteel meet demand in 2003 despite the fact that the average growth rate exceeded 40 percent in the car-making, electrical appliances, mechanics, logistics, and telecommunications industries.

Thanks to the integration strategy and alliances along the value chain, Baosteel built strong foundations and could move toward new objectives, such as becoming a world-class company in the iron and steel industry and being listed internationally. Baosteel ranked 300 among global 500 firms in 2006 with revenues of US$22,700 million. [*Fortune* Global 500, 2007. The company's assets reached RMB147billion (at end of the 3rd quarter, 2006)].

Case 2: Horizontal Integration at Tsingtao Beer

Tsingtao Brewery Co., Ltd. was founded in 1993 and is listed on both Hong Kong and Shanghai Stock Exchanges. US company Anheuser-Busch first made an investment in Tsingtao Beer in 1993 and the two companies formed a strategic alliance in 2002 to share their expertise in management and technology. This enabled Tsingtao Beer to become China's leading brewer. The Qingdao State-owned Assets Supervision and Administration Commission of the State Council (Qingdao SASAC) is the largest shareholder in Tsingtao, holding a 30.6 percent share. Anheuser–Busch is the largest nongovernment shareholder with 27 percent.

As described by a senior manager of Tsingtao Brewery Group (Tsingtao Beer), the company' development is based on a very clear strategy focus: "We focus on

Table 1.1: Tsingtao Beer Operating Revenue and Assets (RMB millions).

	Operating revenue	Total assets
Year 1998	1,760.95	4,119.76
Year 1999	2,503.44	5,447.05
Year 2000	4,068.45	7,577.43

Source: Development report on China's major companies (2001–2002), Association of Chinese Businesses Appraisal, Chinese Personnel Press.

the beer business because we believe that concentrating our resources and capabilities in this industry is the only way to develop our competitive advantage at an international level."

Tsingtao Beer decided not to diversify but to grow in the beer business through a strategy of integration which was mainly achieved through a series of M&As. Between 1998 and 2000, the total assets of Tsingtao Beer increased by 83.9 percent, while the operating revenue increased by 131 percent (Table 1.1).

Tsingtao Beer M&A Strategy

As early as 1994 and 1995, Tsingtao Beer started its integration strategy by the acquisition of Yangzhou Brewery and Xi'an Hans Brewers. Unexpectedly, it was not an immediate success. The company lacked experience, management skills and technology, and the environment was not favorable. Tsingtao learned from these lessons and accelerated the pace of its acquisitions. Since 1997, Tsingtao Beer has acquired as many as 40 breweries, including Pingdu, Rizhao, Pingyuan, Heze, Xuecheng, Rongchen, Ma'anshan, Huangshi, Yingcheng, Penglai, Wuhu, and Shanghai breweries.

Tsingtao Beer now controls a broad portfolio of subsidiaries:

— Heilongjiang Kaiku and Beijing Five Star breweries in the North,
— Xi'an Hans and Weinan breweries in the West,
— Sino-Japanese joint venture Shenzhen Tsingtao Asahi Breweries Ltd. and Zhuhai Sanshui breweries in the South,
— Sichuan Luzhou and Huoju breweries in the Southwest,
— Shanghai, Yangzhou, Wuhu, Ma'anshan in Central China and
— Huangshi and Yingcheng breweries in Hubei province.

The production capacity reached 2.5 million tons annually and Tsingtao Beer was one of the top breweries in China.

By the end of the first half of 2004, sales had gone up rapidly and production exceeded 1.2 million tons, which was a 40 percent increase from the previous year. Profit tax increased by 82 percent, and 60 percent of its profits came from the 38 companies that had been acquired. The 40 companies acquired by Tsingtao Beer are profitable with the exception of three or four which are in a process of reorganization. In 2004 Tsingtao sold 3,71 million kiloliters, being the No. 1 brewer in terms of volume, production, market share, sale income, gross profit and foreign exchange in China.

This strategy of integration was closely associated with a broader policy developed by Tsingtao Beer and defined as Development from a Strategic High Point and Expansion at Low Cost.

Tsingtao Beer Strategy Framework

Focusing on beer as the core business   Although Tsingtao Beer was a latecomer to the market economy, it did not "follow the tide" by diversifying into related or unrelated sectors, at least in the short-term.

Instead, it kept its focus on beer brewing as its core business and built its competitive advantage by concentrating all of its financial, human, material, and technological resources in order to enlarge its market share and to become a leading force in the industry.

Expansion at low cost   There were internal and external reasons to develop a low cost expansion strategy. In the early 1990s, Tsingtao Beer's production lagged at 200 to 300 thousand tons. In 1996, Tsingtao Beer's market share shrank to a mere 2 percent. One could infer that Tsingtao Beer had a brand name, but not much production. The company had to fight in order to survive. At the same time, foreign brands were entering China's market scale *en masse*, transforming domestic competition into an international beer war. Many small and medium-scale breweries went bankrupt. As a result, a few large brewery groups emerged and became the key actors in China's beer industry.

At that time, companies that would not grow quickly enough would rapidly lose market share and become bankrupt. Keep pace with competitors, or, if possible, take the lead, was the only way to survive the fierce competition.

Tsingtao Beer evaluated each of its acquisition targets on a case-by-case basis in order to minimize the investment. The company used several methods to grow: acquisition of a bankrupt company, M&A, and creation of a joint-venture.

Based on Tsingtao's estimate, the investment made in more than 40 newly acquired companies, plus the cost of renovation and upgrading, was two-thirds less than what it would have cost to build these companies from scratch. For each target company, Tsingtao Beer had defined specific criteria and conducted a detailed analysis of the company situation, the feasibility of the acquisition and the company growth potential.

One criterion was that the company should have a specific advantage in terms of human resource, technology, and equipment. It should also have an acceptable debt ratio. Another requirement was that the company should be able to stop losing money and become profitable after capital and management expertise being supported by Tsingtao's. These criteria ensured the quality of the acquisitions and the smooth running of the entire group.

Financial integration and management control   After acquiring a company, Tsingtao Beer would make the necessary capital injections, nominate a chief financial officer, and create an effective financial and management control system. They would also appoint a manager in charge of operations to introduce Tsingtao Beer's up-to-date production technologies and modernize the existing management system based on Tsingtao beer expertise.

Brand policy and local cultures   Tsingtao Beer maintained a strict control over the use of the "Tsingtao Beer" brand name in order to avoid problems at the level of the newly acquired subsidiaries. The subsidiaries would continue to use their local brands, which had a strong reputation in the local markets. Simultaneously, Tsingtao Beer introduced its production technology and management system to these companies so as to enhance their product quality and management expertise. Once they were up to Tsingtao standards, they would be authorized the use of the trade mark of "Tsingtao Beer series" and the logos of Tsingtao Beer.

Such measures protected the value of Tsingtao Beer's brand name and created the opportunity to build well-known local brands. When the technological and management level was reached by the local subsidiaries, the parent company would introduce its major brand "Tsingtao Beer" to the local markets. As a result of this process, Tsingtao Beer successfully penetrated domestic markets and increased its market share.

Tsingtao Beer has been able to create synergies between its corporate identity and local cultures by building on the loyalty of local consumers. The group adapted its own management culture to local specificities while disseminating its management expertise and promoting harmonious interpersonal relationships. This led to extraordinary brand loyalty from local consumers and explains why demand exceeded supply a few months after Tsingtao Beer first launched its marketing strategy. The strategy was to keep the original brand name of the local beer while also promoting the Tsingtao Beer series. By respecting cultural differences, Tsingtao Beer managed to spread its corporate culture to its acquired subsidiaries and, at the same time, inherited and enhanced the existing local cultures, thereby achieving a successful cultural integration.

Post-acquisition Integration and Project Teams

To transfer its management culture and implement its management philosophy in newly acquired subsidiaries, Tsingtao Beer would send three project teams to the subsidiary. The first team was in charge of implementing Tsingtao Beer's management philosophy and spreading its management model of "one center, six systems, two supports". This team introduced up-to-date and effective management techniques such as competition among executives for management positions, optimization of work organization, tendering and bidding procedures for large procurements, marketing methods, and cost management.

The second team was in charge of the enhancement of production technology by introducing Tsingtao Beer's brewing technologies and processes.

The third team was in charge of quality. This team introduced a quality assurance system based on ISO9000, as well as strict standards of quality management. Three vice-directors were in charge of leading the three project teams and were responsible for the transfer of management expertise and performance enhancement.

Establishing Distribution Channels

Tsingtao Beer marketing policy is to sell directly to the consumer and to exert a strict control over the distribution network. This policy included door-to-door service for example, which means direct selling to final consumers. Another policy was "carpet bombing", which means not ignoring a single marketing outlet. Acquired subsidiaries had to follow this model in order to increase control over the final user. The distribution network of Tsingtao Beer was classified according to three levels of population density: urban area — where the subsidiaries are located, the periphery, and special markets. Market share rose to 90 percent in urban areas and to 80 percent in small and medium cities after several months of network building.

2.3. Lessons from Integration

Integration is the common trait between these two strategies. Baosteel implemented a horizontal and vertical integration strategy, and, through low cost acquisitions, expanded into an integrated group, aiming at being publicly listed on an international market.

Tsingtao Beer implemented its strategy of Development from a Strategic High Point and Expansion at Low Cost, focusing on core business and increasing its market share.

Baosteel and SOEs' Reform

The upward integration strategy is an interesting characteristic of Baosteel. The investments made by Baosteel to secure raw materials helped the company to grow in its domestic market and limit the growth of its foreign competitors. Penetrating foreign markets could be a second phase of development, after creating a powerful domestic basis.

The restructuring of Baosteel is also quite unique. As a large SOE, Baosteel, through the implementation of an internal integration strategy, was able to complete its capital restructuring and transform itself into an independent market-oriented enterprise. Its listed subsidiary, Baoshan Iron & Steel Co. Ltd. (Baosteel Co.), has been able to acquire the assets of its parent company, generating enough resources to implement the market reforms without external support. Thus, Baosteel has opened a new path for SOE structural reforms and is a good example of a successful integration strategy by a Chinese company. The company has not only protected independent operations but also avoided being acquired by foreign multinationals.

In the framework of Chinese SOE reform, China has seen a wave of creation of groups of enterprises, which is in fact a regrouping of Small or Medium-sized Enterprises (SMEs), bundled together by the local governments. This is done without creating a modern share holding system in the majority of cases. Local governments play a key role in many of these groups of enterprises and in some cases, following government policy, have transformed administrative units into groups of enterprises just by changing their name, which did not give them real unity from a management point of view.

Chinese enterprises wanting to do businesses internationally and compete with foreign multinationals, must establish an independent market-oriented legal status before transforming their management system and improving their competitiveness. From this point of view, the transformation procession of Baosteel and the creation of a real integrated company is an example to follow.

Tsingtao Beer and Branding Policy

By the end of 2000, the total market share of the four largest firms (concentration ratio CR4) in the beer brewing industry was below 20 percent nationwide, which is a typical low market concentration ratio. Tsingtao Beer seized this opportunity to increase its market share through a series of acquisitions. Beijing Yanjing Brewery, China's second largest brewery, followed the same strategy and contributed to the consolidation of the industry. In 2005, the top 10 Chinese breweries represented 61 percent of the national market, a 6 percent increase compared to the year before.

The type of horizontal integration strategy implemented by Tsingtao Beer was well adapted to China's industrial sectors with a low concentration ratio. Many industries such as candies and sweets, purified water, pharmaceutical retailing, and the iron and steel industry still do not have a high concentration ratio. This leaves ample opportunities for growth among companies that have sufficient capital and management expertise to build their strength in the domestic market before expanding internationally.

3. Diversification Strategies

3.1. *The Logic of Diversification*

Diversification strategies involve a process of redeployment of the company's resources, assets, capabilities and human resources. Success in diversifications strategies is mainly linked to the quality of this resource allocation process. Classical typologies of expansion strategies will help clarify the specificities of the Chinese companies' diversification process.

Horizontal diversification refers to developing new products and services in the same economic sector. Vertical integration refers to extending companies' operations upwards or downwards. Concentric or related diversification builds on the company core capabilities and can be further classified into sales-related, technology-related, and sales and technology-related (Ansoff, 1957).

Conglomerate diversification refers to enterprises developing new products and services in an unrelated sector (Table 1.2).

The specialization ratio (Wrigley, 1970) — the percentage of a firm's revenues attributable to its largest single business — is also interesting in the case of Chinese companies. This allows us to define four degrees of diversification (Table 1.3).

In the 1970s, a wave of diversification spread throughout the world. In the 1980s, Chinese enterprises also tried to adopt diversification strategies, looking for new growth opportunities. After the 1990s, there were numerous instances of failed diversification. But despite the failures, the strategy of diversification is still popular among enterprises in China. Meanwhile, more and more enterprises are beginning to realize that it is not good to blindly pursue diversification in order to expand.

Table 1.2: Expansion strategies.

Horizontal	
Vertical integration	Downwards–Upwards
Concentric (related)	Sales related
	Technology related
	Sales and technology related
Conglomerate	Unrelated diversification

Source: Kang Rongping and Ke Yinbin (1999); adapted from Ansoff.

Table 1.3: Specialization ratio.

Degrees of Diversification	Specialization ratio (SR)	Growth pattern
Homogenous products	$0.95 < SR < 1$	Expanding the scope of production in same activity
Dominant products	$0.7 < SR < 0.95$	Focusing on dominant product and conducting minor diversification projects
Related products	$SR < 0.7$	Entering new businesses related to core technology and capabilities
Unrelated products		Entering (usually through acquisition) in businesses not related to core technology and capabilities except finance

Source: Li Jing, 2002; adapted from Wrigley.

They are now inclined to diversify around their core business or capabilities in order to improve their management efficiency, technology, sales and clientele. They employ mature strategies with a greater emphasis on related products or services.

3.2. Cases of Successful Diversification: Haier and Hisense

Case 1: Haier Diversification Strategy

Haier's diversification strategy had two phases: related diversification and unrelated diversification. The former achieved great success, while the latter turned out, to some extent, to be a failure.

In the first phase of related diversification strategy, Haier penetrated into the market of penetrate household electrical appliances soon after it secured a dominant share of the Chinese refrigerator market. After the acquisition of Tsingtao Air Conditioner Factory, Haier launched such products as freezers, air conditioners and washers, one after another. In the air conditioners market, Haier soon over took Chunlan Group to become the market leader. In the washing machine business, Haier replaced Little Swan (Little Swan Group Company Ltd) as the consumer's first choice. It also became the market leader in the freezer market.

The success of Haier's core business of refrigerators, freezers, air conditioners, and washing machines drove the Haier Group forward and stabilized its position as one of China's leading brands. Haier has made a strong impact on the public with its campaign "Try your best and strive to be the number one". This corporate culture is regarded as one of Haier's most valuable assets and the soul of the company's reputation and brand identity. From this perspective, Haier's related diversification was a great success.

In the second phase of the unrelated diversification strategy, Haier entered the market of pharmaceuticals in 1995. The company then entered the food and beverage, television, PC, mobile phone, software, logistics and finance industries. That was, unfortunately, not a good decision. Evidence shows that Haier is still suffering from losses in its pharmacy business. Its pharmaceutical product, Caili, specially designed for the health and fitness market, could never meet Haier's standard of success. Most outlets of the noodle restaurant chain Haier Dasaozi ("elder sister-in-law"), founded in the 1990s, have now closed down. It suffered losses from sales of computers, eversince these were launched. In the mobile phone business with a very competitive market with actors like Bird, Kejian, Xiaxin, Panda, and TCL, Haier did not have a clear competitive advantage and had difficulties building its market share.

Though Haier claims to be the second General Electric, it is still facing great challenges in living up to that model. The move from the refrigerator business to other home appliances and to brown products was quite successful, but further diversification in markets which are less related is questionable.

Case 2: Hisense Diversification Strategy

Hisense is a large-scale Information Technology enterprise with a major shareholder, Hisense Group Corporation. Founded in 1969 as "Qingdao No. 2 Radio Factory" in 1979 the company became "Tsingtao Television Factory", and in 1993 it was named "Hisense Electric Co. Ltd." Hisense, which today is a well-known high-tech company, focused on its core businesses of radio and television in the 1970s and the 1980s. The company launched a wave of diversification in the 1990s when it diversified into new sectors such as household electrical appliances, telecommunications, and information.

Major activities included the production of televisions, air conditioners, computers, mobile phones, refrigerators, software, internet facilities, as well as real estate development (Table 1.4).

Since then, Hisense has developed rapidly with sales increasing from 410 million RMB in 1992 to 27.3 billion RMB in 2004 (Table 1.5).

In the mid-1980s, there were 57 color television manufacturers identified in China, as well as more than 100 local brands. At that time, the color television industry had a low level of market concentration but faced fierce competition and high risks. Large companies dominated the market and having a good reputation was not enough to survive. The only solution for Hisense was to expand its manufacturing volume in order to gain a competitive advantage.

Table 1.4:   Hisense diversification process.

Period	Types of products
1970s	Radios, black and white television sets
1980s	Radios, color television sets
1990s	Color television sets, video, cash registers, computers, air conditioners, information technology, telecommunications, real estate
2000s	TV (plasma, LCD, conventional), VHS, cash registers, computers, air conditioners -information technology, telecommunications, real estate -mobile phones, refrigerators, household electrical appliances

Source: Company data.

Table 1.5:   Hisense revenue (RMB billion).

1981	0.025
1992	0.41
1998	8.25
2000	13.98
2004	27.3

Source: Chinese enterprises appraisal association.

Hisense allocated financial resources and other assets to its diversification process according to two guiding principles:

— First, focusing on growth through product development and being a low cost leader,
— Second, leveraging the financial structure and available stocks to finance mergers, acquisitions and joint ventures.

The major diversification targets outside of the core business of household electrical appliances were the personal computer and telecommunications sectors. In 1996, Hisense invested in a start-up computer company and an optical fiber company. In 1997, it developed the biggest manufacturing base for frequency conversion air conditioners in China. In 1998, it shifted its focus to the high-tech information industry by developing its own software company and an IT industrial park. As a result, the technological wing of Hisense's portfolio of activities and profits increased significantly.

During the interview, Hisense representative pointed out that the company was not considering to increase its degree of diversification. On the contrary, Hisense now attaches great importance to focusing on a few core businesses and nurturing its competitive advantages in these areas. Hisense, which today controls 50 percent of China's television market, has adopted a mature strategy.

3.3. Cases of Unsuccessful Diversification: Apollo and Chundu

Many Chinese enterprises diversify in order to spread their operational risks. However, without an in-depth evaluation of the firm resources, business environment, and characteristics of the target business, the result of diversification can be the opposite: increased risks and potential failure. The dangers of such superficial diversification strategies are explicit in the following cases.

Case 1: Apollo Diversification Strategy

At the end of 1987, the predecessor of the Apollo Group, the Huangjiang Health Products Factory, was set up in Dongguan, Guangdong Province. Later, the factory took part in a national program of evaluation of health products and was awarded gold medal for its product Wanshida, a bio-nutritional food. The event was widely reported in the media. At the beginning of 1988, Huai Hanxin, the holder of the technology for Wanshida quit his job and invested in the production of Wanshida, changing the name of the factory and brand name to Apollo. In the same year, Apollo sales revenue reached RMB 7.5 million. The strategy of the Apollo Group at the time was to focus systematically on vertical integration, with horizontal development as a second alternative. In 1990, the sales revenue increased to RMB 240 billion. Next, Huai Hanxin recruited a group of young elite businessmen at a high salary to take over the firm and introduce information technology-based management. In 1993, sales revenue rose to RMB 1.3 billion and market share rose to 63 percent. Looking for new avenues for growth, Apollo Group implemented a diversification strategy by investing heavily in such industries as real estate, petroleum, international trade, hotels, cosmetics and computers. In two years, the amount invested in these industries reached RMB 340 billion. In 1995, Apollo went public in Hong Kong. It suffered losses of RMB 159 billion in 1997. At one time the share price was as low as HK$0.09, prompting the resignation of Huai Hanxin from his position as the chairman and the recruitment of Wang Zhen, a Harvard MBA graduate, to be the new chairman. However, things did not happen as planned. As he knew little about the nutritional food industry, Wang Zhen's efforts did not improve the situation and the volume of sales continued to decline.

Case 2: Chundu Diversification Strategy

The predecessor of the Luoyang Chundu Group was the Luoyang Meat Processing Factory, founded in 1958. In 1986, after the production of the first western style sausage in China, Chundu became famous throughout the country for its so-called "Dancing Sausage". At the same time its market share rose to 70 percent and assets increased to RMB 2.9 billion. Building on the success of its ham sausage, Chundu Group began its diversification by entering six new businesses: meat processing, frozen meat products, biochemical pharmaceuticals, drinks, packaging materials, and feedstuff processing. From then on, the Chundu Group became a large enterprise. It diversified into many sectors such as industry, commerce, and trade and tourism. The company developed from a meat-processing factory with net assets of only RMB 20 million to a diversified group with net assets of RMB 1.35 billion. Despite its prosperity, the diversification strategy laid the foundation for hidden trouble in the future; the activities were unrelated and this would increase the difficulty in mobilizing financial resources when necessary.

In 1998, the sales volume of its major product — the Chundu sausage — declined, with its market share sliding to 20 percent. The production of jujube tea, in which Chundu Group had invested, was forced to stop. The drinks factories it set up in Luoyang and Zhengzhou (Henan Province) had not begun operations, leaving behind a heap of idle equipment. Even its Lixin brand of health products, which once enjoyed a good reputation, finally collapsed owing to the frequent change of brand names. In 2005, up to 100 production lines had been stopped and the Group was suffering a loss of RMB 670 million as well as a substantive liability of RMB 1.3 billion.

3.4. *Lessons from Diversification*

From the mid to late 1980s many companies diversified. The rapid growth of the consumer market and the excess of demand over supply created lot of opportunities for enterprises. Leveraging these opportunities, some far-sighted enterprises adopted diversification strategies and grew very quickly.

This trend, however, vanished by the late 1990s. In a fast growing economy and with opportunities fully leveraged, profits began to decrease as most companies wanted to retain their market shares. Supply gradually exceeded demand. In addition, many enterprises faced problems of cash flow owing to over-expansion. They had no choice but to drop out and come back with a more focused strategy.

The year 2000 was another turning point. Seeking new avenues of profit, many enterprises re-adopted diversification. For example, Wahaha dealt mainly in nutritional food at first. When this field had been fully exploited it diversified further, into children's clothing, for example. Compared to the diversification strategy in the 1980s, enterprises are now focusing on financial dimension of diversification.

They do not interfere with the management of the projects in which they invest. Instead they employ professionals to take charge of each business, diversifying their investment but also betting on specialized management per industry.

Successful Diversification Experiences

Haier and Hisense had success moving from a single business to related diversification and then to new opportunities, in a virtual circle. Haier became a leader in the refrigerator business in seven years and then expanded into household appliances and finally into unrelated industries. Wahaha began its business of children's clothing after 13 years of dominating the soft drink industry. Hisense first became a leader in China's television industry in term of branding, after-sales service, and management before it entered related industries in the 1990s with freezers and air conditioners. Those products offered synergies with television in terms of core technology, marketing channels, and final consumers. Hisense moved afterwards to unrelated businesses such as information technology and telecommunication.

During the diversification process these companies carefully managed their activities as an integrated portfolio of core businesses and new ventures; they used the cash flows generated by the core businesses to finance the development of new activities that would in turn contribute to profits and diversify risks. Haier's profits in its core household goods business financed the development of the computer, mobile phone, and kitchen segments, which were promising industries. This portfolio management was however less successful in unrelated businesses than in related businesses.

Timing has been key in the art of seizing opportunities. Companies started their diversification process just after achieving relative dominance in their core business in the early and mid-1990s. During the same period, the "reform and opening up" policy at the national level offered ideal conditions for the business environment.

Unsuccessful Diversification Experiences

Companies that faced difficulties were vulnerable in their core business. They entered unrelated businesses before firmly establishing their leadership in their core business.

The companies ultimately did not have enough resources to diversify successfully. They entered blindly into unrelated businesses instead of moving step by step from related to unrelated sectors.

The Apollo Group invested RMB 340 million when sales in the core initial business were reaching RMB 1.3 billion. Since there was no specific knowledge or experience in these unrelated activities at the holding level, the needed financial resources far exceeded the available resources; the new activities faced cash flow problems and soon ran out of steam.

These enterprises also could not keep up with their expansion strategy due to a lack of management capabilities. Chundu Group, for example, did not have the corporate culture or the individual and collective talents to taken on such diversification.

Finally, the companies that failed had neither a clear competitive advantage in the sectors they wanted to enter nor a strong management culture and the necessary capabilities at the corporate level.

4. Globalization Strategies

Chinese enterprises have a strong interest in actively taking part in the international division of labor and in expanding from the domestic to the international market. Having reached an optimal size, they are interested in reorganizing their value chain in a more complex way at a global level. At the corporate level this means increased integration and interaction with the world economy in terms of production factors, capital, technology and human resources, as well as in terms of business functions such as R&D, supply, production, and marketing.

4.1. *The Logic of Globalization*

Since the beginning of the opening-up policy 30 years ago, Chinese enterprises have been exploiting their comparative advantages in production and market potential, thereby attracting multinationals from developed countries to invest in China. These investments have contributed to industry restructuring, enabling Chinese enterprises to enter the global supply chains of multinational enterprises. Such investments have also raised Chinese industries, products, and markets to international standards, enabling China to become an actor in the global economy. In 2005, China had accumulated a total of US$12.3 billion in foreign investments, but its overseas investment was only US$57 million. The "bringing in" policy has been the main form of China's participation in the globalization of the world economy. From a micro-economic perspective, China's international-oriented economy has been rather passive because of the major role played by foreign multinational enterprises in integrating China's enterprises and resources. Nowadays, "bringing in" can no longer satisfy the development needs of the globalization of Chinese enterprises. Chinese enterprises have to "go-out" and actively take part in global economic activities.

The ratio of wholly or partly private large enterprises that have invested successfully abroad is increasing rapidly and firms like the 999 Group (one of China's largest traditional herbal medicine manufacturers), Jiangsu Little Swan Electronic Appliances Company, TCL, and Haier are good examples of successful "going-out" strategies.

The key challenge for these Chinese corporations on the global scene is to increase their competitive advantage in their core business through continuous innovation.

Nevertheless, the current globalization process among Chinese enterprises is still in its infancy. It is taking place in a developing economy, in sharp contrast to the environment of developed economies such as the United States and Japan and newly industrializing countries. Since the opening-up policy, China has been developing its export businesses with the help of foreign investments. Although China has opened quite a number of industries to foreign investments, Chinese enterprises are not fully equipped to face the challenges posed by the international market due to long-time protection by the government. After China's entry into the WTO, Chinese enterprises have had to engage foreign multinational competitors head on. Therefore, a globalization strategy had to be adopted. Meanwhile, multinational enterprises have been moving their production into China in order to reap the benefits of cheap labor and explore the huge market potential. In the face of such severe challenges, Chinese enterprises have to be flexible enough to enter the international market by adapting to the dynamics of globalization.

For Chinese enterprises, the road to globalization is not simply to sell products or services to international clients, but rather to achieve international standards of corporate strategy and management. Only a few companies such as Sichuan Changhong Electric Co., Haier, and TCL have significantly begun this globalization process. Transnational mergers and acquisitions have also begun only in recent years with TCL's acquisition in 2004 of the color television division of Thompson Multimedia in France, BOE's acquisition of the TFT-LCD business of Korean Hyundai, Lenovo's acquisition of IBM's PC division and Shanghai Automotive Industry Corporation (SAIC) attempt in 2005 to buy MG Rover.

With the further opening-up of the domestic market and the development of M&As at the global level, these first steps signal the entry of emerging Chinese MNCs into the business of transnational acquisitions.

The Chinese market is the domestic market with the highest potential, providing sufficient room for both Chinese and foreign enterprises to expand further. As it occupies a key position in the global market, companies that are not present in China cannot be considered fully globalized.

Generally, multinationals have to first achieve sufficient presence in their domestic market to generate the financial resources necessary to enter the global marketplace. But for Chinese enterprises in particular, both domestic and international markets are important because they provide significant opportunities for development and expansion. Thus, Chinese enterprises should actively cooperate with foreign multinational enterprises in the domestic market and, at the same time, seize every opportunity to enter international markets and increase their presence at the global level by leveraging on their strong positions in the domestic market.

4.2. Cases of Globalization Strategies: Wahaha and Wanxiang

All Chinese enterprises participating in the HEC-Tsinghua SEM Research Project on Chinese Multinationals have formulated a specific globalization strategy. They only differ in their stage of development: either preparing for international expansion, entering foreign markets, or structuring a global presence.

Two cases will illustrate the process, stages of development and specificities of emerging Chinese multinationals' globalization strategy.

Case 1: Wahaha Globalization Strategy

Wahaha's strategy is based on two combined principles. The first is to serve Chinese consumers' needs in order to increase the penetration and market share in China's domestic market. From Wahaha's point of view, this was the reason to work with foreign partners in the Chinese market.

The second principle is to internationalize Wahaha's capital structure to facilitate the development of its international operations and globalization. This led to the cooperation with Danone.

In 1996, Wahaha's annual revenues reached RMB 1 billion with RMB 200 million net profit. In order to develop further, Wahaha entered into a joint-venture representing US$ 40 million in foreign investment with the French company Danone, the world's sixth largest enterprise in the food and beverage industry. This decision had two main consequences.

First, Wahaha bought world-class production lines for purified water, fruit-juice milk and soft drinks with this capital injection and housed these production lines in newly built factories of 200,000 square meters.

Second, Wahaha found a technically competent partner. The joint-venture allowed Wahaha to achieve its goal of expansion, while at the meant same time strengthening its brand in the domestic market. This meant that the collaboration between Wahaha and Danone was at the same time cooperative and competitive. Wahaha oversees and manages its own subsidiaries and the Danone–Wahaha joint-ventures. But Wahaha does not sell Danone products because Danone has other activities in China, including products that can be competing with Wahaha's products.

With a growing demand in the Chinese market, it was a win-win strategy for the French partner. The policy for the JV was to have separate branding policies and to exclude Danone from day-to-day management of the operations. Human resource policies of the joint-venture stated that their employees above 40 would not be fired and their compensation would be based on performance. Danone's brand name was not a major issue in the venture and many Chinese clients are unaware of the join-venture between Wahaha and Danone.

The results of the JV have been very good, with sales doubling in the second year of collaboration.

The two companies decided to invest jointly in Indonesia in 2004, Danone controlling 70 percent of the JV and Wahaha as a minority shareholder with 30 percent. The Indonesian factory produced Danone dairy products and biscuits, as well as Wahaha dairy drinks for children. Wahaha sent its engineering teams to manage the production process of dairy drinks, a Wahaha specialty.

Case 2: Wanxiang Globalization

The Wanxiang Group, a privately owned company, is China's biggest auto parts supplier. Wanxiang specializes in auto parts such as universal joints, bearings, constant drive shafts, propeller shafts, shock absorbers, rolling elements, rubber sealers, suspension, and brakes.

Wanxiang's policy incorporates three standards: world-class R&D capabilities, world-class production system, and a global marketing and service network.

Wanxiang Group is one of 120 experimental enterprises supported by the State Council, and the only auto parts manufacturer on the list of 520 key national enterprises as defined by the central government.

Wanxiang started to specialize in the early 1980s by introducing modern production technology and focusing on growth in the domestic market; exports would start in a second phase. The company, which produced universal joints in large quantities, was making profits of RMB 100,000 per day thanks to economies of scale.

The Wanxiang Group took its current form in 1990 when after 20 years of successful operations, the Zhejiang Provincial Government approved the proposal of Lu Guanqiu to formally establish the Zhejiang Wanxiang Machinery & Electronic Group (The "Wanxiang Group").

In 1994 a subsidiary of the Wanxiang Group, Wanxiang Qinghai Co. Ltd., was listed on the Shenzhen Stock Exchange and Wanxiang America was founded in Chicago's Industrial Park to become the center of Wanxiang's overseas strategy.

This was the founding step of Wanxiang's globalization strategy and the beginning of a series of international acquisitions with a clear focus on the USA.

From 1994 to 2006 Wanxiang America took control of Zeller, ID Co, LT C, QAI Co, American Universal Automotive Industries Inc (listed on Nasdaq), and Rockford Powertrain, using a variety of financial techniques, majority or minority shareholding, or cross-shareholding.

For Lu Guanqiu, the founder and, until 2003, the Chairman of Wanxiang, globalization and localization are two sides of the same coin: "We have to become more local in order to become more international. Our guiding policy is to take root in our own soil and make every effort to become as local as possible."

Wanxiang's localization policy includes four dimensions.

The first is the localization of human resources. Wanxiang America employs only five Chinese expatriates among a staff of 60. Wanxiang employs local staff, including general managers, in its European and South American branches. The salary scale is in complete accordance with local standards. A business manager at Wanxiang America earns US$200,000, more than double that of his/her Chinese counterpart.

The second policy is localization of management practice and style. Wanxiang's objective is not only to adapt to local regulations and the business environment, but also to merge with local business culture.

The third policy is localization of capital. Currently, Wanxiang America's financing, which originates in the USA, is twice as much as Chinese funding. Wanxiang America maintains close relationships with leading US financial institutions such as Citigroup and Merrill Lynch, and Wanxiang plans to be listed in the USA in order to have access to a large financial market.

The fourth dimension is localization of quality standards. Wanxiang Group's products achieved the (ISO) 9002 standard to meet the requirements of the three biggest American auto manufacturers and are constantly adapted to new market demands.

Since its foundation, the Wanxiang Group has created, acquired, or invested in 30 companies in eight countries, including the US, Great Britain, Germany, Canada and Australia.

4.3. *Lessons from Globalization Strategies*

In the context of China's late developing economy, Chinese enterprises' globalization strategies differ significantly in their respective experiences. Each company exhibits a specific stance.

Wahaha's major internationalization move is its alliance with the foreign multinational Danone, which allows both cooperation and competition on the domestic market and potential joint activities abroad.

Wanxiang focused on the US market and emphasizes a localization strategy of staff, management, and capital.

The history and the globalization strategies of Chinese companies do not depend only on the internal and external conditions they face today.

Globalization strategies are path-dependant: they depend on the stages of development that companies had followed in the past. They also depend on leaders' vision of the internationalization process at an early stage of development.

Chinese Companies and Localization Policy

A first general trend is that Chinese enterprises are developing an integrated network of production, R&D, and marketing overseas. An international marketing strategy and network, in particular, have become key elements in enterprises' core competitiveness. Huawei has established marketing networks in over 40 countries and regions, leading to a stable growth in the market share of those markets. TCL has established, through its forward integration strategy, an extensive domestic distribution network which multinationals such as Philips and Panasonic have to share before they are able to tap into the Chinese market. Access and control of distribution networks are key in the globalization of Chinese enterprises.

A second trend is based on China's sustainable comparative advantage in specific industries such as consumer electronics. Chinese companies will build on this comparative advantage as they globalize. However, the objectives of acquisitions made by Chinese enterprises overseas still differ from foreign multinationals' objectives. The major motivation for Chinese enterprises is to learn how to manage the internationalization process from their acquisitions. They are especially eager to acquire the ability to upgrade their technology through R&D. For Chinese enterprises that are already globally competitive, further expansion in the international market remains a logical priority.

A third trend is localization, which for Chinese multinationals is the only path to successful globalization. Mature multinationals have reorganized their staff, production facilities, marketing network, and R&D on an international basis. Emerging Chinese multinationals have to employ local staff in host countries, utilize local resources, adapt to local laws and cultures, manufacture locally, develop production, marketing, and R&D locally to reach maturity. They can realise their ambition of going global only through a high degree of localization.

— *Localization of Manufacturing* — Initially Chinese enterprises exported domestic products overseas. Then, when volume increased, they began investing in local factories to manufacture locally so as to reduce the cost of transportation and avoid trade barriers. This allowed them to lower trade tariffs, thereby reducing the product cost and increasing their market share locally,

— *Localization of management* — This goes hand-in-hand with the localization of production. Wanxiang built its top management teams overseas with local managers. Except for one, all Wanxiang America teams, are locals with rich experience in the US car industry. The company is managed American-style.

— *Localization of R&D* — facilitates the intimate coordination of development, production, and marketing to adapt to local demand, and allows local talent to enlarge the company's global knowledge pool. According to the US Department of Commerce, 375 multinational enterprises had established 715 R&D centers in the United States by the end of 1999, supporting the proposition of growing localization of R&D abroad. At the same time, Microsoft, Bell, and other foreign multinational enterprises are doing the opposite, that is localizing their R&D centers in China.

— *Localization of human resources* — This is the core element of the localization process. By the end of 1998, multinationals had some 35 million employees working globally. Experience shows the limitation of an internationalization process based on expatriate employees. This is not only costly, but also fosters imperfect communication with local employees, government, suppliers, and customers. To avoid this weakness, Chinese emerging multinationals will have to seriously invest in the development of local staff.

Chinese Companies Alternative Internationalization Processes

"The Easy Way First"
The "easy way first" means investing first in emerging markets (Figure 1.2). By 2004, there were over 6,000 overseas subsidiaries owned by Chinese enterprises in over 160 countries and regions, with Hong Kong and Macau alone accounting for 2,185 of them — or 35 percent — of the total number. The rest were scattered in developing markets of Asia, Europe, and South America. For example, Huawei set up key subsidiaries in developing countries and regions. China has many SMEs which are good at investing in small-scale, labor-intensive projects. Such projects are easy to handle and production can be shifted locally in virtually no time. They can meet the needs of emerging markets. Large enterprises can first try their hand at directly investing in developing countries. After accumulating enough experience, they can proceed to more developed markets in America, Europe and Japan to further enhance their own competitiveness.

SMEs have more difficulties in implementing global strategies. To minimize these difficulties, they could build strategic alliances with one another, or enter into stable, cooperative relations with large enterprises so as to share resources,

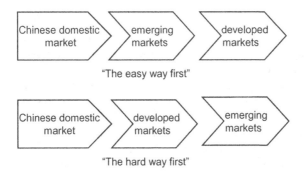

Figure 1.2: Investment priorities: emerging markets versus developed markets.

risks and profits. This would be a shortcut to explore the global market and an important strategy for international specialization. TCL is a typical example of the implementation of such a model. During the early stages of its globalization process, it entered Southeast Asian market such as Vietnam and the Philippines, whose cultural backgrounds are similar to China. It then expanded into developed countries step-by-step, through large-scale acquisitions.

Such a model could be implemented with low risks and high profits for three reasons. Firstly, it enables Chinese enterprises to expand their scale by releasing excess production into the global market. Secondly, it enables Chinese enterprises to accumulate experience in globalization, to recruit and train specialists in international business, and to learn foreign trade rules. Lastly, it avoids any large-scale investment and waste of resources. This model yielded positive results for TCL whose overseas sales grew from US$716 million to US$1.16 billion in 2002.

However, this strategy has two limitations. First, in emerging markets and especially in Southeast Asia, Japanese companies occupy the upper segments of the market, leaving the middle and lower segments to Chinese manufacturers. These segments are less profitable and sometimes Chinese companies are left with little or no profit.

Second, the presence of Chinese companies in emerging markets might have a negative impact on their brand image when they enter the European and North American markets.

"The Hard Way First"

The "hard way first" means investing first in developed markets. That was the case for Haier, which had clear ambitions in the USA and in Europe, as illustrated by the founding of Haier America and the opening of a plant in the USA (1999), and the creation of Haier Europe and acquisition of a factory in Italy (2000).

The Chinese market was saturated, so Haier positioned itself to enter developed markets and face the intense competition there. The success in these countries would then ease entry or growth in emerging markets.

Evidently, not all Chinese companies have the ability to follow this model. It requires a strong brand and capabilities of innovation since brand and products are the key success factors. It requires also strong financial resources because it takes a long time, especially in a country with a different cultural background, to create awareness of new brands among local customers. Without sufficient financial resources, the strategy cannot be sustainable and could lead to serious losses.

Thus the risks arising from this model might be too high for most Chinese enterprises. It is rather difficult for a country which is not a technological leader to export to the most developed markets. On the other hand, a few companies such as Haier are already mastering the necessary combination of resources — brands, product development capabilities, and financial resources — to successfully penetrate the very competitive but mature and regulated European and US markets.

The Gradual Development Process

According to their specific goals and their unique combination of resources, Chinese enterprises can choose different foreign market entry modes.

The traditional stages of the internationalization process cove exporting, licensing, entering strategic alliances, acquisitions, and creating new wholly-owned foreign subsidiaries (Hitt, 2002). Chinese companies in the early stages of their internationalization operate mainly along the first three stages. More mature companies go on to stage four and five if they have higher ambitions of international market share and when they have accumulated the appropriate resources (Figure 1.3).

Generally speaking, most Chinese companies choose the "easy way first" approach by starting to focus on emerging markets before progressively moving up the ladder through acquisitions and wholly-owned subsidiaries in developed markets.

Conclusion: Challenges Faced by Emerging Chinese Multinationals

Emerging Chinese multinationals have successfully entered the first stages of their internationalization process, but will need time to catch up with leading

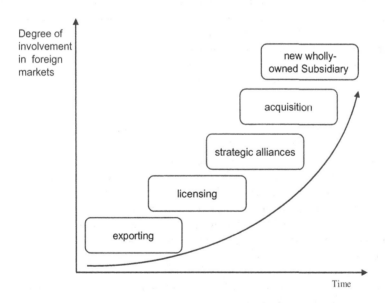

Figure 1.3: The gradual development process.
Source: Adapted from Hitt (2002).

multinationals. Many companies already face serious troubles in their investment overseas. Some of them have not delivered on their announcements, while others are still struggling on the global scene. They still face a series of challenges in their "go-global" strategy.

- Chinese enterprises lack sufficient financing to compete in overseas markets. Abundant financial resources are needed for marketing, advertising, communication, and distribution. Chinese companies do not have the same resources as established multinationals.
- Emerging Chinese multinationals still have difficulties with money transfers because of the restrictions and lengthy foreign exchange procedures. Managers of private companies such as Huawei are not even able to travel easily for business due to visa procedures.
- Emerging Chinese multinationals are not yet fully familiar with the foreign investment environment and thus face high risks. The majority of Chinese companies target emerging markets which are characterized by relative instability in economic policy, credit, and security. This results in higher risks than developed markets. Furthermore, insurance mechanisms are not yet sufficiently developed in those countries.
- Emerging Chinese multinationals do not always have a sustainable competitive advantage. They have less management experience and R&D capabilities than other multinationals. Additionally, only a few companies are mastering their core technology. The majority of the companies are still competing on low cost, which is not sustainable in the long term because of increase in Chinese labor costs and competition from other countries.
- China's competitiveness is limited by its lack of high technology and innovation. Among non-trade overseas investments, nearly 40 percent are labor-intensive projects with low added value and technology. The demand for such projects is not growing in the global market, which leaves little room for expansion. In China's large and medium-scale enterprises, R&D expenses account for only 1 percent to 2 percent of sales. The 500 biggest companies spend between 5 percent and 20 percent on R&D. Currently, two thirds of the large and medium-scale SOEs have not set up their own R&D departments.
- Emerging Chinese multinationals do not have many well-reputed brands. According to a survey completed by the United Nations Industrial Development Organization (UNIDO), famous brands represent only 3 percent of brand names but have a market share of over 40 percent. There is no Chinese brand among the top 50 brands worldwide.
- Chinese emerging multinationals lack management professionals and have to further develop their entrepreneurial and managerial skills.

References

Chen Qingtai (2005). Shishi zouchu qu zhanlue de jige wenti (Several Problems with the Implementation of Going-Out Strategy). *Guoji gongcheng yu lao wu, 6 qi* (International Project Contracting and Labor Service), Issue 6.

HEC Paris – Tsinghua SEM (2005–2008). *Chinese Multinationals*, Company interviews, Tsinghua SEM.

Hitt M.A. (2002). *Strategic Management: Competitiveness and Globalization: Concepts*; *6th Edition*, Beijing: Mechanical Industry Press.

Jin Zhanming (2004). *Zhanlue guanli chao jingzheng huanjing xia de xuanze*, di 2 ban (Strategic Management — the Only Choice under the Environment of Fierce Competition, 2nd edition). *Qinghua daixue chubanshe*, Beijing: Tsinghua University Press.

Kang Rongping and Ke Yinbin (1999). *Qiye duoyuanhua jingying* (Diversification Strategy of Enterprises). *Jingji kexue chubanshe*, Beijing: Economic and Science Press.

Kang Rongping and Ke Yinbin (2004). Zhongguo qiye zhanlue 20 nian (20 Years of Chinese Corporate Strategy). *Jingji guancha bao* 8 yue 21 ri. *The Economic Observer*, August 21.

Li Ya (2004). *Min ying qiye fazhan zhanlue, di yi ban* (The Development Strategy of Private Enterprise 1st edition). Zhongguo fangzheng chubanshe, Beijing: China Fangzheng Press.

Li Rong (2004). Jizhong du di cuo shang zhongguo gangtie ye (Low Concentration Ratio Damages Chinese Iron and Steel Industry). *Zhonghua gongshang shibao. China Business Time.*

Liu Yingqiu (2003). Kuaguo jingying: min ying qiye xin zhanlue xuanze (Multinational Operations: New Strategies by Private Enterprises). *Jingji cankao bao*, 2 yue 19 ri. *Economic Information Daily*, Feb 19.

Mang Jingshi (2001). Hou fazhan jingji de/di guandian: yige hexin gainian jiexi (The Point of View of Late Development Economy: An Analysis of a Key Concept). *Riben yanjiu* di 5 qi, zong di 65 qi, Japanese Studies, 5(65).

Sun Ming (2005). Quanqiu 500 qian zai zhongguo (Top 500 in China), *Beijing qingnian bao* 2 yue 17 ri. *Beijing Youth Daily*, Feb 17.

Wang Qin (2004). Zhongguo qiye guoji hua zhanlue xuanze mubiaoshichang, jinru fangshi yu jingzheng zhanlue (Globalization Strategies by Chinese Enterprises: Target Markets, Entry Routes, and Competition Strategies), *Gansu shehui kexue.*

Ye Bingxi and Pang Yahui (2003). Hai er zhanlue VSTCL siwei (Haier Strategy versus TCL Thinking), *hongguo jingying bao*, China Business.

Zhongguo renmin daxue jingzhengli yu pingjia yanjiu zhongxin yanjiu zu (Research Center for Competitiveness Appraisal Renmin University of China) *zhongguo guoji jingzhengli fazhan baogao (2001). shiji fazhan zhuti yanjiu* (Report on China's International Competitiveness — Research Project on Development in 21st Century), *Zhongguorenmin daxue chubanshe*, Beijing: China Renmin University Press.

Chapter 2

CHINA'S GO GLOBAL POLICY

Li Zhaoxi

Enterprise Research Institute —
Development Research Center of the State Council (DRC)

1. China After WTO Entry

1.1. *National Goals and Company Objectives*

The growth of Chinese multinationals is directly linked to Chinese economic development and China's international competitiveness. The "opening-up" policy reached a turning point in 2001 when China entered the World Trade Organization (WTO) and opened its market further. Chinese enterprises then had to face much more severe competition in their home markets. It was the moment for some to go abroad — with the support of government — in order to enhance their international competitiveness.

The internationalization of Chinese companies has accelerated since then and we now see the emergence of Chinese multinationals (MNCs). Their number, size and nature are good indicators of Chinese economic progress.

The Chinese government's support for companies to reach beyond their national borders has three major objectives:

— Securing natural resources.
— Contributing to China's economic adjustment.
— Improving the international competitiveness of Chinese enterprises.

Securing Natural Resources

China is a developing country with a large population and relatively scarce resources: it is short of some important mineral resources and depends on a large amount of imports including oil, natural gas, iron, manganese, chromites, alumina, gold, silver, copper, and potash. In the context of increasing globalization, China's internationalization strategy follows other countries' example and aims to secure the resources, especially energy and raw materials, which are necessary to achieve sustainable economic development.

Contributing to China's Economic Adjustment

China's national objective of building a "moderately prosperous society" by 2020 is based on sustainable industrialization, the establishment of a sound socialist market economy, as well as a more vigorous, more open economic system. Even if the country has managed to maintain high growth in value and volume, China faces the urgent task of readjustment of its industrial chain and transformation of its growth mode in order to insure sustainable development.

To rapidly achieve this objective, China needs to further extend its internationalization policy. Moreover, if the adjustment was only conducted inside the country, it would be relatively limited in scope. So China's internationalization policy has to be accelerated and companies have to increase their overseas investment. The promotion of overseas investment by the Chinese government contributes to company growth and profitability when there is an excess of supply over demand on the domestic market. It will also contribute to capital accumulation and accelerate the path of technological innovation, thus producing a positive effect on China's economic adjustment.

Improving Chinese Enterprises' International Competitiveness

Most Chinese companies are exposed to globalization and are developing various forms of international activities. The priorities, however, vary from one company to another in developing a worldwide, sales, production, and supply network or in promoting their brand internationally. It is China's "world famous brands" policy.

China's WTO membership means that China has truly begun the process of globalization. China's comparative advantage in manufacturing is increasingly transforming the country into a global resource pool. Owing to the ever expanding liberalization of the Chinese market, many large multinational companies are able to benefit from China's low cost labor through localized production and distribution. If, however, China were to limit its ambition to comparative advantage in manufacturing — at the bottom of the industrial structure — Chinese enterprises would not be able to compete globally.

After 30 years of the "reform and opening up" policy, some Chinese enterprises have built sufficient strength to expand abroad. The growing presence in China of foreign MNCs and the large volume of exports of Made in China products have resulted in these products reaching international quality standards. The abundance of cheap labor give Chinese enterprises an obvious competitive advantage over their competitors' cost structure. Thus, WTO membership provides Chinese companies the opportunity to optimize their resource allocation at a global level.

But Chinese enterprises still face many difficulties in maximizing this opportunity to develop internationally. They need to gain more experience in international competition, establish overseas distribution networks, train international management talent, and promote their brand internationally.

Lu Guanqiu, the chairman of Wanxiang Group — China's largest car component manufacturer — once said:

"The most difficult part of a Chinese enterprise's internationalization process is to enter foreign markets and build brand recognition."

For most Chinese enterprises, the key international strategy objective now is the development of a sales network and the creation of distribution channels to enter foreign markets. To face the globalization challenge, Chinese companies must actively participate in international competition and develop both their global vision and local presence. This gradual internationalization process demands changes in investment modes and geographic targets.

By building on their international business experiences, step-by-step Chinese companies are entering a phase of multinationalization.

1.2. The Chinese Economy and International Investments

China's Level of Development and Outward Foreign Direct Investment

At a macroeconomic level, the introduction of the "reform and opening up" policy in 1978 has resulted in sustained rapid growth of the Chinese economy. China's GDP has increased from RMB364.5 billion in 1978 to RMB10.9 trillion in 2001, with an annual growth rate of 9.4 percent. From 1989 to 2001, the economy had to face adverse conditions at home and abroad, but China maintained a relatively high rate of economic growth with an annual growth rate of 9.3 percent. This rate was far higher than the 3.2 percent growth of the world economy, the 2.7 percent growth of developed countries, the 5.2 percent growth of developing countries, and the 5.8 percent growth of the newly industrialized countries in Asia. China's development had become one of the fastest in the world.

By the end of 2002, China's GDP per capita reached US$1,000. In the most developed regions such as Shanghai and Beijing as well as in the provinces of Guangdong, Jiangsu and Zhejiang, the GDP was between US$3,000 and US$5,000. China's economy and foreign trade ranked No. six in the world and the total value of China's import and export trade was US$621 billion. By March 2003, China's foreign exchange reserve had reached US$316 billion. These economic conditions created a favorable context for Chinese companies' internationalization strategy between 2001 and 2003.

According to Dunning, the flow of Foreign Direct Investment (FDI) of a country is closely correlated to its level of economic development and follows typical stages of development. At the time of Dunning's first investigations, four stages of development could be identified according to the level of GDP per capita of the country

— Stage 1: the country receives little inward FDI and makes no overseas invest-ments (GDP per capita below US$400).
— Stage 2: inward FDI begins to increase, and the country also starts to make a small amount of investment overseas (GDP per capita between US$400 and US$1,500). At this stage, the country's outward FDI is low compared to the inward FDI.
— Stage 3: inward FDI still surpasses the country's overseas investment, but the gap is narrowing (GDP per capita between US$2,500 and US$4,500).
— Stage 4: outward FDI surpasses inward FDI; the country is a main FDI con-tributor. (GDP per capita above US$4,600).

In 2001 China was typically at the second stage with a large amount of FDI entering the country. With China' entry into the WTO, the "reform and opening up" policy entered a new phase. China had to further open its market to foreign products to fulfill its obligations.

Since 2002 China has drastically reduced its import tariffs on more than 5,000 goods. The general tariff rate dropped from 15.3 percent to 12 percent and in one case — information technology products — the tariff was cancelled altogether. Controls over quotas, licensing, and tendering for some products were also can-celled. In 2002 its WTO commitments also led China to enact and improve laws and regulations for tertiary industries including finance, insurance, telecommuni-cations, foreign trade, business, transportation, construction, tourism, and agency services. Tertiary industry became a new hotspot of foreign investment. Foreign investors became more confident about investing in China which enjoyed a new upsurge in foreign investment.

The flow of inward FDI grew rapidly. China attracted US$54 billion FDI in 2002 and was the largest FDI recipient that year. The inward FDI continued to grow in 2003 and 2004; 508,941 foreign enterprises had registered in China by the end of 2004. This was a demonstration of China's attractiveness to international investors based on its large market potential and good investment climate. On the other hand, there was still very little overseas investment consistent with China's new economic weight. China's overseas investment only took off significantly in 2004. It was the opening of a new phase of development for Chinese companies: investing internationally in order to build their competitive advantage and optimize their resource allocation on an international basis.

China's Enterprise Reform

The reform of state-owned enterprises (SOEs) has always been a key element in China's economic restructuring. Since the beginning of reforms and the liberalization of the economy, the Chinese government has executed various experiments, trying by every means possible to solve the problem of long-term, extensive losses incurred by SOEs.

During the 1990s, China's SOEs made headway in implementing the standard "Modern Enterprise System": by 2000 most large and medium-scale SOEs had received a new legal status conforming to the "Modern Enterprises System".

According to the follow-up investigations by China's National Bureau of Statistics, of the 2,473 SOEs that had started reform on a trial basis in 1994, 81.5 percent had been converted to companies in accordance with the Company Law by the end of 2000. Of these, 29.9 percent had been transformed into limited liability companies, 35.4 percent into shareholding companies limited, while 34.7 percent were still state-funded. Among successfully reformed companies, 82.2 percent have regular shareholder meetings, 95.1 percent have a board of directors, and 84.5 percent have a supervisory board. All of them had validated their legal status.

The non-state-owned economy, that is the private sector economy, is developing rapidly and has become an important factor in the growth of China's economy. Private enterprises and foreign-invested enterprises are contributing more to China's foreign trade than SOEs. The latest statistics show that, in the first quarter of 2003, the export value of non-state-owned enterprises was 51 percent of the total and had increased 1.5 percent over the 4th quarter of the previous year, surpassing the export value of SOEs. Foreign-invested enterprises, collective enterprises and other enterprises contributed respectively 51.9 percent, 2.2 percent and 1.1 percent to total export value. In provinces such as Guangdong, Jiangsu, Shangdong, Zhejiang, as well as the municipality of Shanghai where the private sector dominates the local economy, private enterprises have been actively involved in international competition. They have developed various forms of international operations and started building their international reputation.

Chinese companies have developed their competitive advantage through various forms of collaborative agreements: they had to compete and cooperate with foreign MNCs actively operation in the country and had the opportunity to learn from their experience. They have improved their technology, accumulated management experience, cultivated management talent, and enhanced their capacity for innovation thanks to joint-ventures, collaborative agreements, and joint projects with foreign multinationals.

Thus, after 30 years of development, China has a number of enterprises with a good level of technology and familiarity with international management, and experience of fierce international competition. China is finding new avenues for growth, new opportunities for resource allocation, and new ways of improving their international competitiveness to help these companies invest internationally.

China's Reform and Opening Up Policy and the International Environment

Comparatively speaking, international and domestic factors had independently influenced China's foreign trade before the 1990s. After the 1990s, following the globalization trend and the broadening of China's "reform and opening up" policy, international and domestic factors have had a combined influence on China's foreign trade.

The evolution of the international environment

In the 1990s, international relations had two key characteristics: globalization and the unipolar versus multipolar political debate. These elements had many economic consequences such as: the acceleration of the free trade process, the development of regional blocs, the growing influence of multinational companies on world trade and industrial policy, the rapid adjustment of world economic structures, the growing role of science and technology, and the intensification of world competition.

This new kind of world economy not only increased the mutual dependence of each country's economy, but also increased greater pressure from the challenges of international competition and structural adjustment on their respective industries. Thus, the question of the sustainability of economic development became increasingly acute with the orientation of the Chinese economy increasingly focused on international competition.

China's gradual "reform and opening up" policy

After the adoption of the "reform and opening up" policy, China gradually undertook economic globalization and experienced three historic breakthroughs:

— the adoption of the reform and reform and opening up policy,
— the establishment of the principles of the socialist market economy system,
— China's entry into the WTO which set a starting-point for China's globalization.

This meant that China shifted its policy from the liberalization of selected economic sectors to a broad liberalization covering a full range of activities. It moved from the unilateral opening up of China's domestic market to multilateral exchanges in the framework of the WTO. It moved from passively accepting international trade rules to actively participating in their formulation. It moved from depending solely on bilateral negotiations to harmonize trade relationships to multilateral negotiations. These changes have had a major influence on the Chinese economy at a domestic level, and have also been the key factors influencing the internationalization process of Chinese enterprises.

The Internationalization Process of Chinese Enterprises

There are currently 30,000 Chinese companies operating internationally. Among them are large-scale manufacturing companies, high-tech companies, SOEs, private enterprises, enterprises focusing on overseas contracted projects and labor cooperation, as well as businesses making their first investments overseas as the beginning of their internationalization process. Key actors of China's overseas FDI are large diversified companies and groups taking the lead in internationalization, such as China National Petroleum Corporation (CNPC) — China's largest producer and supplier of crude oil and natural gas, Sinopec (oil and petrochemical products), China Worldbest Group (pharmaceuticals, health care, biotechnology), and the Haier Group (home appliances).

The 10 mainland China companies listed in the top 100 non-financial transnational corporations from developing countries are state-owned or state-controlled enterprises (UNCTAD, 2006).

Non-governmental businesses like Huawei Technologies and Wanxiang have followed SOEs in the internationalization process. However, compared to SOEs, the majority of these companies are smaller in size.

Being the original emerging Chinese multinationals, SOEs have been key actors of the broadening of the "reform and opening up" policy. Hence, the internationalization of Chinese companies and amount of investment overseas are closely related to the change of government policy, the transformation of the economic system, and the accumulation of capital in the domestic market.

The development of Chinese multinationals is rooted in China's economic development and modernization process, as well as in the pursuit of national objectives.

Thus, Chinese enterprises still face several problems of the first stage of international development even if they have successfully begun the internationalization process. These include the relatively small volume of overseas' investments, the lack of development sustainability, the lack of transparency in ownership structure, and weak international competitiveness.

2. Overseas Investment Policy and Administration

2.1. *Developments Stages of China's Overseas Investment Policy*

Following the adoption over 30 years ago of the "reform and opening up" policy, China has developed a complete system of policies for the "Deliberation and Approval of Project Proposals", as well as policies for administration and promotion of outward FDI. This system, which accelerated the gradual development of China's overseas FDI, has four stages.

Stage one: 1979–1983

This trial period was characterized by a high level of central control and a very limited number of authorized overseas investments. The earliest Chinese outward FDI official regulation was included in the 15 economic reform measures formulated by China's State Council in August, 1979. Although Act 13 specified that "It is permitted to set up enterprises in foreign countries", in practice foreign investment was strictly controlled due to lack of experience in investing overseas and limited foreign exchange reserves. From 1979 to 1982, all Chinese enterprises' foreign investment projects — regardless of the amount or type of investment — had to report to the State Council for examination and approval.

In 1983, the State Council authorized the Ministry of Foreign Trade and Economic Cooperation (MOFTEC) to manage the approval process for Chinese enterprises' outward FDI. The administration worked mainly on individual cases and there was no standard procedure. In order to establish a joint-venture overseas (apart from Hong Kong and Macau) which would require investments exceeding US$1 million, the Chinese investor had to first go through the supervising authority at the level of the municipal, provincial, or autonomous regional government. The supervising authority would then refer the case to the MOFTEC which would seek the opinion of the Chinese Embassy and relevant government departments after which the MOFTEC would decide whether to approve it or not. For smaller projects (less than US$1 million), the investor's supervising authority could directly seek approval from the Chinese Embassy. During this period, Chinese foreign investment per year was limited to only US$9.2 million.

Stage two: 1984–1992

To address the international investment needs of Chinese enterprises, MOFTEC promulgated a Notice on the Authorization and Principle of the Approval of the Establishment of Non-commercial Overseas Enterprises (1984). The organization also issued a new regulation called the Trial Regulation on the Approval Procedure and Administration of Establishing Non-commercial Overseas Enterprises (1985).

The basic administration system of Chinese outward FDI was established when the examination and approval of individual cases was changed to a standardized approval procedure. The new rules specified the conditions for overseas investment and that the right to invest overseas was not limited to only a few enterprises. From 1984 to 1991, China witnessed a marked increase in FDI of up to US$0.2 billion per year, while the amount of investment per enterprise also increased to US$1.4 million.

The increase of Chinese outward FDI led to unfocused and unrealistic investments, and often resulted in failure and key personnel fleeing abroad with the capital. These incidents exposed both the weaknesses of international management at the company level, and the imperfections of China's outward investment administrative system. To solve these problems, as well as to overcome the severity of China's lack of foreign exchange reserves, the Notice on Strengthening the Control of Foreign Investment (1991) revised the approval procedures for FDI (including investment in Hong Kong and Macau).

Accordingly, the State Planning Commission (now the National Development and Reform Commission — NDRC) — China's top economic policy-making body — and other relevant departments examined all proposals and feasibility reports for foreign investment projects that either applied for government financing, sought a government guarantee in order to obtain a loan from overseas banks, or represented an investment of over US$1 million on the Chinese side. MOFTEC examined and approved the contract and statutes of such projects. When projects involved foreign investment by Chinese companies of over US$30 million, the NDRC and other relevant departments initially studied the proposal and feasibility report, after which the State Council examined it again. When the foreign investment was less than US$1 million, the project was in line with the existing foreign investment policy, and its funding or product distribution did not need government support, then the project proposals and contracts could be examined by the departments appointed by the State Council, the provincial government or the autonomous regional government.

Compared to the system established in 1985, the new examination and approval system of 1991 strengthened the control over outward FDI, especially large-scale foreign investment. The review system included more steps: small projects (less than US$1 million) were reviewed by three departments instead of two, and larger projects (more than US$1 million) reviewed by five departments instead of three. The content of the examination was also more detailed to include project proposals, feasibility reports, contracts and statutes.

Stage three: 1993–1998

In 1993, owing to the growing demand for overseas investment, the MOFTEC began to draft the Regulation on the Administration of Chinese Overseas Enterprises to improve the administration of such investments. The MOFTEC was to manage the examination and approval process and be responsible for the administration of overseas enterprises and outward FDI policies. The NDRC was in charge of the examination and approval of the project proposal and feasibility report for such investments. For other ministries and commissions, the provincial-level Foreign Trade Departments were the governing bodies of overseas enterprises. The MOFTEC's authorized the economic and commercial department in Chinese embassies which, in turn, coordinated the administration of Chinese overseas enterprises. This management system is still in use, following the Administration of Overseas Companies and Their Offices policy of 1997.

The clear-cut division of duties among different government departments and the establishment of relevant policies constituted the basis for China's FDI administrative system. This system resulted in the rapid development of various types of foreign investment. During this period, China increased its FDI to US$0.7 billion per year, while the scale of investment per enterprise dropped to US$1.06 million.

Stage four: 1999–present

In order to encourage foreign investment in the more developed light, textile, and household electric appliance industries, the State Council authorized enterprises to set up processing of investor's raw materials and assembling operations abroad (MOFTEC 1999). The State Council also introduced independent examination and approval processes for these international projects.

When a company wishes to invest abroad, the State Economic and Trade Commission (SETC) examines the proposal and feasibility report to determine its merits. After that, the MOFTEC conducts a final examination and grants approval of the project based on appraisals by the SETC and China's commercial departments within the relevant Chinese embassies. The approval contract formulates the detailed polices and measures put in place to support the enterprise in its expansion beyond China's borders. This document also sets down the five aspects that are the guiding principles for foreign investment: an emphasis on work, policy priorities, the examination and approval process, and implementation. The new measure was a breakthrough in the examination and approval process because the approving authority had shifted from the NRDC to the SETC. The latter is more generous with its approvals than the former. Hence the measure meant a loosening of restrictions over the outward FDI in overseas processing or assembly projects.

From then on, these operations became the core of overseas investments and accelerated the internationalization strategy.

From 1999 to 2001, Chinese outward FDI maintained almost the same volume as in the third stage, which was US$678 million per year. Yet the scale of investment per enterprise doubled to US$2.18 million.

Given the shift of influence from the NRDC to the SETC at the central administration level, a similar shift of influence from the central government to the local level made small investments (less than US$1 million) more easily obtainable.

2.2. The Chinese System of Administrative Examination and Approval

The Approval System and China's Internationalization Strategy

Why is China still not ready for a totally free overseas investment system and the further reduction of its administrative controls?

There are several reasons:

First, even if Chinese GDP per capita reached US$1730 in real terms (US$7598 at Purchasing Power Parity) in 2005, China's economy has not reached a sufficient level of economic development to generate a really important flow of outward FDI. Among large-scale Chinese enterprises, only a few have the capabilities to handle transnational mergers and to manage a multinational network. Many Chinese enterprises still rely on the advantages of low cost domestic labor and concentrate primarily on the development of sales networks and production facilities abroad.

Second, among the Chinese enterprises involved in overseas investment, SOEs still represent a high percentage. As the economic system is still in a stage of transition, many SOEs do not have a clear status in terms of legal personality, governance, and property rights. As they do not operate fully according to market rules, this might lead to unrealistic foreign investment decisions.

Third, the liberalization of transactions for capital repatriation has to be managed progressively. Today, the balance of international income and expenses and the level of foreign currency reserves are very limiting factors of outward FDI. Other weaknesses still exist however, such as the maturity of the financial market and the quality of financial control on foreign investments.

The fourth reason for the control of overseas investment is China's *de facto* capital-surplus economy. However, there is a paradox. As a consequence of the experimentation and reforms of the financial system and of the restrictions preventing banks to finance specific industries, deposits far exceed loans in Chinese banks. Nevertheless, this does not mean that China really has a surplus of capital in all dimensions of its economy. The planned economy and market economy still coexist and capital shortage remains a problem, specifically in less developed sectors and regions.

In most countries, the control over foreign investments has moved historically from strict control to a complete liberation through a gradual loosening of the procedures. However, the principal objective of China's internationalization strategy is not to give up management control, but to improve the efficiency of outward foreign investment. Currently the system is not satisfactory.

The weaknesses of China Overseas Investment Approval System

The Chinese government exercises its function of macroeconomic regulation, but also intervenes at a micro economic level as an investor of state-owned assets. This leads to a series of disadvantages:

— The numerous levels of control make the process inefficient. Overseas investment proposals of above US$1 million are examined and approved by five departments — the Chinese embassy, the local government or local branch of the State Council, the NDRC, the MOFCOM, and the State Administration of Foreign Exchange (SAFE). Chinese overseas investments under US$1 million are examined and approved by three departments — the Chinese Embassy, the local government (or branch of the State Council), and the Provincial Adminis-tration of Foreign Exchange. Within each department, there is also a bottom-up reporting system which drastically lowers efficiency and increases delays.
— The examination is too detailed: all government departments involved in the process pay excessive attention to the risks.
— There is a lack of transparency. The policies and regulations are treated as internal documents and are not made public, so companies have no clue about the real requirements. Quite often, when an enterprise has failed after several attempts, the correct way is gradually "discovered" by trial and error. The time limits for the procedure are seldom respected.
— Inadequate follow-up is also a problem. Once the investment is approved, the follow-up phase is neglected. Companies are regularly submitting financial reports, but there is no real monitoring process.

The negative consequences at the company level

First, companies can miss opportunities because of the uncertainty and delays of the procedure.

Second, before the approval of the feasibility report, companies face a dilemma in not being able to sign documents — including a legal commitment towards their foreign counterpart. If the project is not approved before the negotiations, the Chinese enterprise is not in a position to negotiate with its foreign partners and its reputation might be endangered if its project is rejected by the government. If the project is approved before negotiations, Chinese enterprises are in a negotiating difficult position to obtain a fair deal from the foreign partner.

Another negative consequence is that Chinese companies might be tempted to minimize the total amount of the investment or to split it into smaller separate projects in order to avoid examination by the NDRC. Alternatively, they might be tempted to invest first before submitting the project examination. In every case the system has a negative impact on corporate behavior.

The negative consequences at the government level

First, the evaluation of the business risk at a micro economic level which should be conducted at the company level, is conducted by the government, which takes the limited resources of each government department. Hence, the government cannot concentrate its resources and energy on the macroeconomic administration of foreign investment.

Another criticism is that the government fails to obtain sufficient knowledge and information on foreign investment, making it difficult to monitor the macro economic policy, and even more difficult to evaluate the risks of investment.

Furthermore, the overlapping of the government's examination and investment functions causes conflicts of interest among government departments. In order to safeguard its own interests, no department is willing to give up its examination authority. This phenomenon becomes an obstacle for the implementation of the internationalization strategy.

Finally, this system may mean that enterprises rely more on their personal connections, *guanxi*, eventually leading to corruption in order to circumvent the legal process.

2.3. *The Need for Reforms*

In order to execute the internationalization strategy, the system must be reformed. Although China has not reached the stage of a complete opening up of foreign investment, some enterprises are able to effectively invest abroad after many years of international experience. These enterprises are strong in innovation and product development, have achieved a large volume of domestic production, enjoy a large market share, and at the same time have a deep understanding of the international market through their export business. These enterprises have reorganized their ownership structure, separated management from ownership, and developed a modern managerial decision-making process. They have also assumed sole responsibility for their profits or losses. In addition, these enterprises have the drive to invest abroad. In the context of economic globalization and China's entry into the WTO, Chinese enterprises face severe international competition. Many enterprises realize that they need to grow internationally to survive, and that foreign investment can contribute to this goal.

How does investing in foreign countries help Chinese enterprises? First, foreign investment allows the circumvention of trade barriers. It can also make available first-hand information on market demand. Moreover, the best way to open up export markets for most consumer products is to set up a local after-sales service network, which necessitates foreign investment. Finally, foreign investment permits Chinese companies to acquire advanced technology and management expertise from foreign countries.

The essence of China's internationalization strategy is the combination of attracting foreign investment and investing abroad. These strategies optimize resource allocation and support China's economic development.

Many factors of China's development are interdependent and complementary, such as: the internationalization strategy, the diversification of geographic targets, the emphasis on quality and value addition, and the strategy of "Revitalizing Trade through Science and Technology", which is strengthened in China's 11th Five-Year Plan.

In the context of economic globalization, a country's international competitiveness is in some way determined by the strength of its multinational enterprises. Therefore, besides making up for the shortages in domestic resources and limitations of the domestic market, promoting the export of Chinese products, and learning foreign expertise, the internationalization strategy also aims to cultivate China's own multinational enterprises.

To sum up, China presently can invest abroad, and it is clear that China needs to do so.

However, the foreign investment administration system is still based on the 1991 policies that restrict large projects. It is true that the 1999 notification made foreign investments easier for projects like raw material processing, which is a partial breakthrough. Nonetheless, FDI is not limited to raw material. China's examination and approval system still needs to be reformed.

2.4. Promoting China's Outward Investment

Foreign Exchange Policy and Overseas Investment

The State Administration of Foreign Exchange (SAFE) is in charge of checking the origin of funds used for FDI. In 2003, the decision was made to simplify and decentralize the procedures for overseas mergers and investments by implementing the Notice on Furthering Reform of Foreign Exchange Administration of Overseas Investments, which led to the following system.

All investors making overseas investments must obtain foreign exchange approval from SAFE or its local counterpart, the Administrative Bureau of Foreign Exchange. Companies have to provide information about the planned purchase, the purchase agreements, and evaluation reports written by mediation agencies. Enterprises that have already made overseas investments and plan to increase their investment are required to submit the following the appraisal by the project's supervising department, the approval from the local Administrative Bureau of Foreign Exchange for the origins of the funds when the overseas enterprise was established, the approval for the remittance of the foreign exchange, the foreign exchange registration certificate of the overseas investments, the registration certificate of the overseas enterprises, and the business license. Put simply, the required materials and documents for examination are specified, so that it is easier for the enterprise planning on overseas investment to prepare accordingly for the administrative examination.

Since October 2002, SAFE instituted a pilot program in 14 provinces and cities in order to further simplify the procedure and manage it at a local level. In 2005, this measure was expanded to include all of China. SAFE has also defined guidelines to simplify and standardize the foreign exchange procedures in order to facilitate foreign investment and enhance China's economic development and "reform and opening up" policy.

China's Outward Investments Promotion Policy

China has always employed strict foreign exchange control on overseas investment. Starting in the 1980s, however, China loosened control of certain areas of foreign exchange control according to its economic plan, at the same time formulating policies to encourage overseas investment. Consequently, there was an upsurge in overseas investment in the 1980s. The poor financial performance of these overseas projects resulted in a return to tight control of overseas investment. After the Asian financial crisis in 1998, China adopted the strategy of encouraging enterprises to set up raw material processing plants abroad, in order to increase exports. This was China's first movement towards a policy of promoting outward FDI.

Economic Intelligence and Technical Support

Chinese embassies are the major source for information on overseas investment opportunities for Chinese companies. This information — which includes a description of the economic environment, the market, and the necessary legal structure — is disseminated through multiple channels such as international trade magazines and the MOFCOM's various web sites. The embassy is also in charge of reviewing the projects and sharing information with the companies involved on projects eligible for government funding, such as foreign trade development funds and foreign aid funds.

Some local governments in China also organize trade missions abroad and provide technical support to companies. The Fujian provincial government, for example, has an annual subsidy of RMB 100,000 to compensate companies for their feasibility studies and travel costs related to raw material processing projects.

The Chinese government has been providing this information service for overseas investment since the early 1980s. However, the quality of information remains limited in comparison with the US or Japan's trade organizations, where information is also provided by private companies. Thus, many Chinese companies are not sufficiently aware of the available sources of information on international investment opportunities, nor are they able to assess the quality of this information.

This might be due to the absence of a central organization responsible for information dissemination.

China's Financial Support and Overseas Investment Insurance System

To encourage raw materials processing and assembling projects, the People's Bank of China and the MOFTEC have passed a special regulation called the "Guidance for Granting Loans to Support the Overseas Processing of the Investor's Raw Materials and Assembling Operations."

Employing Article 4 of this regulation, the Commercial Bank and the Export-Import Bank of China (China Eximbank) can grant long-term and short-term loans to companies investing in such projects. Long- and medium-term loans (over one year) are given for the domestic purchase of the equipment and technology necessary to build the factory.

On the other hand, short-term loans (less than one year) are made to purchase raw materials, components, and parts needed for overseas processing, as well as for production expenses.

Loans are usually in Renminbi, but when overseas projects need foreign currency, the bank will grant short-term loans in foreign currency.

These loans are granted at a preferential interest rate, according to Article 6 of the regulation. The standard interest rate for domestic activities is generally applicable though it can be lower if, for instance, the host country benefits from China's foreign aid program. The central government foreign trade development fund subsidizes interest payments for both Renminbi and foreign exchange loans.

Priority is given to loans related to exports, such as credit for the export of all equipment, technology, components, parts, and raw materials required for the overseas processing projects.

Apart from loans, financial support is also available for Chinese enterprises involved in resource-seeking projects to buy Chinese equipment and technologies and to establish joint-ventures with local companies. These projects are evaluated by the China Eximbank and financed by two central government funds: the Foreign Trade Development Fund and the Foreign Aid Joint-Ventures and Cooperative Fund.

The same policy is conducted at a provincial level. The Fujian provincial government allocates 10 million RMB annually for loans at subsidized rates from its Provincial Foreign Trade Development Fund. Shenzhen provides an interest rate deduction of 2 percent on long- and medium-term loans for overseas trade involving processing.

Finally, according to the guidance provisions, Chinese investors normally have to be provided with a risk guarantee when they suffer economic losses because of political and non-commercial risks like war, currency exchange ban, requisition, or breach of contract by the host country government.

This system is still at an early stage of development and has many shortcomings. Financial support and insurance coverage are limited for the moment to overseas processing projects. Projects oriented towards technology, market expansion, or enhancing competitiveness are not eligible. Only SOEs can benefit from the system.

For ventures that are eligible, the budget is limited. China Export & Credit Insurance Corporation (SINOSURE), for instance, which was founded in 2001 and specializes in overseas investment insurance, has a registered capital of only RMB4 billion.

In addition, the administrative review process is too complex, time-consuming and costly. If a company wants to get a loan or insurance coverage even for a small project, it will have to go through many procedures and different administrative departments including the Ministry of Foreign Trade, the Foreign Trade Commission, and China Eximbank — each of which will repeat the whole examination process. Companies report that it may take at least six months to complete all the processes and sometimes the potential financial support does not even cover the administrative cost of the procedure.

Tax Policies and Overseas Investments

Two strategies are worth noting as part of the Chinese government's policy to encourage overseas processing projects: The first is to help companies to increase the scale of their operations and profits during a period of five years. After this time, the profits can be reinvested locally. The second strategy is that there is no value-added tax (VAT) levied on the sales of equipment or components necessary for the project, so the related input VAT is refunded.

Apart from the nation-wide VAT tax exemption and refund policy, China has not yet developed proactive measures to support outward FDI compared to other countries, where we see benefits like tax privileges and tax-loss benefits.

International Investment Agreements

In the past, China signed bilateral investment treaties (BITs) with 101 countries. When it signed these agreements, it was focusing on promoting inward FDI in China and not protecting outward FDI. In July 1986, China applied for admission to the WTO's predecessor, the General Agreement on Tariffs and Trade (GATT). Since entering the WTO in 2001, international Chinese investors have been protected by the Trade Related Investment Measures (TRIM).

Meanwhile, statistics show that from 1979 to 2001, overseas investments approved or filed by MOFCOM reached US$8.36 billion, and China had nearly 6610 enterprises in over 160 countries and regions. In order to support this growth,

China has to develop a new generation of BITs that offer more protection to its own international investors.

References

Cheng Siwei (ed.) (2001). Zhongguo jingwai touzi de zhanlue yu guanli (Strategies and Administration of China's Overseas Investment) *Minzhu yu jianshe cubanshe.*
Dunning, J.H. (1981). Explaining the International Direct Investment Position of Countries: Towards a Dynamic or Developmental Approach. *Weltwirtschaftliches Archiv,* pp. 30–64.
Dunning, J.H. (1988). *Explaining International Production.* London: Unwin Hyman.
Li Wenfeng (2001). Zhongguo kuaguo gongsi xianzhuang, wenti ji duice (Status, Problems and Countermeasures of China's Multinational Enterprises), *Gaige,* (5).
Lu Tong (2003). Zhongguo qiye kuaguo jingying zhanlue (Chinese Enterprises' Multinational Management Strategy) *Jingji guanli chubanshe.* Economy and Management Publishing House.
MOFCOM (2005). Provisions on Issues Concerning the Approval of Overseas Investment and Establishment of Enterprises.
MOFTEC International Cooperation Department and International Trade and Economic Cooperation Research Institute (2004). Zhongguo duiwai zhijie touzi xianzhuang yu fazhan qianjing (Current Status and Developmental Prospects of China's Foreign Direct Investment). *International Trade.*
MOFTEC, MOF and General Office of the State Council (1999). Circular No. 17 on Suggestions on Encouraging Enterprises to Develop Overseas Business in Processing and Assembling Business the Supplied Material.
Nan Zhenghua (2001). Zhongguo qiye kuaguo jingying de sikao yu jianyi (Reflections and Suggestions for Chinese enterprises' Multinational Management). *Guoji Jingji Hezuo,* (4).
National Bureau of Statistics of China (2006). *China Statistical Yearbook.*
UNCTAD (2006). *World Investment Report 2006 FDI from Developing and Transition Economies: Implications for Development.* New York and Geneva: United Nations.
Wang Zhile (ed.) (2003). Zouxiang shijie de zhongguo kuaguo gongsi (China's Multinational Companies Go Global) *Zhongguo shangye chubanshe,* Beijing: China Commercial Press.
Yan Dong, Jiang Ning, Liang Maolei (2004) in Beijing Xinhua Trust Consultation Co., *Zhongguo qiye haiwai shangshi diaocha baogao* (Investigation report on China's overseas listed enterprises in 2004) *21 Shiji Jingji Baodao* (21 Century Economic Report).
Zhang Xiaoji (ed.) (2003). Zhongguo duiwai kaifang de qianyan wenti (Leading Edge Problems Concerning China's Opening-up). *Zhongguo fazhan chubanshe* Beijing: Development Press of China.

Chapter 3

CHINA'S OUTWARD FOREIGN DIRECT INVESTMENT

Li Zhaoxi

Enterprise Research Institute —
Development Research Center of the State Council (DRC)

1. China's International Presence and Investment

The scale and scope of China's overseas investments are growing continuously and Chinese companies are enthusiastically implementing the internationalization strategy. Thus, China is increasing its international presence in all key dimensions of international business: foreign trade, contracted overseas projects, labor service cooperation, foreign direct investment, overseas M&A, international financial investments, creation of overseas Research and Development centers, agricultural cooperation, development of overseas resources, and investment in international high-tech ventures.

1.1. *China's Foreign Trade*

China's foreign trade volume increased from US$20.6 billion in 1978 to $509.8 billion in 2001. It grew continuously even when the world economy was growing slowly, during which time China moved from the 32nd most active trading nation position to the sixth the country upon growth accelerated entry into the WTO. In 2004, total imports and exports broke the US$1,000 billion level, reaching $1,150 billion.

China was becoming the world's third largest trading country after the United States and Germany, and before Japan. In 2005 the trend was confirmed when China's foreign trade reached US$1,422 billion. The country kept its position among the world's top three largest trading nations in 2006, when foreign commerce reached US$1,761 billion (+23.8 percent).

As for the structure of exports (Table 3.1), high-tech products and high value-added commodities which have good export potential continue to grow as a proportion of total exports. In 2003, over 50 percent of Chinese exports were high-tech commodities, such as electronic products. Foreign-owned companies contribute most to these results, even if Chinese enterprises are also progressing in the export of high-tech and high value-added products.

Table 3.1: China's Export Value Major Commodities (2007 January to June).

Commodity	Value (*)	Percent of change 2007/2006
Machinery and Electronic Product	309,946	27.1
New and hi-tech Product	152,870	23.9
Automatic data processing equipment and components	54,609	35.2
Accessories of garment and dress	48,307	21.7
Yarn, fabric and products	25,218	9.8
Steel	22,399	136.4
Agricultural Product	17,241	22.6
Telephone set	17,033	11.7
Spare parts for automatic data processing equipment	14,977	3.1
Footwear	11,961	17.2
Integrated circuit	10,924	21.2
Furniture and parts	10,144	22.5
Plastic products	7,105	12.5
Auto accessories	5,516	33.9
Shipping	5,424	60.7
Travel goods and bags	4,971	22.6
Components of TV, radio and telecommunication equipment	4,624	−59.5
Insulated wire and cable	4,415	43.2
Air-conditioner	4,390	23.6
Product oil	4,366	30.5
Printed circuit board	4,352	29.6
Device and parts for circuitry	4,246	29.2

Source: MOFCOM.   Unit: US$ million

Table 3.2: China's Top Ten Export Markets (2007–6 first months).

Rank	Country (Region)	Jan.–Jun.	Percentage
	Total Value	546, 7	100.0
1	European Union	107, 9	19.7
2	U.S.A.	107, 2	19.6
3	Hong Kong	83, 9	15.3
4	Japan	48, 0	8.8
5	ASEAN	42, 5	7.8
6	Republic of Korea	26, 3	4.8
7	Taiwan	11, 0.	2.0
8	Russia	10, 7	2.0
9	India	10, 2	1.9
10	Canada	8, 9	1.6

Source: MOFCOM 2007.   Unit:US$ billion

China's foreign trade is also progressing in terms of geographic diversity. China's foreign trade partners are mainly developed countries. Among them, the European Union (EU) is China's number one trade partner and export market (Table 3.2). China's trade with South-east Asia, Latin America and Africa is growing rapidly. In 2004, the trade value between China and South-east Asian countries exceeded US$100 billion.

Since China's adoption of the "reform and opening up" policy, China has maintained a 14.5 percent annual foreign trade growth rate. This exceeds the average growth rate of the world economy and world trade. The reasons for such continuous rapid growth are described below.

First, China seized the opportunities created by the three rounds of adjustments to the world economic structure. The Chinese government has always emphasized seeking opportunities, strengthening reform and widening the opening up policy. The first opportunity occurred in 1980. The worldwide adjustment of industrial structures enabled. China's foreign trade to enter the rapid development stage. At the beginning of the 1990s, China put great effort into the exporting of manufactured goods, especially electromechanical products. Hence, China's export composition was further improved. Since the 1990s, the export of China's high-tech products, represented by the IT and electronic industries, has increased notably, and now makes up over 30 percent of total exports. The composition of China's export commodities continues to be optimized.

Second, China has always paid great attention to the improvement of the investment environment and the attraction of foreign investment. The country has achieved a lot in both respects. Since China's reform and liberalization, the inward Foreign Direct Investment (FDI) has grown steadily, especially in the processing sector. In recent years, the international specialization of industry has increased, and foreign investment has advanced the development of China's foreign trade.

China's adjustment of foreign trade polices was timely in view of the foreign trade system reform. This can be seen with the reform of the foreign trade contract system, the transfer of foreign trade management rights, the reforms of the examination and approval system, and the fact that non-governmental companies can manage foreign trade directly. Factors such as China's entry into the WTO and China's new foreign exchange policies contributed to China's economic growth. Until 2004, SOEs were responsible for 30 percent of total imports and exports; private enterprises, 17 percent, and the growth rate was 70 percent. Generally speaking, the government stimulated all levels of economic activity to boost foreign trade.

Finally, over the 30 years of China's reform and opening up, the Chinese economy has maintained continuous growth, with an annual growth rate of 9 percent. This laid a solid foundation for the development of foreign trade.

1.2. *International Contracting Projects and Labor Export Services*

China's overseas contracted projects started at the end of the 1970s and contributed to China's foreign aid policy, becoming an important element of the country's opening-up to the outside world. After 25 years of development, China's overseas contracts have experienced phenomenal growth (Table 3.3).

From 1985 to 2003, the turnover of contracted projects increased from US$663 million to US$13.837 billion. This represents a more than 20-fold increase. The value of contracted projects continued to grow, reaching US$17.47 billion in 2004 and US$21.76 in 2005.

The scope of such operations has also expanded. In the beginning, the contracted projects consisted mainly of construction work, such as building of houses and roads. Now, operations are diversified and include not only traditional operations such as construction, but also more technologically-demanding operations such as telecommunications, power plants, infrastructure, water supply, sewage disposal, and petrochemicals.

The nature of contracts also changed from subcontracting to general contracts, then gradually developed into fund-raising contracts, and finally dominated by BOT, BOO, and BOOT contracts.

China's contracted projects are conducted in over 180 countries and regions.

China has nearly 2,000 enterprises that are qualified to carry out overseas contracted projects and labor cooperation. In 2001, the American magazine *ENR* listed 39 Chinese enterprises among the world's 225 largest international contractors. Eleven of these Chinese enterprises were among the world's top 200 design firms and China was among the top 10 project-contracting countries in the world.

Table 3.3:   China's Overseas Contracts.

Year	Number of contracts	Contract value (US$ billion)	Annual turnover value (US$ billion)
1985	465	1.116	0.663
1989	776	1.781	1.484
1990	920	2.125	1.644
1991	1171	2.524	1.97
1992	1164	5.251	2.403
1993	1393	5.189	3.668
1994	1702	6.028	4.883
1995	1558	7.484	5.108
1996	1634	7.728	5.821
1997	2085	8.516	6.036
1998	2322	9.243	7.769
1999	2527	10.199	8.522
2000	2597	11.719	8.379
2001	5836	13.039	8.899
2002	4036	15.055	11.194
2003	3708	17.667	13.837
2004	n.c.	23.840	17.470
2005	n.c.	29.600	21.760
2006	n.c.	66.000	30.000

Among these large Chinese contractors, specialized companies such as China State Construction Engineering Corporation (CSCEC) or Shanghai Construction Group have acquired a real advantage over their international competitors in construction and labor export services. CSCEC —- a state-owned enterprise established in 1982 — was the largest construction enterprise and the largest international contractor in China in 2005 (Table 3.4). Among design firms, two Chinese firms were listed among the top ten world-wide: China Railway Engineering and China Railway Construction.

Since the 1990s, the scale, means, structure, and content of international contracted projects have all changed fundamentally. New conditions offer new opportunities for China's overseas contracted projects, while posing new challenges at the same time.

Opportunities and Challenges for Chinese Construction Enterprises

Chinese companies benefit from three positive factors:

Table 3.4:   Top 10 Chinese International Contractors (2005).

Rank	Enterprise	Turnover US$ million
1	China State Construction Engineering Corporation (CSCEC)	2076, 1
2	Huawei Technologies Co., Ltd	1925, 3
3	China Petroleum Engineering & Construction (Group) Corporation	552, 5
4	Great Wall Drilling Company	538, 7
5	China National Machinery & Equipment Import & Export Corporation	482, 2
6	Sinohydro Corporation	460, 2
7	Shanghai Bell Alcatel Business System Co., Ltd	352, 2
8	China Harbour Engineering Company Ltd	34, 9
9	China National Petroleum Corporation BGP	329, 3
10	Shanghai Zhenhua Port Machinery Co., Ltd	316, 4

Source: MOFCOM.

1. The construction market is growing faster than the commodity sector and is a relatively open market at the international level. Thus, according to WTO regulations, member countries — especially developed countries — will have to further open their domestic construction market to foreign enterprises.

2. There is strong demand in both developed markets and emerging economies for national infrastructure construction projects. The demand is mainly driven by new technologies in developed markets while the necessity to create the appropriate infrastructure for economic development drives demand in emerging markets. Asian countries have largely recovered from the financial crisis of 1997 and have reopened their construction markets. Most governments have taken advantage of globalization in changing their method of contracting to prevent corruption, enhance efficiency, and lower costs. Governments have adopted international public bidding for construction projects which offer Chinese construction companies good opportunity to enter the international market.

3. The development of outward FDI also creates opportunity for construction companies, especially in greenfield projects which require building the appropriate infrastructure and manufacturing facilities from scratch, as well as installing and adjusting the equipment. Chinese construction companies also benefit from the internationalization strategy, including support in terms of loan and guarantees for the development of overseas processing and assembling plants

However the companies also face several new challenges:

1. Competition has become more severe due to the growing number of contract projects and the globalization of the sector. This has led to a transformation of the nature of the contracts and their technologic sophistication, as well as a transformation of financing abilities in cases where contractors have to provide financial solutions. There is also a tendency to combine project design and consulting services. More and more mergers and regroupings are occurring among international construction companies, and the degree of professionalism is increasing with the use of IT, e-networks and e-commerce. Such technology simplifies the bidding process and enhances the efficiency of project design and management.
2. The reform process of Chinese SOEs has put new constraints on Chinese government-controlled construction and engineering companies. At the company level, the board of directors is more careful about investments in high risk areas. At the banking level, state-owned banks and financial institutions are also much more cautious about loans and guarantees for potentially risky projects.
3. In 2001 when China signed the agreement to join the WTO, it did not sign the multilateral WTO Government Procurement Agreement (GPA) — which has 40 signatories including a large majority of WTO developed member states. Hence, Chinese construction enterprises have not been able to enter the government procurement market. However, China started negotiations for its accession to the WTO GPA in 2007.
4. The management of China's international contracts is facing severe constraints due in part to the administrative process, especially the examination and approval system and the foreign exchange control regime.

China's Overseas Labor Cooperation

By the end of 2003, the total value of China's foreign labor cooperation was US$32.6 billion, with a turnover of US$27.1 billion. In 2003, the value of new contracts was US$3.1 billion, with revenues of US$3.3 billion (Table 3.5).

The major markets for China's foreign labor services are in developing countries. Three-quarters of the labor is sent to Asian countries, and a small percentage to developed countries. The main components are medium or low-level labor such as construction and sewage workers. But high-level labor is increasing continually, such as sailors, computer software engineers, project consultants, and doctors. China's international competitiveness is gradually being enhanced.

Sending labor abroad not only provides job opportunities for the people and create a large amount of foreign exchange income for the country, but also enhances the quality of labor and improves the development of relevant industries such as domestic airlines and telecommunications. Sending labor abroad has become the most competitive export pattern for China's service sector. By the end of

Table 3.5: China's Export Labor Service Cooperation.

Year	Number of contracts	Contract value (US$ billion)	Turnover (US$ billion)
1985	458	0.149	0.172
1989	2324	0.431	0.202
1990	4255	0.478	0.223
1991	7267	1.085	0.393
1992	8241	1.335	0.646
1993	10212	1.611	0.870
1994	15789	1.960	1.095
1995	17397	2.007	1.347
1996	22723	2.280	1.712
1997	25743	2.550	2.165
1998	23191	2.390	2.276
1999	18173	2.632	2.623
2000	20474	2.991	2.813
2001	33358	3.328	3.177
2002	30163	2.752	3.071
2003	38043	3.087	3.309
2004	n.c.	3.500	3.750
2005	n.c.	4.250	4.800
2006	n.c.	5.230	5.370

Source: China Statistical Yearbook, China Statistics Press (1985–2007).

April 2007, accumulated turnover of China's labor service overseas amounted to US$42.84 billion, with a contract value of US$47.38 billion. The total number of Chinese overseas workers at that time was 392,600.

1.3. *China's Outward Foreign Direct Investment (FDI)*

Rapid Growth of China's Outward FDI

China's outward FDI has grown rapidly from 1978 to 2002 (Table 3.6). The stock of outward FDI which was US$131 million in 1985 reached US$35 billion by the end of 2002.

China already ranked sixth among 118 emerging economies in terms of outward investment (Table 3.7).

The annual flow of FDI has increased more rapidly since China' entry into the WTO; in 2005 it reached US$12.3 billion, of which US$3.8 billion capital stocks,

Table 3.6: China's Outward FDI Flows (1979–2006) Non financial investments sector.

Year	Annual outward FDI (US$ million)	Average investment value per enterprise (US$ thousand)
1979–1983	9.2	800
1984–1992	208	1400
1993–1998	705	1060
1999–2001	678	2180
2002	2700	2810
2003	2850	4090
2004	3620	4367
2005	6920	6485
2006	17630	n.c.

Source: Ministry of Commerce — National Bureau of Statistics State.

Table 3.7: Ranking of Outward FDI Stock Among Developing Economies.

Rank	Region/Country	Stock (US$ million)	Share (percent)
1	Hong Kong	370, 296	(43.59)
2	Singapore	71, 336	(8.40)
3	Taiwan	59, 553	(7.01)
4	Brazil	53, 227	(6.27)
5	Republic of Korea	43, 500	(5.12)
6	China	35, 538	(4.18)
7	South Africa	28, 755	(3.39)
8	Virgin Islands	23, 722	(2.79)
9	Malaysia	20, 194	(2.38)
10	Cayman Islands	20, 026	(2.36)
Other Developing Economies		123, 317	(14.52)
Total Developing Economies		849, 464	(100)

Source: UNCTAD (2003), World Investment Report 2003, Annex Table B.4., pp. 262–265.

US$3.2 billion reinvested profits, and US$5.26 billion other forms of investments. This represents an increase of 123 percent over 2004 (UNCTAD, 2006).

At the end of 2005, China's total net stock of FDI was US$57.2 billion and 6,426 mainland companies were investing abroad (NBS). Chinese investments accounted

Table 3.8: Outward FDI by Provinces and Cities, 2005.

Rank	Provinces and cities	Outward FDI (US$ billion)
1	Shanghai	6.7
2	Zhejiang	1.8
3	Shandong	1.6
4	Guangdong	1.1
5	Jiangsu	1.0
6	Hebei	0.8
7	Beijing	0.8
8	Fujian	0.7
9	Henan	0.6
10	Heilongjiang	0.5

Source: MOFCOM.

respectively for 1.68 percent of the global annual net FDI flow and 0.59 percent the global net FDI stock (UNCTAD, 2006).

According to China's 11th Five-Year Plan, the country's overseas investment stock (other than banks, insurances and securities enterprises) will reach the US$60 billion level between 2006 and 2010.

The contribution to outward FDI varies considerably from one region to another, with Shanghai and Zhejiang province leading the pack in 2005 (Table 3.8).

China's Overseas Investment is Still at the Take-Off Stage

Although China's outward FDI has grown rapidly since 2001, China's FDI capital stock is still very low compared with developed countries such as the United States and Japan. By the end of 2002, Japan's FDI capital stock was US$3,450 billion, and that of the United States was US$6,891 billion. China's FDI stock was US$35 billion — which equals to only 1 percent of Japan's FDI stock and 5/1000ths percent of US FDI stock.

In terms of stage of development, Chinese FDI in 2003 could be compared to the level of Britain and France at the end of 19th century. In comparative financial terms, Britain in 1882 and France in 1892 had an equivalent volume of outward FDI stock abroad, but their investment started to surge only at the beginning of the 20th century. China is still at a very early stage of investment and does not have a major role at the global level.

However, China's outward FDI has already had extremely positive effects on the Chinese economy. It helps to expand production capacities and enter new markets, thus creating new job opportunities and increasing exports. It also creates the opportunity to start building the image of Chinese companies abroad. FDI has also provided new sources of financing for international expansion. Overall, it laid the foundation for the advancement of the internationalization process of Chinese companies.

Orientation of China's Outward FDI

In terms of geography, Chinese FDI in the eighties focused on Hong Kong and Macao and had little presence in developed markets such as the United States, Europe and Japan. In 2000, outward FDI went to new frontiers, especially the emerging economies of Asia, Latin America and Africa.

In 2005, Chinese companies were present in 163 countries and regions, with Hong Kong being the favorite destination, followed by the Cayman Islands and British Virgin Islands. China's presence is especially strong in Asia with Hong Kong and Republic of Korea as leading destinations, representing 71 percent of cumulative investments. Latin America follows at 20 percent (mainly the Cayman Islands), then Africa (3 percent), Europe (3 percent), North America (2 percent) and Oceania (1 percent) (Tables 3.9 and 3.10).

With regard to industry and type of international operations, China has also diversified its portfolio of activities to include international trade, shipping, international contracting, mining, manufacturing. Resource-seeking investments including oil and mining projects have increased especially rapidly.

Table 3.9: China's Net Outward FDI, by Region, 2005.

Country or region	Net outward FDI 2005 (US$ billion)	Cumulative net outward FDI — end of 2005 (US$ billion)	Share of total (percent)
Asia	4.4	40.6	71
[*Hong Kong*]	[*3.4*]	[*36.5*]	[*64*]
[*Republic of Korea*]	[*0.6*]	[*0.9*]	[*2*]
Africa	0.4	1.6	3
Europe	0.5	1.6	3
Latin America	6.5	11.5	20
[*Cayman Islands*]	[*5.2*]	[*8.9*]	[*16*]
[*Virgin Islands (UK)*]	[*1.2*]	[*2.0*]	[*3*]
North America	0.3	1.3	2
Oceania	0.2	0.7	1
Total	12.3	57.2	100

Source: *China Statistical Yearbook* 2006.

Table 3.10:   China's Top 20 Outward FDI, by Country or region, 2005.

Country or Region	Cumulative net outward FDI — end of 2005 (US$100 million)
1 Hong Kong	365.1
2 Cayman Islands	89.4
3 Virgin Islands (UK)	19.8
4 Republic of Korea	8.8
5 United States	8.2
6 Macao	6.0
7 Australia	5.9
8 Russia	4.7
9 Sudan	3.5
10 Singapore	3.2
11 Germany	2.7
12 Vietnam	2.3
13 Algeria	1.7
14 Japan	1.5
15 Thailand	2.2
16 Mexico	1.4
17 Indonesia	1.4
18 South Africa	1.1
19 United Kingdom	1.1
20 Canada	1.0

Source: *China Statistical Yearbook* 2006.

Since 1999, the Chinese government has strongly encouraged investments abroad of processing and assembly enterprises. The most active industries have been textile, household electrical appliances, electromechanical products, chemicals, and pharmaceuticals. Chinese enterprises were present in a wide range of industries in 2005. Leasing and business services ranked first (29 percent) followed by wholesale and retail trade (20 percent), Mining (15 percent), Transportation (12 percent), and Manufacturing (10 percent). China also started developing international agricultural cooperation and deep-sea fishing projects, (Table 3.11).

In terms of ownership structure, China's outward investment is more and more diversified, with large-scale enterprises playing the most significant part. China has 30,000 enterprises involved in international investment and operations, of which 1,600 enterprises are in the international contracting and export labor services. Limited-liability companies have overtaken SOEs to become China's largest investor in the overseas market. Their cumulative investment represents 32 percent of investments, while SOEs account for 29 percent.

Finally the type of investment has also changed considerably, and Chinese companies are entering the Mergers and Acquisitions (M&A) game.

Table 3.11: China's Outward FDI (Non-financial), 2005.

Sector	Net overseas direct investment 2005 (US$ billion)	Accumulated net overseas direct investment — end of 2005 (US$ billion)	Share of total (percent)
Leasing and business services	4.9	16.6	29
Wholesale and retail trade	2.3	11.4	20
Mining	1.7	8.7	15
Transport, storage and post	0.6	7.1	12
Manufacturing	2.3	5.8	10
Real estate	0.1	1.5	3
Information transmission, computer services and software	0.0	1.3	2
Services to households and other services	0.1	1.3	2
Construction	0.1	1.2	2
Other	0.2	2.3	5
Total	12.3	57.2	100

Source: *China Statistical Yearbook* 2006.

1.4. *Cross-Border M&A*

Recent Evolution

Chinese overseas M&A have taken off only in recent years. Before 2003, SOEs mainly went abroad to acquire energy and raw material companies in order to provide natural resources for the country. Chinese enterprises began to make acquisitions overseas beginning in the early 1980s. Typical cases included the Shougang Group which acquired the Hierro Peru iron ore mine from the Peruvian government (1992); the Ministry of Railway and China Minmetals Corporation that jointly purchased the Sydney Steel Factory (1994); CITIC Group that acquired the Jiahua Bank, listed in Hong Kong.

At that time, the Chinese economy was still at the early transitional stage, changing from a planned economy to a market economy. Thus government played a decisive role in overseas M&As and the country's national interest was the major motivation for overseas acquisitions (Table 3.12).

After 2003, mainly non-governmental businesses went abroad to acquire foreign companies, developing their international strategies according to market rules. Large scale M&A appeared only gradually (Table 3.13).

Since 2003, overseas acquisitions by Chinese enterprises have maintained a high growth rate. According to MOFCOM, M&A accounted for half of China's

Table 3.12:   Crossborder M&A by Chinese Companies (US$ million).*

Year	1990	1995	2000	2001	2002	2003
	60	249	470	452	1,047	1,647

Source: UNCTAD, 2004.
*The data cover the deals involving the acquisition of an equity stake of more
than 10 percent.

outward FDI in 2005. Other sources estimated that it could have exceeded US$14
billion (DRC, 2006).

Chinese Government and Company Attitudes Towards M&A

A key preoccupation of the Chinese government in 2000 was the restructuring
and reform of SOEs to reduce their share of the national economy. A second
objective was to increase Chinese companies' competitiveness and facilitate the
emergence of top-quality enterprises through various forms of cooperation with
foreign companies. This objective was even more important after China's entry
into the WTO.

At the same time, the strategy of Chinese companies started to focus more on
core business than on size. They began to seize opportunities to grow more quickly
in their core business through acquisitions of foreign assets in China and abroad.

Acquiring resources and brands are the two main objectives of Chinese cross-
border M&A. Relatively speaking, China lacks natural resources and the gap
between demand and supply has widened since China became the world's manufacturing center. This explains the resource-seeking investments of Chinese companies. They need such natural resources for production in industries such as oil
and gas, mining, steel, electricity, and the consumer durable goods industries.

1.5. Overseas Listing of Chinese Enterprises

China's Overseas IPOs

In 2004, 84 Chinese enterprises were listed on overseas stock markets. This
represents an increase of 75 percent from the previous year, and amounts to a
paid-up capital of US$11.15 billion (Sinotrust Consulting, 2004). At the same
time, the Shenzhen and Shanghai exchanges listed 98 new shares and collected
US$4.3 billion, the lowest amount taken since 1997. The capital pooled by Chinese
enterprises through Initial Public Offerings (IPOs) in other countries was three
times the amount on the Chinese mainland.

Table 3.13: Major overseas M&A by Chinese Enterprises (Jan. 2002–Jan. 2005).

Industry	Date	Acquiring corporation	Acquired company	Country or Region
Petroleum	Jan. 2002	China National Offshore Oil Corporation (CNOOC)	86 percent Repsol-YPF Indonesia assets	Indonesia
	Apr. 2002	PetroChina	10 percent Devon Energy Corporation	Indonesia
	Oct. 2003	CNOOC	13 percent oil & gas assets (Gorgon Liquified Natural Gas Field)	Australia
	June 2005	PetroChina	100 percent Petrokazakhstan	Kazakhstan
Mining	June 2002	Shanghai Baosteel Group Corporation	46 percent Hamersley	Australia
Automobile	Sept. 2004	SAIC (Shanghai Automobile Group)	48.9 percent Ssangyong Motor	Republic of Korea
Household electronic appliances	June 2001 to Sept. 2002	BOE Technology	100 percent Hyundai Display Technology — Hydis	Republic of Korea
	Sept. 2002	TCL Group	Schneider Electronics	Germany
	Nov. 2003	TCL Group	67 percent Thomson SA	France
Information Technology				
	Nov. 2002	China Netcom Group	Asia Global Crossing	USA/Bermuda
	Nov. 2004	Shanda Entertainment	28.96 percent Actoz Soft Co. Ltd	Republic of Korea
	Dec. 2004	Lenovo	100 percent IBM's PC business	USA
	Jan. 2005	China Netcom Group	20 percent PCCW	Hong Kong

Source: Company sources and drcnet.com.cn.

Although the number of listed companies was increasing rapidly (up 75 percent), the growth rate of the capital collected (59 percent) was lower than the growth rate of the number of companies compared to 2003. Many Chinese enterprises had to lower their IPOs and reduce collected funds in order to satisfy international investors.

Overseas expansion has been characterized since the beginning by a series of difficulties:

— Class actions against China Life Insurance Co, the country's biggest insurer, at the time of its Initial Public Offering (IPO) in Hong Kong and the USA in 2003.
— The 2004 scandal of insider trading at China Aviation Oil Corporation listed in Singapore, a subsidiary of Chinese SOE Aviation Oil Holding Company.
— Extended scrutiny by the US Committee on Foreign Investment of Lenovo's proposed acquisition of IBM's PC division in 2005.

Around this time, the Chinese government started to monitor overseas listings more closely in order to ensure better transparency, better governance, and the prevention of losses of state assets.

Chinese Companies Listed in Hong Kong, Singapore and the US

For years, Hong Kong, the United States, and Singapore have been the most popular destinations for mainland China's state-owned companies to raise funds.

In 2004, most Chinese enterprises chose to be listed in Hong Kong, then Singapore, followed the United States. Forty-Three Chinese enterprises were newly listed in Hong Kong, 31 in Singapore and 10 in the United States (Table 3.14).

Although SOEs accounted for only 18 percent of newly listed Chinese overseas enterprises, they accounted for 75 percent of the total of capital in 2004. Large IPO projects were basically all from SOEs. Their first choice was to be listed in New York, though sometimes they wanted to be listed in both New York and Hong Kong.

The Hong Kong Stock Exchange had just revised its listing rules to attract large-scale mainland China SOEs, while Singapore was not very attractive because of procedures and limitations for these companies at that time.

In 2004 the largest amount of capital collected by Chinese enterprises through overseas IPOs was from Hong Kong, totaling nearly US$7 billion. The United States contributed the next largest amount with US$3.5 billion. Singapore listings collected only USD$589 million. However, the United States contributed the most in terms of average capital investment in Chinese enterprises' IPOs, followed by Hong-Kong and Singapore.

Though the regulations were more severe in the USA, and the listing cost was higher, the American markets were more attractive than Hong Kong because it was

Table 3.14: Characteristics of Chinese Enterprises Listed in Hong Kong, Singapore and the United States.

Characteristics	Hong Kong	Singapore	USA
Capital collected	US$6.99 billion	US$0.589 billion	US$3.57 billion
Number of newly listed companies	43	31	10
Price-earning ratios	10–20 times	10 times	30–50 times
Investors' preference	Manufacturing, IT — communication industry	Manufacturing, IT — communication industry, food/agriculture	High-tech companies, IT — communication industry
Percentage of newly listed state-owned enterprises	30%	0	20%
Fund raising situation	Easy	Relatively easy	Average
Market liquidity	High	Relatively high	Average
Time needed for to be listed	Short	Short	Very short

Source: Sinotrust Consulting Co. Research Report 2004.

possible to raise large amounts of money and benefit from a higher price-earning ratio, especially for high-tech operations in the IT and communication sectors.

In 2005, 32 Chinese enterprises were listed on the New York Stock Exchange (NYSE), including 17 from mainland China, 10 from Hong Kong, and five from Taiwan (Table 3.15).

These enterprises are listed through the American Depositary Receipts (ADR) program on the NYSE where their shares can be traded.

Relatively speaking, Chinese enterprises were not as familiar with the United States and Singapore markets as with the Hong Kong market. That has changed though. Since 2004 the number of companies listed in Singapore has grown rapidly and the Singapore Stock Exchange strengthened its publicity in China, encouraging China's small and medium-sized enterprises to be listed in Singapore.

Singapore positioned itself as a Pan-Asian stock exchange market so Chinese enterprises obviously were the major clients that Singapore wanted to recruit. Yet, compared with Hong Kong's stock exchange, Singapore's was relatively small.

In 2004, the newly listed Chinese enterprises in Singapore were all small and medium-sized non-governmental business. The percentage of food/agriculture, environment, and textile industries was higher in Singapore than in Hong Kong, probably owing to the relatively small scale of enterprises in this sector. Conversely, companies in the financial, energy and real estate sectors chose Hong Kong.

Table 3.15: Chinese Mainland Companies Listed at New York Stock Exchange (Feb. 2005).

Aluminum Corp. of China Ltd.
China Eastern Airlines Corporation Limited
China Life Insurance Company Limited
China Mobile (Hong Kong) Ltd.
China Netcom Group Corporation (Hong Kong) Limited
China Petroleum & Chemical Corporation
China Southern Airlines Company Limited
China Telecom Corporation Limited
China Unicom
Guangshen Railway Co. Ltd.
Huaneng Power International Inc.
Jilin Chemical Industrial Company, Ltd.
PetroChina Company Ltd.
Semiconductor Manufacturing International Corporation
Sinopec Shanghai Petrochemical Company Limited
Suntech Power Holdings Co., Ltd.
Yanzhou Coal Mining Co. Ltd.

Source: New York Stock Exchange (NYSE).

Hong Kong has been the first-choice listing destination for mainland Chinese companies since the late 1990s. At the end of 2006, 96 Chinese companies were listed on the main board in the Hong Kong bourse H-share, while 47 smaller Chinese companies were listed on the GEM, the second board of the Hong Kong stock exchange (China Securities Regulatory Commission, Jan 2007).

At the end of 2006, China Securities Regulatory Commission (CSRC) began to promote the Shanghai and Shenzhen stock markets for listing private companies, while State-owned Assets Supervision and Administration Commission of the State Council (SASAC) on the SOE's side was recommending Hong Kong as the first choice for overseas listing.

2. Chinese Companies' International Challenges

2.1. *Large Corporations*

China's overseas investment is dominated by large companies. Their presence is very strong in all dimensions of China's international activities: overseas engineering contracts, overseas labor cooperation, and overseas investment — all activities that have been growing at high volumes since 2001.

The annual turnover of Overseas Engineering Contracts increased to US$13.8 billion in 2003 and the average contract value climbed to US$50 million. In this sector dominated by large companies (especially SOEs), the Engineering, Procurement and Construction (EPC) contracts still form the majority of deals, but more advanced forms of contracts such as BOT are becoming more popular, such as:

— oil and natural gas exploration projects in Kazakhstan (US$140 million),
— digital telecoms project in Bangladesh (US$214 million),
— the Merowe Dam project in Sudan (Euro 556 million),
— the Subiya water supply project in Kuwait (US$109 million).

Overseas labor-cooperation projects have faced difficulties from external conditions such as the SARS epidemic, the war in Iraq, the instability of some financial markets, as well as a recession in the labor market. In some countries the market was saturated with very intense competition on price. In response, the Ministry of Commerce introduced measures to improve the efficiency of sectors dominated by large companies and to explore new markets. This activity continued to increase through 2006.

China's outward FDI grew tremendously and became more country-diversified after the entry into the WTO.

Asia remains the main target of overseas investments, but China's presence is growing both in developed economies such as the USA and Europe, and in markets such as Africa, Russia, Central Asia, Latin America and Asian countries.

Chinese investment is based on three pillars: resource seeking investments (oil, gas, and mining), overseas processing and assembling business, and wholesale and retail.

The number of resource-seeking projects has increased continuously as well as the amount of investment per project. Typical examples are:

— China National Fishery Corporation (CNFC): fisheries in West Africa,
— China International Trust and Investment Corp. (CITIC): aluminum projects in Australia,
— China Metallurgical Group Corp. (MCC): iron ore mining in Australia

These investments have helped reduce the risk of resource shortage, increased the nation's strategic resource reserves, and helped safeguard the nation's economic stability and security.

The main players of China's globalization are large or very large corporations, SOEs or publicly owned companies in which the state has a relative majority of share control:

— Large SOEs are key in the international contacting business, the overseas labor services, and the energy and raw material overseas investments. Their share of outward FDI was 29 percent in 2005 compared to 43 percent in 2003.

— State Foreign Trade Corporations (FTCs) and large-scale trading corporations, which have been the pioneers of Chinese exports, have kept an important place in China's international operations.
— Large production-oriented enterprises have the specific advantages necessary to enter the internationalization process: huge domestic production facilities and sales networks, relatively mature production technologies, R&D capabilities, and full foreign-trade rights. These companies are late-comers of international management experience, but they have the resources of funding, technology, access to markets, and management skills to expand rapidly in international markets.
— Large-scale insurance and financial service companies such as Ping An Life Insurance Company of China, Ping An Insurance Co. and PICC Property and Casualty Co. have the financial resources and the management capabilities to make large overseas investments. Such investments have been encouraged since 2007 by the new regulations issued by China Insurance Regulatory Commission.

2.2. *Private Companies and SMEs*

The growing presence of non-governmental business in the internationalization process is an important phase of development for the Chinese economy. Private companies represented 14 percent of Chinese outward FDI in 2004. A number of private enterprises have thus already developed and managed their international operations successfully in a variety of industries. Examples of such enterprises are: Haier and Jiangsu Little Swan Company (home appliances), Wanxiang (automotive components), Broad Air-Conditioning Co., the New Hope Group, or Chongqing Lifan Industry Group (the largest Chinese private motorcycle manufacturer).

At this early stage of development, some companies that wanted to internationalize had to retreat in face of difficulties.

The Motivation to Go Abroad

In the past, China encouraged mainly large SOEs to go abroad and develop their international operations, strictly limiting the investments of non-governmental business. Few of them had clear competitive advantages over their foreign rival and they lacked international business experience. They usually met with more difficulties and risks than SOEs. The Chinese government did not offer them information, legal assistance, or consulting support.

After 2001 Chinese private companies still had difficulties successfully developing their internationalization process, but the domestic market was at a stage of over-capacity and companies were looking for new outlets. Thus, Chinese entry into the WTO was a major opportunity to find new markets overseas.

Many companies followed the same sequence of moves in international markets:

— Exporting first, then investing. Exporting helped them analyze foreign markets and business environments, accumulate experience, and generate capital. They would then consider investing and setting up production facilities locally.
— Entering first in joint-ventures, then looking for 100 percent ownership and control. Joint-ventures helped Chinese companies gain experience on how to do business locally, before exercising full control and investing in greenfield projects to increase their presence in the local market.
— Starting first with labor-intensive products, and then moving to technology-intensive products. Chinese private enterprises first build their production capacity in China for their low labor cost advantage. After accumulating financial resources and developing competitive advantages, then they go abroad with more technology-intensive products.
— Starting first with foreign technology, and then developing proprietary technology. The first phase generates the capital and the capabilities making it possible to invest successfully in new proprietary process or product innovation.
— Starting first in emerging markets, and then investing in developed economies. Based on the evaluation of their competitive advantages, the majority of Chinese firms have focused first on emerging markets of Asia, Latin America or Africa in order to reduce the cost of management and organization, and to minimize the risk of failure.

Chinese private companies, especially small and medium-sized enterprises (SMEs), face administrative difficulties in developing their international activity compared to SOEs.

They suffer from the complexity and rigidity of the approval process. Frequently, they have to seek coverage under the umbrella of a SOE or collective enterprise by paying a fee in order to operate internationally. This situation is unsatisfactory for the company and administration of overseas investments.

SMEs suffer from the restrictions on import and export rights. Since 2002, SOEs and collective enterprises have been "self-operated enterprises": they enjoy import and export rights and are free to establish import and export organization when and where appropriate.

The majority of private companies still have to use the services of a foreign trade agency which increases cost and the risk of leaking business secrets.

They also lack financial support. Import and Export banks have a key role in financing outward FDI, but the China Eximbank's loan policy traditionally focuses on international investments for large companies of outstanding reputation, excluding in a sense many SMEs.

Finally, SMEs lack information about foreign markets and foreign investments opportunities, and have consequently invested without sound intelligence.

Considering the key role private companies and SMEs should have in Chinese overseas investment, Chinese government policy is changing in order to create the same conditions for all companies, independent of their legal status of ownership. The policy is thus changing to promote FDI, including FDI from SMEs.

2.3. *Challenges Ahead*

The internationalization process of Chinese companies implies transformation at three different levels:

— The creation of the appropriate international organization at the company level to serve the needs of international demand and markets.
— The internationalization of management practices in terms of investment decision-making process, finance, production, and distribution.
— The institutional support for the internalization process at macroeconomic policy level.

Along with these three dimensions, China is facing a series of challenges:

— The structure of overseas Chinese business is still unbalanced. Trade-oriented investment accounts for 60 percent of total overseas investment, while manufacturing and resource-oriented investment together account for only 30 percent.
— Compared to developed countries, China's overseas investments are generally smaller in scale. Chinese enterprises do not have the financial resources to develop their investments and are weak in managing investment risks. The average Chinese overseas investment in the processing trade project is US$2.2 million, compared to US$6 million for average overseas investments by developed countries, and US$4.5 million for average investment by developing countries.
— As a large number of Chinese enterprises operating internationally are SOEs or holding companies with the state as the biggest shareholder, the administrative influence on their decision-making process and management system does not create the best conditions to compete efficiently with private foreign MNCs.
— Sometimes Chinese overseas investments do not have a clear objective and lack detailed investment appraisals. Some enterprises invest overseas in order to enjoy the preferential policies offered by the government. Some invest overseas in order to transfer state-owned properties. Market research has not always been seriously conducted, risk has not been properly evaluated, and many companies are overestimating their capacities of implementation. These errors lead to unsound investments.

— Enterprises have problems raising funds for international operations and they undertake large-scale overseas investment because of limited company resources and because of the foreign exchange system. The development of overseas engineering contracts is limited. Two examples of such limitations are the difficulty getting loans from China Eximbank and restrictions imposed by the international market.

— Chinese enterprises have not always protected their legal rights abroad, lacking experience in international business law and information on the local legal and administrative environment. Normally, companies have to register with China's foreign embassies, but sometimes some of them have been found in a very difficult defensive position without a solid legal framework.

— Chinese companies' international development is limited by a shortage of international managerial talents: professionals with business experience, management skills, legal background, foreign languages skills, etc.

— Chinese policy towards outward FDI lacks unity and transparency. It is implemented by different administrative departments which have their own procedures. The consequence is that some outstanding enterprises cannot enter the internationalization process because they have not been able to meet the approval process, while other companies have been able to elude the government' system of supervision and "sneak out" through illegal means, causing the loss of state-owned assets in foreign countries.

— The approval procedures for overseas investment projects are too complex, too detailed, and too lengthy. Companies are tempted to escape the system by breaking the project into parts so as not to lose the momentum and investment opportunities.

— The legal framework for overseas investment is not unified and streamlined. China has to develop a standardized system so that companies can easily proceed from one step to another. Such a framework should include information services, foreign exchange, and insurance.

— Finally, the functions of the foreign investment-related agencies have to be strengthened in the areas of international law, accountancy, evaluation, and consulting services.

2.4. *Chinese Emerging Multinationals*

Multinational companies are key player in the world economy. They occupy a dominant position in international trade and investment and play a significant role in the growth of the world economy. In China, which is a developing country at a transitional stage, the very nature of emerging multinational companies is still a question mark: what is the objective, to which companies would this apply, and what kind of management model should they follow?

Strategic Goals and Criteria for Success

To succeed internationally, Chinese companies have to define reasonable goals and strategies based on their competitive advantages, capabilities, and resources. The priority for them at this first stage of their internationalization process is to learn from other countries' technology and experience. There is an initial investment, and companies might have to accept potential losses as part of the learning process of implementing their strategy and building profitable operations.

The criteria for success vary from one company to another and combine different objectives:

— trade-oriented companies want to maximize their export potential,
— resource-seeking enterprises want to secure their access to raw material,
— learning-types of enterprises want to acquire advanced technology and experience,
— market-seeking enterprises want to increase their international market share,
— companies with a clear competitive advantage want to penetrate new markets.

Multinationals from developed countries rely on their advantages in capital, technology, and market networks to allocate their resources globally and develop their presence in key markets. On the contrary, multinationals from developing countries have relatively less capital, fewer technological skills, and few specific assets that they can leverage on internationally. Thus, especially for China the learning-curve of internationalization is key to accelerate the technology-accumulation process.

Large or Small Multinationals?

In 2006 there were 22 Chinese enterprises on the *Fortune* 500 Global List. However, their organization at the headquarters level differed strongly from the organization of their foreign subsidiaries. In most Chinese multinationals, the structure at the top was more like a holding company controlling different legal entities than a well integrated corporate management team. It could be compared more to a coalition of allied fleets than to an aircraft carrier.

Besides, one should not neglect the fact that the majority of multinationals are not necessarily among the largest companies in the world; on the contrary, some 60,000 small or medium-sized multinationals are active on the international scene. This is clearly an opportunity for Chinese medium-sized companies that have already started their internationalization process.

The Management Model of Chinese MNCs

China's emerging MNCs can base their learning process both on their own experiences in the first steps of internationalization, and on the experience of the first Chinese MNCs. Additionally, they also have to adapt their management system to international management practices and international standards.

At the company level it means not only expanding successful international strategies, but building a new innovative organization with the appropriate structure in terms of legal personality, financial structure, governance principles, and human resource management.

Companies are at different stages of the transformation process.

— companies — SOEs and private — which already have the appropriate organization and legal personality to invest internationally. They work with foreign partners in China, they manage an international organization, and they compete efficiently in international markets.
— companies which operate internationally but do not have the appropriate management system: it is the case of state-owned foreign trade enterprises and some overseas subsidiaries of processing trade enterprises.
— companies which have the appropriate management system but occasionally invest internationally and focus mainly on the domestic market.

At the government level it means developing a supportive legal environment to serve the internationalization process.

2.5. Policy Issues

Since 2001, the Chinese government has defined new policies and step-by-step measures to facilitate the support of the internationalization process for overseas investment, overseas processing trade projects, overseas resource exploration, and overseas contracted projects. Major measures have been taken regarding financial support, foreign exchange administration, export tax reimbursement, financial services, and insurance. However, in order to further promote the "go global" strategy, new schemes have to be considered.

Tax Policy

In order to encourage domestic enterprises to invest overseas, many governments have introduced tax exemption or reductions in their tax laws. For example, in Britain enterprises engaged in FDI are entitled to a 25 percent reduction of their income tax; in France, there is no value-added tax on revenues generated abroad; in Germany companies investing in developing countries and regions enjoy exemptions from value-added tax for 12 to 18 years. Similar policies of tax exemptions and reductions are followed in Asia (for example Republic of Korea, Singapore, and Malaysia) to promote outward FDI.

Many countries, such as Australia, Belgium, Canada, France, and Germany, have also signed bilateral tax agreements to avoid double taxation between partner countries. These policies could be followed by the Chinese government which had already signed 115 Bilateral Trade Treaties (BITs) by the end of 2006.

Financial Support, Foreign Exchange and Insurance

Developed countries usually have special funds and foreign exchange support for domestic companies investing in developing countries. Half of the Organization for Economic Co-operation and Development (OECD) member countries have these funds. China could implement a similar strategy, following the different stages of development of its companies in the domestic and international markets. Companies themselves could organize the financing of their international operations and be responsible for managing their debts. Control over the way Chinese companies raise funds overseas could be relaxed.

Companies which need to invest to increase their export sales of technology products and equipment should have no restriction on foreign exchange. Export loans could be extended to more economic sectors. Government subsidies could be made available to support companies participating in international bids, fact-finding missions and exhibitions of international investment projects.

The interest rates on loans and the insurance fee for FDI should be reduced, and companies should be able to work with international insurers in order to reduce their cost.

China could create an overseas investment fund or an overseas investment corporation to support companies' internationalization process with low interest loans, guarantees and capital. A special fund such as a "market and investment development fund", financed by both central and local government budgets, could be especially oriented towards companies investing internationally in resource exploration and technology development.

Investment insurance could be developed further, with a special scheme for overseas investment insurance. Japan has an investment insurance system, and a similar system would protect Chinese companies, particularly against political and non-commercial risks.

Information and Guidance

Chinese embassies abroad constitute the front line of information collection and host country analysis. Other departments and agencies also contribute information and guidance, but the information needs of Chinese enterprises "going international" are growing in quantity and quality. Companies need quick access to information, wide connections, and professional services.

China's existing chambers of commerce, which are government-controlled institutions, differ from most of their foreign counterparts. They are in a sense not related closely enough to the companies' interest. Thus, private institutions or trade associations could play a stronger role in terms of information, guidance and consulting services. Companies could also share information at the regional or industrial level.

If we refer to Dunning's investment development theory, China is at a stage where it can build its international presence using specific advantages, even if there is still a great gap between China and developed countries in international management skills, technology and funding. In the past, China developed its competitive advantages mainly in light industry, textile, chemicals, electronics, and medicine. However, in recent years it has also demonstrated its potential in relatively advanced high-tech sectors, such as space-flight technology, nuclear energy, bioengineering, and PC software.

In both traditional and high-tech industries, Chinese companies will be able to go global successfully by increasing their competitiveness and innovation capabilities.

References

MOFCOM (2005). Foreign Market Access Report 2005.

MOFCOM (2005). Guidelines for Overseas Investment Industries.

National Bureau of Statistics of the PRC (2007). *China Statistical Yearbook*.

Sinotrust Consulting (2004). Chinese Companies Listed in Overseas Markets, Research Report, Beijing.

UNCTAD (2003a). *World Investment Report 2003: FDI Policies for Development: National and International Perspectives*. New York and Geneva: United Nations.

UNCTAD (2003b). *E-Brief China: An Emerging FDI Outward Investor*. Research Note.

UNCTAD (2004). *World Investment Report 2004 Annex Table B.8*, pp. 416–419. New York and Geneva: United Nations.

UNCTAD (2006). *World Investment Report 2006, FDI from Developing and Transition Economies: Implications for Development*. New York and Geneva: United Nations.

Chapter 4

THE INTERNATIONALIZATION PROCESS
OF CHINESE MULTINATIONALS

Kang Rongping

Institute of World Economics & Politics —
Chinese Academy of Social Sciences (CASS)

The internationalization process of Chinese companies and their evolution towards the status of multinational or transnational companies can be evaluated according to three major dimensions:

— the initial investments of these companies, the nature of the investment, the geographic orientation, the timing;
— the long-term goals and vision pursued by Chinese companies at the corporate level;
— the internationalization pattern of Chinese companies and their specific stages of international development.

These dimensions will be illustrated by the analysis of the major overseas investments of 16 selected Chinese companies belonging to eight broad economic sectors from January 2000 to June 30, 2007.

The companies are the following: Baosteel Group, BOE Technology Group, China National Petroleum Corporation (CNPC), China National Offshore Oil Corporation (CNOOC), China Worldbest Group, Haier Group, Hisense Group, Holley Group, Huawei Technologies, Jincheng Group, Lenovo Group, China Nonferrous Metal Industry's Foreign Engineering and Construction Co., Ltd.(NFC), Shanghai Electric, Shougang Group, TCL Corporation, and the Wanxiang Group (Annex 1).

1. Initial Investments and Goals of Chinese Companies

Before investing internationally, most Chinese companies have had the opportunity to develop their international experience though exportation, foreign investors in China, and technological partnerships with foreign companies.

However, the real turning point in the history of these companies is when they have made their first investment abroad, usually in manufacturing or in R&D. Such companies often then move on to other countries and in some cases build a global presence.

In order to enter this internationalization process, China's domestic players had to face great challenges in terms of both resources and management capabilities.

The analysis of their initial foreign investments gives a good idea about the motivations and conditions of the internationalization of these companies, their new needs in term of resources, as well as the differences between their domestic and international operations (Table 4.1).

There is of course a close relationship between three elements: growth on the domestic market, getting prior international experience through foreign JVs and collaborative agreement, and exports of core products.

Haier, before investing abroad in 1996, had from the very beginning built on foreign technology with Liebherr (Germany), registering the "Qingdao-Liebherr" trademark for its refrigerators and technology partners such as Mitsubishi Heavy Industry and Matsushita Electric.

TCL, before investing in Vietnam in 1999, had developed technology partnerships with Hong Kong and Taiwanese companies. The Holley Group, before investing in the USA and in Thailand in 2000, had collaborated with an Italian partner in a joint-venture in Zhejiang.

Similarly, China Worldbest had been working with Dupont, BASF, and Hearst before investing abroad in 1997. Shanghai Electric, before investing in Japan in 2002, had cooperated with over 100 multinationals such as Westinghouse and Carrier (United States), Siemens and ABB (Germany), Mitsubishi and Hitachi (Japan), Schneider Electric and Alsthom (France), and set up 125 joint-ventures.

Shougang started exporting in 1980 and created its first joint-venture with a foreign partner Shougang-Kanthal in 1985. It made its first investment abroad in 1988. Baosteel started exporting in the 1980s and made its first overseas investment in Brazil in 2001.

Wanxiang — which had experienced exporting in the USA since 1984 — created Wanxiang America in 1994 and made its first overseas acquisitions in the USA in 2000.

Jincheng Group started exporting in 1988 and made its first international investment in Indonesia in 1996.

Table 4.1:   Initial Foreign Direct Investment of Selected Chinese Companies.

Name of company	Business	Year	Country	Project
Baosteel Group	Steel	2001	Brazil	Creation of a joint-venture with CVRD : Baovale Mineração S.A, each company contributing US$38 million, to mine iron ore in Brazil — Contract to supply 6 million tons of iron ore annually to Baosteel.
BOE Technology Group	Display technology	2001	Republic of Korea	Acquisition of 45 percent of Hydis (a subsidiary of Hynix Semiconductor Inc.) units specialized in small-sized flat-panel display technologies (STN-LCD and OLED) for US$380 million.
CNOOC	Oil and gas	1994	Indonesia	Acquisition of 39.51 percent of the equity in the Malacca Strait Production-Sharing Contract (PSC) for US$190 million from the ARCO/Nippon Oil Corporation — an oil reserve of 16.4 million barrels.
CNPC	Oil and gas	1997	Sudan	Acquisition of 40 percent of the Great Nile Petroleum Operation Company (GNPOC) and the operational rights in zones 1, 2, and 4 in Sudan oil fields.
China Worldbest Group	Textile	1997	Niger	Acquisition of 80 percent of Sonitextil, renamed Enitex, the state-owned textile and dyeing company. An investment of US$3 million.
Haier Group	Home appliances	1996	Indonesia	Creation of PT. Haier Sapporo Indonesia Haier to manufacture refrigerators (Haier 51 percent).
Hisense Group	Home appliances	1996	South Africa	Taking over a Daewoo television factory near Johannesburg (Hisense 60 percent).
Holley Group	Electricity meters	2000	Thailand	First overseas plant in Bangkok to manufacture and sell electricity meters.

(Continued)

Table 4.1:   (*Continued*)

Name of company	Business	Year	Country	Project
Huawei Technologies	Telecom equipment	1993	USA	Creation of a research institute in the Silicon Valley to collect technical information and develop chips.
Jincheng Group	Motorcycles	1996	Colombia	Creation of Jincheng de Colombia (Jincol), a 50-50 joint-venture with Colombia Easter Auto Trading Company to manufacture motorcycles.
Lenovo Group	Personal computers	1988	Hong Kong	Creation of a joint-venture — Hong Kong Legend Technology — and acquisition of Quantum, a company specialized in PC mother boards.
NFC	Nonferrous metal	1995	Thailand	Creation of a joint-venture to recycle non-ferrous metals. The JV sells the lead alloy extracted from recycled used batteries to battery manufacturers.
Shanghai Electric	Power generation equipment	2000	Japan	Acquisition, along with Morning Side Group (Hong Kong), of Akiyama Machinery Manufacturing Corporation.
Shougang Group	Steel	1988	USA	Acquisition of 70 percent of Mesta Engineering and Design Inc. (Pittsburgh) for US$3.4 million — a company specialized in steel mill machinery and equipment.
TCL Corporation	Consumer electronics	1999	Vietnam	Creation of TCL (Vietnam) Co — a 100 percent subsidiary of TCL Corp. — to assemble color TV sets for the local and South Asia market.
Wanxiang Group	Automotive parts	1994	USA	Foundation of Wanxiang America Corporation in Chicago with a registered capital of US$500,000.

Source: CASS and HEC Paris.

1.1. *Three Internationalization Paths*

There is a major difference between Chinese multinationals, which are latecomers, and their Western counterparts. When the first American and European multinationals started their internationalization process they were competing with only few multinationals in their industry and they owned proprietary technology.

On the contrary, when latecomers — including Japanese companies and emerging market multinationals — started their internationalization process, many multinational players were already active in their industry and they depended on foreign technology (Kang Rongping *et al.*, 1996).

Chinese companies are in this situation and, moreover, their international process differs according to the following criteria:

— When was the company founded?
— When did it start its internationalization process?
— What are its international objectives?

Based on these criteria the internationalization paths of Chinese companies fall into three major categories (Figure 4.1):

A first group of companies is following a "transitional path". These companies were created when the Chinese economy was closed and they achieved a considerable size on the domestic market before investing internationally. When the Chinese economy started to open up, these companies were large or medium-sized and had accumulated more resources than their domestic competitors. Companies like Shougang (steel industry), CNPC and CNOOC (oil and gas industry) are examples.

A second category of companies have followed a "normal path": These companies grew steadily during the phase of opening-up of the Chinese economy despite

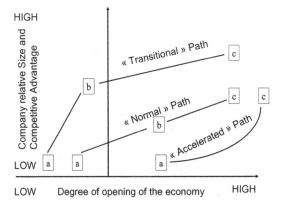

Figure 4.1: Internationalization paths of Chinese companies.

the growing competition of foreign products. These companies began the internationalization process step-by-step. Some examples are: Baosteel, Haier, Hisense, Holley, Huawei Technologies, Jincheng, TCL Corporation, and Wanxiang.

There is a third category of companies following an "accelerated path": These companies have been created during the period of the open economy and have been fighting for resources and markets from the beginning. Thus, they have almost immediately started their internationalization process. BOE, China WorldBest, NFC, and Shanghai Electric fall into this category.

Companies following the "transitional" path through the internationalization process hope to gain a complement to their already relatively large size and historical competitive advantage.

Companies following the "normal path" grow internationally at a slow but steady rhythm according to their size and current competitive advantage.

Companies following the "accelerated path" internationalize in order to increase their relative size and develop their competitive advantage.

1.2. *International Vision and Corporate Goals*

The way companies define their overall mission, vision, and goals gives us interesting indications about the link between the internationalization process and goals at the corporate level (Table 4.2).

Of course, the process of developing an international strategy differs strongly from one company to another and evolves over time.

China National Petroleum Corporation's (CNPC) key responsibilities defined in the eighties included: stabilizing production in the east of China and investing in the west, developing production overseas, and diversification. Five policies formulated in 1988 put the emphasis on growth, restructuring, cost reduction, technological innovation, and market expansion, especially internationally. Finally, the strategic plan of CNPC in 2001 defined CNPC as "a typical multinational oil and gas company" with the objective of being among the top 10 oil companies worldwide.

Lenovo's first international strategy — defined in 1988 — included three steps:

— creating an international trading company to develop sales in international markets,
— creating an international network of R&D, manufacturing and sales units,
— being listed on the international financial markets.

NFC, in a report prepared with the China Association for the Promotion of Investment in 2000–2001, defined its objectives as: resource-seeking foreign investments for the period of China's 10th five-year plan. This strategy was

Table 4.2:   International Vision and Corporate Goals.

Name of company	Business	Vision and goals
Baosteel Group	Steel	— to focus on "premium products" to become the leading company in China's iron and steel industry for new processes, new technologies and new materials — moderate diversification; — to rank among the top three steel enterprises in China and among the world's top 500 companies; — to achieve revenues of 150 million yuan by 2010 and to be listed internationally; — to become the most competitive multinational steel firm within five years (2003 objectives).
BOE Technology Group	Display technology	— to be a world-leader in display industry, with at least three leading brands on the domestic market; — to be number 3 in terms of market share worldwide; — to achieve revenues over US$10 billion for core business, with a net Return on Assets of over 15 percent, ahead of domestic competitors.
CNOOC	Oil and gas	— to become an internationally competitive, comprehensive energy company by 2008 and a first rate international player.
CNPC	Oil and gas	— to transform the company into a competitive multinational: increasing resources, market expansion, expanding the businesses overseas; — to be among top ten oil companies worldwide.
China Worldbest Group	Life sciences and Textile	— to focus on the life science and textile sectors; — to develop "high-technology, export-oriented, industry-based and transnational" strategies.
Haier Group	Home appliances	— historically three successive stages: internationalization, diversification, and brand strategy; — currently: the "global brand stage" — enhancing Haier's leadership in Chinese and global markets and strengthen the reputation of Haier's brand worldwide.
Hisense Group	Home appliances	— three successive stages: brand building in China (1994–2000), internationalization — brand building

(Continued)

Table 4.2: (*Continued*)

Name of company	Business	Vision and goals
		on international markets (2000–2010) — (third stage): a global company offering internet facilities and value-added services (2010–2020).
Holley Group	Electricity meters	— to become a multinational with global presence; — to establish manufacturing bases world-wide; — to become the world's top manufacturer of electricity equipment; — to realize by 2010 50 percent of its operations on the domestic market and 50 percent overseas.
Huawei Technologies	Telecom equipment	— to become a world-class equipment supplier.
Jincheng Group	Aviation & motorcycles	— to become a multinational in the four core businesses: aviation products, motorcycles and gasoline engines, engineering hydraulic pressure machines, and services; — establishing a world-class enterprise and creating an internationally well-known brand in the motorcycle business.
Lenovo Group	Personal computers	— historically: building R&D capabilities, international presence, and financial resources; — currently:a global leader in the PC business.
NFC	Nonferrous metal	— focusing on two core businesses: copper and aluminum oxide overseas) and three geographic area (Central and South Africa, peripheral nations, and Australia and Canada); — to be a leading international mining corporation integrated with financing, investments, exploration, constructing, processing, and merchandising.
Shanghai Electric	Power generation equipment	— focus on core business, high technology innovation, global sourcing; — to become one of the largest and most competitive equipment manufacturers world-wide with number 1 ranking in China; — "Shanghai Electric" as a global brand.

(*Continued*)

Table 4.2: *(Continued)*

Name of company	Business	Vision and goals
Shougang Group	Steel	— Relocating all steel-related operations by 2010 out of Beijing to a new manufacturing base (Tangshan, Hebei Province); — diversification in non-steel-related businesses: mining, machine production, building, real estate, service and foreign trade, etc.
TCL Corporation	Consumer electronics	— four core businesses: multimedia, mobile communications, information and electric engineering; — objective 2003: to be among the top five companies worldwide in the fields of color TV and communications equipment in three to five years.
Wanxiang Group	Automotive parts	— focusing on automotive parts; — an export base and the most competitive manufacturing centre in China; — following internationally its global clients.

Source: CASS and HEC Paris.

confirmed in 2003 with an emphasis on two businesses — copper and aluminum — and three regions: South Central Africa, peripheral countries, and Australia and Canada. The overall goal is and to transform NFC into an "international integrated mining corporation" which would cover finance, investments, exploration, construction, processing, marketing, and sales to provide sustainable, long-term, overseas, nonferrous metal to China.

The "international strategic guidelines for the 21st century" of the Holley Group were defined in early 2000 for the period 2000–2010 in the document: "WTO & Holley Group". The guidelines included:

— to achieve sales of RMB 30 billion: 50 percent on the domestic market and 50 percent overseas.
— to establish manufacturing bases all over the world, and to become the world's top manufacturer of electrical equipment.
— to be a multinational company with global allocation of resources (market, personnel, capital and technology) by 2010.

In terms of overall vision, half of the companies studied say they want to be "a world-leading" company. Huawei wants to be "a world-leading enterprise",

Shanghai Electric "a leading conglomerate" and Baosteel "the most competitive multinational steel firm". As latecomers, Chinese enterprises dream of becoming world leaders, hence they focus on catch-up strategies.

With regard to the portfolio of activities at the corporate level, most of the companies mentioned demonstrate a clear focus on specific economic sectors: Baosteel (iron and steel), BOE (display technologies), Huawei (electronics and information equipment supplier), Shanghai Electric (power generation equipment supplier), CNOOC (oil and gas), CNPC (oil and gas), NFC (aluminum and copper), Wanxiang (auto parts).

A diversified group like Jincheng clearly identifies its four core businesses: aviation products, motorcycles and gasoline engines, engineering hydraulic pressure machines, and finally services.

TCL identifies five businesses: multimedia, mobile communications, information, electrical engineering, and culture. This is a limited spectrum of diversification and the "culture sector" outlined in TCL's "Tiger Plan" has not yet materialized.

China Worldbest focuses on two major activities: life sciences (biology, pharmacy and healthcare) and textile (clothing, decorative and industrial fabrics).

Hisense, which has currently a limited scope of activities, mentions internet facilities as an avenue for growth in the future.

Other companies seem to be more tempted by diversification. Haier, for instance, does not define its core business, which probably means it will go on with its diversification strategy.

International strategies have a strong relationship with key growth strategy options: the nature of the portfolio of activities and the degree of diversification.

Some companies treat overseas operations as a totally separate set of activities, which suggests problems of coordination between the international strategy and overall growth strategies. In some cases, it is even difficult to evaluate the performances of foreign subsidiaries as well as the impact of their performance on results at corporate level.

The rationale for Chinese's first foreign investments and the first formulation of an international strategy varies from one company to another.

Since its founding in 1992 Worldbest Group has made clear its ambition to develop a "transnational strategy", though that was well before making its first overseas investment in 1997. Other companies, like CNPC and Hisense, have also been anticipating or preparing their international process before seizing opportunities.

On the other hand Haier, Holley, and Jincheng, facing the opportunities of international acquisitions or partnership, formulated an international strategy and made it explicit at the moment of their acquisition.

2. The Internationalization Pattern of Chinese Companies

Many Chinese companies have the ambition to become multinational players. But what are the conditions of their transformation into multinationals or transnational companies? The internationalization process of corporations has been studied in depth from a theoretical point of view, but do these theories apply to latecomers, especially Chinese companies?

Let us first review briefly what can be learned from former experiences and research before looking at the internationalization process of Chinese companies specifically.

2.1. *Lessons from the Experience of Foreign Multinationals*

After the Second World War, the rapid growth of MNCs and their direct investments abroad caught the attention of many Western scholars who have proposed different theories regarding MNCs based on different research targets, methods and hypotheses.

According to Hymer's monopolistic advantage theory (Hymer, 1976), multinationals invest abroad because they possess unique resources in term of technology and size, unique products, trademarks, patents and proprietary technologies, financing and management skills, etc.

Raymond Vernon developed the product life cycle theory (Vernon, 1966): the FDI decisions of US companies were a response to the changing production and competitive conditions during a product's lifetime. During the first stage when the product is new, companies are exporting. As the product becomes more popular, they invest abroad, for example from the USA to Western Europe. Finally, at the stage of maturity of the product, they invest in emerging markets.

Knickerbocker (1973) introduced the oligopolistic reaction theory to explain why most large FDI made by US multinationals took place at the same time. Investment can be offensive or defensive, with firms following and countering rivals in foreign markets.

Buckley and Casson (1976) followed by Rugman (1981) developed the *internalization theory* (e.g. intra-firm trade) based on the study of Western MNCs. Their observation was that the international division of labor was more the result of firm-based decisions than market-based decisions. This helped multinationals explore the alternative choices offered in terms of exporting, licensing and investing internationally.

The eclectic paradigm proposed by Dunning (Dunning, 1977) explores the conditions of successful internationalization of US, European and Japanese MNCs. The paradigm focuses on three conditions for successful international

investment: conditions in term of ownership (O), location (L), and internalization
(I) advantages:

— Ownership (O) advantages are firm-specific competitive advantages such as
  natural resources and tangible or intangible assets such as technology,
— Internalization (I) advantages refer to the ability of a firm to manage and coordinate internally the activities along the value-added chain.
— Location (L) advantages refer to the institutional and productive factors which
  are present in a particular geographic area.

The study of these variables allows a firm to choose between strategic options:
exporting, franchising or investing locally, and choosing the appropriate product
and country targets.

Finally among non-mainstream theories, Kojima provides an interesting
Japanese model of foreign direct investment based on the principle of compar-
ative costs in the international division of labor (Kojima, 1978, 1987). Historically
Japanese FDI presented interesting differences:

— Japanese FDIs were export-oriented. FDI and foreign trade complement each
  other.
— Japanese FDIs focused more on natural resources and labor intensive sectors
  such as textile and components manufacturing.
— Japanese FDI investors were mostly SMEs, much smaller than their European
  and American counterparts, the technologies transferred were mainly applied
  ones, and usually the investment was made in the form of joint-ventures.

2.2. *Chinese Multinationals in the Age*
of Globalization

Most of the existing theories on multinationals are based on the experience of
Western companies. The monopolistic advantage theory, the product cycle theory,
and the "oligopolistic reaction theory" are based on US firms. The eclectic paradigm
focuses on US and European companies.

Few studies have been conducted on latecomers such as multinationals based in
emerging markets. More than that, the environment in which latecomers are operating has changed dramatically in terms of technology and economic environment.
The last decades have been characterized in particular by the development of information technologies and the beginning of the age of globalization.

These transformations pose many challenges to existing theories on multinationals and specifically Chinese emerging multinationals (Kang Rongping, 2001).

One of the most important premises of mainstream multinational theory is that
investing abroad implies higher costs than investing in the domestic market, and

consequently that a company should possess a clear competitive advantage over its rivals before investing abroad: they should possess a "prior competitive advantage" (Child and Rodrigues, 2005).

Another hidden premise in previous studies is that before the era of globalization most companies could survive and grow normally in their domestic market, thus internationalization was not a condition of survival and growth.

Globalization and the development of information technology have changed radically these conditions:

— Globalization has removed the barriers preventing the international flow of production factors, and all countries compete to attract Foreign Direct Investment.
— Information Technology, especially the internet, has contributed to a radical reduction of transaction costs, especially for international operations. Thus, the cost of operating abroad compared to operating in the domestic market has been reduced significantly and, in some cases, has disappeared.

In this new context, possessing a "prior competitive advantage" might no longer be a prerequisite for internationalization.

More than that, firms have to reorganize their value chain on a global basis to survive and grow in a global business environment.

A study by the Conference Board on the performance of 1,000 American manufacturers during a 10 year period demonstrated that companies with global operations had a higher Return on Investment. They grew faster with a 50 percent higher survival rate than their domestic counterparts (The Conference Board, 1992).

In the era of globalization, internationalization was becoming the norm of corporate growth. For emerging market multinationals, the question is not so much whether to go-global or not, but rather how to create or increase competitive advantage through globalization.

Thus the internationalization process of latecomer multinationals suggests the existence of different kinds of players in the international scene:

— companies building and maintaining a clear prior competitive advantage through their internationalization process,
— companies with a clear prior competitive advantage gaining new advantages through their internationalization process,
— companies without a prior competitive advantage who must build their competitive advantage through internationalization.

For this third type of company, the principle of building on a clear prior competitive advantage in the domestic market is replaced by a new doctrine: building competitive advantage through internationalization. To pursue this route, companies can benefit from the opportunity to control elements of the value chain (Porter,

1985) which are key success factors in their industry and which can be acquired internationally if they do not own them.

They exploit in that case an important consequence of globalization: the global disaggregation of the value chain and relocation of activities from one country to another according to comparative advantages.

2.3. *The Experience of Overseas Chinese Corporations*

The internationalization process of overseas Chinese corporations operating from Singapore, Thailand, Indonesia, Malaysia, the Philippines, Hong Kong, Macao and Taiwan, offers useful clues to the understanding of the internationalization process of Chinese mainland multinationals (Kang Rongping and Ke Yinbin, 2001).

A first group of companies ("building prior advantage first") have built their competitive advantage first in their home market before using this competitive advantage to gradually enter foreign markets (Table 4.3).

It is a technology advantage in the case of Creative Technology, founded in Singapore in 1981 and a worldwide leader in digital entertainment products for the personal computer and internet.

Acer, founded in 1976 in Taiwan, is today among the world's top five branded PC vendors. Its competitive advantage is based on cost and volume.

Table 4.3:   International Investments of Overseas Chinese Corporations.

Category	Type of competitive advantage	Company
Building prior competitive advantage	Technology	Huachang, Creative Technology
	Low-cost	Zhengda, Acer
	Combined advantage	Hutchinson Whampoa, Sanlin Group
	Acquisition of technology	Eupa, VTech
International first		
	Acquisition of distribution network	Wing on, Semi Tech Group, Midway
	Supply of raw material	Formosa Plastics

Source: Kang Rongping and Ke Yinbin (2001).

In the case of the Sanlin Group, one of the largest conglomerates in Indonesia and Southeast Asia (agribusiness, chemicals, financial services, etc), it is a combination of advantages.

A second group of companies ("international investment first") developed a strategy which is more beneficial to latecomers: investing first internationally in order to build their competitive advantage, then acquiring natural resources and technology, before perhaps getting access to the market.

Vtech, founded in Hong Kong in 1976, is a technology-driven company that went international quite quickly. After it was founded, Vtech began to develop its R&D capabilities through partnership with top international laboratories. Headquartered in Hong Kong, VTech currently has a presence in 10 countries and approximately 30,000 employees, including around 1,000 R&D professionals based in Canada, Hong Kong and mainland China. It is one of the world's largest suppliers of traditional and cordless telephones as well as electronic learning products.

This distinction between "building prior competitive advantage" and "international investment first" helps us to understand the growth strategies of mainland China's emerging multinationals.

2.4. Building "Prior Competitive Advantage" versus "Internationalization First"

BOE developed its low cost advantage first in the traditional display area of the domestic and foreign markets and thus had the financial resources to acquire technology abroad. Through successive partnerships and acquisitions abroad, the company was able to master the small-sized flat-panel-display TFT-LCD technologies.

It then developed an industrial park near Beijing dedicated to production and R&D in TFT-LCD display business: the BOE Display Technology Park.

Combining low cost and technology advantage, BOE was becoming a global display supplier with high potential: a new technology, a huge domestic market, competition limited to Asian competitors, and potential Chinese government support.

Haier also first developed its low cost advantage in the white goods appliances industry before starting its internationalization process. It kept its low cost advantage in international markets while its strategy in the home market was based on top quality and service. Haier's sources of competitive advantage were not only inexpensive labor, but also productivity, managerial skills and corporate culture. So when Haier moved successfully to the USA and Europe, the company was able to master a combination of advantages which created a real superiority over its international rivals.

China Worldbest, Hisense and Holley also first developed a low cost advantage. China Worldbest did it through export and volume, Hisense by expanding its manufacturing base in emerging markets to keep the cost at the lowest level, and Holley through exports and manufacturing in low cost areas (at least for its electricity meter division).

Other firms like Huawei Technologies, Shanghai Electric, and Jincheng Group have been investing to build their technology advantage first.

Among motorcycle manufacturers, Jincheng Group has pursued a prior-technology advantage with a well structured sequence of absorption of the most advanced international technologies, product development, production on the domestic market, and export. The status of Jincheng (a state-owned enterprise) might not facilitate its internationalization process in the short term, but the company has the potential to become a global player in the motorcycle business.

One group of Chinese companies has invested abroad to acquire and secure a regular supply of raw materials to serve their own domestic operations and nurture their core business.

These resource-seeking investors include steel makers such as Baosteel and Shougang, oil and gas companies such as CNPC and CNOOC, and metal producers such as NFC. In terms of growth, the Chinese market will be a priority over foreign markets for a rather long period for these companies,

A second category is composed of companies that have looked for opportunities of developing simultaneously their technological and marketing advantage through a potentially significant foreign acquisition. Lenovo's acquisition of IBM's PC division in late 2004 and TCL's takeover of Thomson Multimedia from France are examples of this trend.

The case of Wanxiang is less clear-cut. The company initially benefited from its low cost advantage in its manufacturing activities, such as the production of universal joints and bearings. Then, thanks to its technological know-how, the company had the opportunity to enter the international scene by following its most demanding clients, particularly in the USA, where it entered with its American car manufacturers' clients operating in China.

2.5. *The Acceleration of Chinese Companies' Internationalization Process*

Since the foundation of the new China in 1949, the Chinese government has established a few enterprises overseas, such as the Hong Kong Branch of the Bank of China, China Merchants Group, China Resources, Ltd., and the China Travel Service. These companies were founded to support China's key import and export trade. As these institutions were limited in number and in focus, they did not attract much attention.

In the mid 1950s, China's foreign-aid policy began in the form of large projects, technology, equipment, and cash to help third world countries gain and safeguard their independence. These economic and technological projects, financed by non-interest loans and donations, were a major vector of China's international presence and provided a preparatory experience for Chinese enterprises that would later go international.

In the late 1970s, the development of China's overseas contracted projects led to the founding the China State Construction Engineering Corporation (CSCEC) which became the first contractor for foreign engineering projects in 1978. This grew enormously and served as a prelude to the birth of Chinese multinationals.

In 1979, the State Council — in the framework of economic reform — began to encourage companies to manufacture abroad. For the first time since 1949, outbound FDI was part of China's policy. This was the beginning of the internationalization process. Beijing Friendship Store Service Company and Japan's Maruichi Shoji created Kyowa Co., the first Chinese joint-venture abroad since the "reform and opening up" in 1978. From 1979 onwards, the internationalization process of Chinese enterprises increased regularly in three successive phases.

The phase of transition (1979–1995) is particular to China because, unlike Western, Japanese, or Korean multinationals, the Chinese companies which embarked on the internationalization process after the opening up of the economy were state-owned enterprises and had built their strength in the planned economy system, such as Shougang in the steel industry.

These companies differed radically from foreign MNCs in term of objectives, sequence of moves and overall strategy. Lacking experience, they sometimes made bold moves which sometimes resulted in problems in their foreign ventures.

The phase of normal development occurred from 1996–2003. Companies that had been created after the opening up policy also started the internationalization process. Investment abroad by manufacturers of home appliances and motorcycles were typical of that period, because there was an overcapacity on the domestic markets and companies were looking for new markets abroad (Table 4.4).

The third period, from 2004 onwards, was a phase of acceleration.

Table 4.4: Initial FDI of Selected Chinese Companies (1995–1997).

Company	Year	Location	Industry
Little Swan	1995	Malaysia	Home appliances
Haier	1996	Indonesia	Home appliances
Hisense	1996	South Africa	Home appliances
Huawei	1996	Hong Kong	Telecom
Jincheng	1996	Colombia	Motorcycle
Wanxiang	1997	U. K	Car bearings
Holley	1997	Nepal	Textile mills

Source: Kang Rongping and Ke Yinbin (2001).

Since China's entry into the World Trade Organization (WTO) at the end of 2001, Chinese firms faced increasing international competitive pressure, forcing them to accelerate their internationalization process. Cross-border mergers and acquisitions (M&A) have rapidly become one of the most significant entry modes into the international market. Compared to the first phase, projects were also more technology-oriented and capital intensive.

This trend reached its first peak in 2004 and can be regarded as "the year of Chinese firms' cross-border M&As", a symbol of this phase of the "Go-Global" strategy.

2004 was the year of three major acquisitions:

— Shanghai Automotive's acquisition of Ssangyong Motor Company (Republic of Korea)
— TCL's acquisition of Thomson Multimedia's global television business (France)
— Lenovo's acquisition of IBM's PC business (USA).

Compared to greenfield projects, M&As had the advantage of speed, but would also create a new challenge to Chinese companies: how to manage multinational operations?

2.6. *Lessons from the China–Japan Comparison*

An interesting parallel can be made between the internationalization process that Japanese MNCs experienced after World War II and the same process that Chinese companies went through in the eighties.

China's Unique Phase of Transition

This phase was unique for China due to the gradual process of Chinese reform policy and the "great leap forward" of Chinese firms during the transition period.

On the contrary, in Russia and Central Europe, most companies were restructured and privatized before going international.

China's Policy of Promoting Inward Investment First

Japanese policy after World War II and for a long time afterwards was to limit inward foreign investment and to support the internationalization of Japanese companies. Japan began to encourage foreign inward investment only in 2000. The contrary was true in China where the government welcomed inward FDI for a long period and only in 2000 did it start to encourage companies to go global.

Compared to Japan, Chinese companies started their internationalization process with much less international marketing experience than their Japanese counterparts. However, China had a larger home market and more experience than the Japanese in facing international competition at home.

Different Entry Modes

At the beginning of their internationalization process, US multinationals were focusing on wholly-owned subsidiaries. In a survey done in 1951 on a sample of 180 US MNCs, 58 percent had created wholly-owned subsidiaries (UNCTAD, 1978). Japanese companies, on the other hand, put emphasis on joint-ventures and building factories abroad. A survey conducted in the late 1970s on 562 overseas subsidiaries of 60 Japanese multinationals found that 94 percent were JVs and only 6 percent were wholly-owned subsidiaries (Li Wenguang *et al.*, 1993).

Chinese companies have followed the Japanese pattern. A survey conducted in 1995 found that 79 percent of Chinese investment abroad was in the form of JVs with only 21 percent as wholly-owned subsidiaries (Kang Rongping *et al.*, 1996).

As overseas M&As pose greater managerial challenges than building new factories, both Japanese and Chinese multinationals started their internationalization process with greenfield investments. They maintained this approach during a rather long period before launching cross-border M&As. The period of time, however, differed from one country to another: 35 years for Japan and 25 years for China. The growing competitive pressure felt by Chinese companies after China's accession to WTO probably increased their motivation for M&As.

First Movers Versus Followers' Advantage

Studying the characteristic of the largest companies based in leading industrial countries, Chandler pointed out that a vast majority of them were operating in capital intensive industries and possessed a strong advantage in the form of economy on scale. In a chapter on Scale and Scope (Chandler, 1990) about first movers advantages and oligopolistic competition, Chandler stresses the fact that most first movers have been concentrating in capital intensive sectors and have built strong barriers to entry through manufacturing, management know-how, and marketing. Thus, it was very unlikely for followers to compete successfully against them in the same industries.

This explains why challengers, Japanese and later Chinese multinationals, have had to avoid head-on competition and focus on the weakest links of first movers.

Domestic Market Versus International Market

In terms of size, China's domestic market is bigger than Japan's, which is in turn bigger than Republic of Korea's. The primary motivation for a local company to enter the internationalization process is in a sense inversely proportional to the size of its domestic market. However, we have seen that globalization and more interdependence and freedom of movement between the domestic market and the international market have been strong factors pushing Chinese companies to invest abroad.

Sony, founded in 1946, grew slowly at first due to the limitation of its home market. It began to move into the US market in 1955. Afterwards, Sony launched its new products first in the US market before selling them at home. When the balance between the domestic and international markets was achieved in the 1980s, Sony had become a leader in its business sector.

Lenovo — Legend at that time — founded in 1984, had to open a branch in Hong Kong because of administrative constraints at home which made it difficult to get a computer manufacturer license. Being successful abroad, Lenovo obtained this license and shifted its attention back to the domestic market. Thus, after acquiring a dominant market share of the Chinese PC market in 1996, Lenovo almost abandoned its international market. Then, in 2000, the average profits in the PC sector in China began to drop and Lenovo faced major drawbacks in its diversification strategy. Priority was again placed on the internationalization strategy. The acquisition of IBM's PC business took place in late 2004.

The Key Role of Integrated Trading Companies

The internationalization process of Japanese companies came along with the development of integrated trading companies — the Sogo Sosha — which have played a key role in the internationalization of the Japanese economy. During the seventies, when Korean companies entered the internationalization process, similar forms of integrated trading companies emerged and were very successful. Chinese state-owned foreign trade corporations have not seized the same opportunity during the phase of transition, mainly for institutional reasons. Later on they did not seize such opportunities because they suffered heavy losses during the phase of normal growth when they lost their monopoly position.

This explains partly why in these early stages Chinese emerging MNCs have been mainly small and medium-size SOEs.

Finally, there might be another difference between the two countries in terms of the learning process.

During their internationalization process, most Japanese companies relied more on their own management principles, policies, and processes than on foreign experience. Chinese companies on the other hand, especially those in the phase of cross-border M&A, have been built on foreign managerial expertise (Kotler, 2005). From this point of view, Chinese companies might be closer to their Western counterparts than to Japan.

References

Child, J and Rodrigues, S.B (2005). The internationalization of Chinese Firms: A Case for Theoretical Extension? *Management & Organization Review*, 1(3), 381–410.

Kang Rongping *et al.* (1996). *Zhongguo qiye de kuaguo jingying* (Multinational Operation of Chinese Enterprises), *Jingji kexue chubanshe*. Beijing: Economic Science Press.

Kang Rongping and Ke Yinbin (1999). *Zhongguo qiye pinglun: zhanlue yu shijian* (A Review of Chinese Enterprises: Strategy and Practice), *Qiye guanli chubanshe*. Beijing: Enterprise Management Publishing House.

Kang Rongping (ed.) (2001). *Daxing kuaguogongsi zhanlue xin qushi* (New Trends in Strategies of Transnational Corporations), *Jingji kexue chubanshe*. Beijing: Economic Science Press.

Kang Rongping and Ke Yinbin (2001). *Huaren kuaguogongsi chengzhang lun* (On the Growth of Chinese Multinational Companies), *Guofang daxue chubanshe*. Beijing: National Defense University Press.

Kojima, K. (1978). *Direct foreign investment: A Japanese model of multinational business operations,* London: Croom Helm.

Kojima, K. (1987) *Direct Foreign Investment*. New York: Praeger.

Li Wenguang *et al.* (1993). *riben de kuaguo qiye* (Japanese TNCs), *zhongguo jingji chubanshe*. Beijing: China Economy Publishing House.

UNCTAD (1978). *Transnational Corporations in World Development*. New York and Geneva: United Nations.

UNCTAD (1995). *Transnational Corporations and Competitiveness*. New York and Geneva: United Nations.

UNCTAD (2002). *World Investment Report: Transnational Corporations and Export Competitiveness*. New York and Geneva: United Nations.

UNCTAD (2005). *World Investment Report: Transnational Corporations and the Internationalization of R&D*. New York and Geneva: United Nations.

Chapter 5

INTERNATIONAL MARKETING STRATEGIES OF CHINESE MULTINATIONALS: THE EXPERIENCE OF BIRD, HAIER, AND TCL

Hu Zuohao and Wang Gao

Tsinghua School of Economics & Management

Since the 1980s, China's economy has been going through a transition from being a planned economy to a market economy, from a closed economy to an open economy. The result has been rapid development. In 2006, China's GDP reached 20.94 trillion RMB (US$2.72 trillion), and its imports and exports amounted to US$1.76 trillion. Accompanying China's rapid economic development, one group of Chinese enterprises has grown up amid intense market competition and has started marketing activities in the international market.

Founded in 1984, the Haier Group is China's biggest manufacturer of household electronic appliances. In 2005 its total global sales were 103.4 billion RMB. Haier has established design, manufacturing, and marketing centers in its main markets worldwide, including the United States.

The TCL Group, founded in 1981, is China's second biggest household electronic appliances producer. TCL became the world's biggest color TV manufacturer through the acquisition of the French TV manufacturer Thomson in 2003. TCL, whose sales topped US$6.7 billion in 2006, is adopting a multi-brand strategy to sell its products in the world's four largest markets.

Bird Corp, founded in 1992, is China's biggest manufacturer of mobile phones. In 2004 its sales totaled 10.4 billion Yuan and its volume of mobile phone exports was 3,370,000 units, which accounted for 24.7 percent of its total sales volume of 13,640,000.

Why do these Chinese enterprises carry out international marketing activities, and what is their main motivation? How do these Chinese enterprises choose their overseas markets and what are their strategies for entering such markets? What are the characteristics of an enterprise that endeavors to enter foreign markets? What kind of international marketing strategies do these Chinese enterprises adopt in the overseas market, and what are the characteristics of these strategies?

This chapter attempts to answer these questions based on the experience of the three key actors of China's consumer-electronics industry: Haier, TCL and Bird.[1]

1. Motivations for International Marketing

The main motivations for Chinese enterprises which are entering a foreign market and conducting international marketing activities are the following:

1.1. *Competition in the Domestic Market and the Need for Growth*

Although China is the world's largest manufacturing and consumer market of household appliances and telecommunication products, it is also the most competitive market. For example, in 2004 73,000,000 color television sets were manufactured in China, accounting for 44 percent of global color television sales. Thirty-seven million color televisions were sold on the domestic market, which makes up 23.4 percent of total global color television sales by volume. China's domestic color television market is maturing, and the intense market competition has reduced the number of color television brands in the market from about 100 to about 50 brands, including internationally famous brand names such as Sony, Panasonic, Philips, etc.

At the same time, the market share of the top 10 brands has reached 80 percent. It has become very difficult for both the big-scale and the small-scale television manufacturers to enlarge their market share in the domestic market. This is also the case with mobile telecommunications. After rapid development, China's mobile phone market entered a mature stage. In 2002, the total number of mobile phone users was 0.206 billion, of which 61,390,000 sets were used by new subscribers; in 2003, the total number was 0.258 billion, with 51,380,000 sets being used by new subscribers. The number of new users is beginning to drop as the market

---

[1]The authors would like to thank particularly the managers of Bird, Haier and TCL who contributed to the study: Mr. Zhu Zhaojiang, General Manager of Bird's international department, and Mr. Shangguan Yanyun, General Manager of Bird's planning department; Mr. Chen Weiyan, senior analyzer of TCL and Mr. Deng Rui, the department head of TCL's strategic planning department, Mr. Zhou Xiwen, president of Haier University.

reaches maturity. In 2003, 0.186 billion mobile phones were produced in China, accounting for 35 percent of the global output. Of these, 73,786,000 sets were sold in China. In 2004, three out of the top five brands occupying the mobile phone market were foreign, namely Nokia, Motorola and Samsung. At present, there are more than 50 mobile phone manufacturers and the competition in the mobile phone market is extremely intense. In order to cope with the need for further development, many enterprises in the household appliances and telecommunication business are actively engaged in penetrating overseas markets and carrying out international marketing activities.

1.2. *Opportunities Offered by the Global Market*

The enormous overseas market offers great opportunities for international marketing by Chinese enterprises. For example, in 2004 the global sales volume of color televisions was 0.166 billion, of which 37,000,000 sets were sold in China, 33,000,000 in the United States, 33,000,000 in Europe, and 63,000,000 in other places. Furthermore, the emerging market is growing rapidly. In 2003, the global sales volume of air conditioners and refrigerators reached 0.105 billion and 700,000,000, respectively. In that same year, the global sales volume of mobile phones reached 0.52 billion. The upgrading of the industrial capacity of multinational enterprises has provided great opportunities for Chinese enterprises. For example, in the color television industry, multinational enterprises such as Panasonic and Philips have almost totally given up the manufacturing of medium and low level CRT color televisions; instead they have Chinese enterprises handle such production.

1.3. *Economies of Scale and Relative Cost Advantage*

Compared with other multinational enterprises, the greatest advantage of Chinese enterprises is to sell good quality products at a lower price.

After enduring 10 years of severe testing in the intensely competitive domestic market, many Chinese enterprises, and especially large enterprises such as Haier and TCL, have adopted international standards of manufacturing technology and quality control and developed an enterprise culture that responds promptly to the market. At the same time, they benefit from economies of scale and the relative cost advantage based on the huge domestic market. The cost advantage based on good quality is the main competitive advantage of Chinese enterprises in the overseas market. Taking the television manufacturing industry as an example, in the first half of 2004, 18,920,000 color televisions were exported. At

an average unit price of US$111.5, this represents an export value of US$2.11
billion. In TCL's case, 6,800,000 color television sets were sold domestically in
2002, of which 1,300,000 were sold overseas. In 2004, TCL's domestic sales
volume reached 8,870,000 sets and the export volume was 5,120,000 sets, meaning
an increase of 30.4 percent and 285 percent, respectively. Cost savings from
economies of scale in purchasing, manufacturing, and research and development
have provided TCL products with a relative cost advantage. On the other hand,
large-scale export enables the enterprises to fully utilize their production capacities, further expanding the effect of economies of scale and enhancing the cost
advantage. For example, in 2004 the mobile phone production capacity of Bird
Corp. reached 20,000,000 sets; the domestic sales volume was 10,000,000 sets,
and the export volume was 3,370,000 sets. Large-scale exports increased the rate
of Bird's utilization of its capacity, giving Bird mobile phones a greater cost
advantage.

1.4. *Building World-Famous Brands*

Having grown up in market competition, Chinese entrepreneurs are generally
willing to undertake new ventures. Many entrepreneurs set their sights on the international market, aiming to make their brands world famous and their enterprises
multinational. In 1999, Mr. Li Dongsheng, CEO of TCL, stated that "our goal is
to establish a world-level enterprise." He believes that "China must have a group
of world-level enterprises which have global competitiveness and world famous
brands. These enterprises must have their own brands, must have their own operating networks, must have their own independent and complete supply chain. China
must develop its own global enterprises."

TCL's goal is an increase in sales volume from 42.1 billion Yuan in 2004 to
150 billion Yuan in 2010 (US$20 billion). Between 2007 and 2009, TCL wants
its two main businesses, multimedia display terminals and mobile telecommunications terminals, to become internationally competitive, allowing the company to
be among the top five world leaders. TCL plans to become the domestic market
leader in three core businesses: multimedia electronics, mobile communications
and digital electronics. This includes home appliances, key components (modules,
semiconductor chips, displays and power supplies), electric lighting and audio-
visual equipment. Its market strategies are:

— to rely on China's big market, establish its lead in the domestic, medium-high
   technology industry, then delve into the international market;
— to promote its brand in developing countries (emerging markets);
— to open up Original Equipment Manufacturing (OEM) and Original Design
   Manufacturing (ODM) businesses in developed countries, using locally known
   brands to expand in the local market.

Haier's CEO, Mr. Zhang Ruimin, pointed out in 1997:

"Accompanied by the rapid progress of economic globalization, and faced with formidable international competition, the survival and development of Chinese enterprises depend on a radical change of the traditional system, taking part in market competition, and internationalizing. As for the ultimate goal, to achieve internationalization is the route that enterprises must go through in order to survive and develop."

In 1997, the Haier Group's management goal was to create China's own world famous brand and to become a world famous multinational corporation. To reach that goal, Haier wants to become a strong competitor among the world's top 500 enterprises by 2010. For its market strategy, Haier formulated the management strategy called "three one-third". "Three one-third" means that one-third of its products will be produced and sold domestically, one-third will be produced domestically and sold overseas, and one-third will be produced in its overseas factories and sold overseas. Bird's chairman, Mr. Xu Lihua, also points out that in order to achieve Bird's long-term goal of becoming the leader in the global telecommunications area:

"Bird must maintain its No. 1 status among Chinese-made mobile phones in the next few years and, at the same time, Bird must endeavor to further develop the overseas market."

Other Motivations

The government's export promotion policy, as well as other policies that encourage enterprises to grow internationally, gave momentum to the launch of Chinese enterprises' international marketing activities.

There is also the need to cope with overseas trade protectionism. Chinese enterprises are often faced with protectionist measures against overseas trade, such as an anti-dumping policy, when entering a foreign market. For example, in the late 1980s televisions made in China were faced with anti-dumping measures by the European Union and, up to now, the quota for television exports to the EU is limited to 400,000 sets each year. In May 2004, the United States also began anti-dumping investigations into China's television trade, which made the export of televisions made in China to the US market uncertain. In order to cope effectively with overseas trade protectionist behavior, and to develop and maintain their volume of sales in the local market, Chinese enterprises started to invest abroad (either by building factories locally, or purchasing local enterprises) to carry out their international marketing activities.

The enterprises also carry out international marketing activities in order to improve their management abilities. For example, by exporting to developed countries, especially through the OEM processing export mode for international enterprises, Chinese enterprises not only acquire information about local markets and borrow their partners' brands and marketing networks, but also learn product planning and design, management of the supply chain, and quality control techniques from their counterparts.

2. Foreign Market Entry Strategies

Chinese enterprises consider two broad aspects, when deciding which foreign market to enter, when to enter, and in which sequence to enter. First, there is the environmental issue, including factors such as politics, economy, social culture, market, and trade competition in the homeland and in the host country. These issues could include: relevant policies of the government, customs and trade barriers, the degree of economic integration in the region, structure of the international industry and the competitive situation, the market scale and potential of the host country, customer requirements and characteristics, the degree of competition and of psychological distance, and the degree of market similarity. Second, there is the enterprise factor, including: the extent of the enterprise's involvement and experience in internationalization, the quantity and nature of the enterprise's resources, its trade and business characteristics, its internationalization goal and strategy, its network of international relationships, the level of technology complexity and the diversity of its products, and its comparative advantages. Based on these factors, the enterprises choose their target markets, the timing, sequence, and mode of entering the international market.

In this chapter, we will continue our study of Haier, TCL, and Bird, and see how they chose their international market and their strategy for entering it.

2.1. *Bird's Foreign Market Entry Strategies*

Bird was founded in 1992 as a manufacturer of Chinese language pagers. In 1999, it allied with the French company Sagem to enter the mobile phone manufacturing field by adopting Sagem's mobile phone R&D technology and using Sagem's mobile phone production lines. China's mobile phone market has always been mostly dominated by foreign brand names. In 1999, the market share of foreign brands in the Chinese mobile phone market was 99 percent. Foreign brands continued to occupy 57 percent of the market share in 2004. Ever since it entered the mobile phone industry, Bird has paid attention to the overseas market. Accordingly, it set up a company branch in Hong Kong in 2000 and started to export a limited number of mobile phones to Southeast Asian and Middle East markets through traders in Hong Kong and Malaysia. To prepare for internationalization, it established an international department in 2001.

From 1999 to 2002, Bird focused on the domestic market to establish itself more securely. Bird sold 6.78 million mobile phones in 2002, occupying 9.95 percent of market share. This was the number three position in China's mobile phone market, and the number one position among mobile phones made in China. Bird's really big export volume came from the French company's Sagem OEM orders in 2002 (from 2002 to 2004, half of Bird's exports came from Sagem's OEM orders). Sagem provided Bird with mobile phone designs and entrusted Bird to manufacturing the phones. Sagem then sold the mobile phones in France. Through this kind of indirect OEM export, Bird's sales increased with decreased production costs. Bird learned manufacturing and management techniques from its partner. However, the OEM mode is not always advantageous for enterprises in establishing their own brands and has management risks. Therefore, Bird also actively started promoting the export of its own brand from 2003, while at the same time carrying out its OEM exports.

When choosing target markets, Bird evaluates the market in each country based on five factors, namely: market scale, market potential, degree of competition, stability of the political environment, and nature of the market (that is, whether the market is controlled by the operators).[2]

In the European market, for example, Bird chose first to enter the open market instead of the operator-controlled market because it is a newcomer and had invested relatively limited resources both in terms of capital and human resources. That is why Bird picked Russia and Italy as its priority target markets in Europe where it could promote its own brand. In the Asian market, the Japan and Korea markets are two highly mature markets controlled by the operators, so it is very difficult for Bird to establish its comparative advantage in these two markets. Therefore, when choosing international markets, the Japanese and Korean markets were not considered.

Birds' key target markets are the emerging markets in Southeast Asia, the Middle East, and South Asia, in particular countries such as Indonesia and Pakistan. The Southeast Asian market is large with good growth potential. It is located near China. Some countries in this region have cultural customs and consumer habits similar to China. The Middle East and the South Asian markets have great market potential and are growing rapidly. With regard to the American market, at present Bird has not chosen North America as a target market because the markets in North American countries are mature and controlled by the operators. However, owing to its good potential for market growth, Bird has selected Brazil as its target market in South America. In the African market, Bird's target markets are mainly Nigeria and South Africa, because markets in these countries have good growth potential. To sum up, in terms of exporting its own brand, Bird's market entry strategy is a selective strategy, consisting mainly of emerging markets.

Bird has adopted two ways to enter these markets: the indirect OEM method for exports to the developed countries (mainly to France), and its own brand method

---

[2]Interviews at Ningo Bird Corp., 28 April 2005.

for export to emerging markets. Within the OEM method, there are two ways. One is OEM manufacturing for Sagem. This means that, using the core technology and mobile phone module provided by Sagem, Bird proceeds with the research and development of application software and visual design and organizes the manufacturing. After that the mobile phones are exported to Europe under the Sagem brand, where Sagem is in charge of sales. The second is direct custom-made manufacturing for the telecommunication operators. In 2004, Bird started to customize mobile phone orders from the European telecommunications giant Vodafone. In the case of its own export brand, Bird adopts different entry methods according to different market environments. For example, in the Russian market Bird promotes Bird mobile phones through the "bird-fly" method by utilizing a locally well-known distributor who is responsible for the distribution and sales of Bird's mobile phones. In the Indonesian market, two distributors are in charge of Bird's sales. At the same time, Bird sets up offices locally to help the distributors launch and manage the sales network and marketing and promotion activities.

2.2. *Haier's Foreign Market Entry Strategies*

Haier began in 1984 as a refrigerator producer. Before 1998, Haier's strategic focus was the establishment of its brand in the domestic market and greater diversification of its business. During this period, Haier began to export refrigerators to the Middle East and the Southeast Asia market. When exporting to these regions, Haier attached great importance to the promotion of its own brand and the creation of relationships. For the first time, Haier registered its trademark overseas in the United Arab Emirates (UAE) in 1991.

In 1996, Haier set up an overseas joint-venture company in Indonesia — Haier Sapporo Ltd. The JV manufactured refrigerators through the CKD mode and sold Haier products by using its own brand. This was Haier's first foreign factory. The reasons why Haier built factories locally to enter the local market included:

— refrigerators are large in size, so the cost of transportation is high;
— manufacturing refrigerators locally through the CKD mode could help Haier achieve a certain cost advantage;
— Haier could utilize the sales network of its local joint-venture partners.

In 1997, Haier set up two joint-venture companies in the Philippines and Malaysia: the Philippine Haier–LKG Electrical Co. Ltd. and the Malaysia Haier Industry (Asia) Co. Ltd., respectively. In 1999 Haier established the Haier–Middle East Co. Ltd. in Dubai in the UAE to take charge of all its sales in the Middle Eastern region. In the same year, Haier set up a joint-venture company in Iran to manufacture and sell refrigerators and washing machines. After 1999, Haier placed greater emphasis on internationalized management and promoting its own world famous brand name. The company began to target the market in developed countries. Haier compares its internationalization strategy to playing chess. That is, if one wants to improve one's chess skills, one should play with the top players. Haier believes that only by entering the fiercely competitive and large-sized markets in developed countries can it expand its market share and create a world famous brand.

By 1998, Haier's refrigerator export volume to the USA was worth US$17 million. Accompanying the increase in its export volume, Haier set up a Haier–America Co. Ltd. in April 1999 in New York to take charge of its sales in the North American market. At the same time, Haier established a sole-venture plant in South Carolina, manufacturing mini-refrigerators with a capacity of under 180 liters sold under Haier's own brand through the Haier–America Co. The company was targeting a niche in the market which is mainly made up of young people and single persons who have no family obligations.

The reasons why Haier set up factories in the US were:

— to be close to the market and make quick responses to market demands;
— the manufacturing scale in the US market. Haier's export volume to the US has surpassed 280,000 refrigerators. This is the minimum number of units it would need to produce if its refrigerator factory is to be profitable.
— the mainstream US market is for large-sized refrigerators. However, due to their bulk and high cost of transportation, these large-sized refrigerators could not be exported to the US market in large numbers. Therefore, the US factory would provide Haier with access to the mainstream market later,
— to avoid the non-tariff barriers in international trade. In the US market, Haier has achieved a "three-in-one localization" pattern, with a design centre in Los Angeles, a marketing centre in New York and a manufacturing center in South Carolina.

In 2001, Haier bought a refrigerator factory in Italy. The refrigerators are distributed in the European market through Haier European Co. Ltd. using Haier's own brand. Demand from emerging markets in the Middle East and South Asia prompted Haier to set up, in the same year, joint-venture enterprises in Jordan and Pakistan to manufacture refrigerators, washing machines, air conditioners and color TVs. Besides satisfying local demand, household electrical appliances produced in these joint-venture factories are also exported to nearby countries. In June, 2002 Haier set up Haier–Japan Co. By 2003, Haier had 13 factories and many sales companies overseas.

In addition to selling its own branded products in foreign markets, Haier also pays attention to OEM cooperation with multinational enterprises. At present, indirect export to markets such as the Japanese and American markets through the OEM mode still maintains a certain percentage of Haier's exports.

2.3. TCL's Foreign Market Entry Strategies

When it was founded in 1981, TCL was manufacturing tapes for tape recorders. It entered the business of television set manufacturing in 1992, and acquired the Hong Kong-based Luk color television company in 1996. Before the 1997 Asian financial crisis, TCL exported its products through the OEM mode, and began an attempt at internationalization. However, the 1997 Asian financial crisis drastically reduced TCL's overseas (OEM) orders for goods, so its exports dropped substantially. TCL experienced great risk arising from a dependence on the OEM export mode. In these circumstances, TCL began to adjust its passive export strategy and the company set up its overseas business department in 1998, actively promoting the export of its products. In 1999 and 2000, the competition in China's television market was extremely severe, especially on price. This further strengthened TLC's determination to expand into the overseas market.

Southeast Asia and South Asia were the first target markets for TCL's international expansion. TCL believes that "to enter the overseas market, both our own brand export and OEM export are needed. When entering Asian markets like Vietnam and India, priority is given to the export of TCL's own-brand products. When entering the European and the United States market, priority is given to the OEM and ODM mode. Considering the matter from aspects such as actual strength, experience and cost, it may be more realistic to enter Vietnamese and Indian markets, which have a higher degree of product homogeny, than to attempt an entry into developed markets, which have a large economic aggregate and have developed more maturely" (Wang Yuanyue and Ji Jiangyue, 2003). The European Union grants an export quota of only 400,000 units of Chinese-made television sets, which is too small an amount. The United States' market is very big, but it is relatively mature, so growth is slow and the market pattern stable. If TCL promotes its own brand in these markets, the cost is too high and the risk is too great. Vietnam and India are emerging markets and have great potential. Also, these countries are quite similar to China in terms of economic structure and modes of consumption. For TCL, with a fixed amount of capital, marketing strength, and number of brands, the possibility of success is much greater when entering such markets.

TCL's first choice of overseas markets is Vietnam because of its 80 million population, its rapidly growing economy and its market scale and potential. Located in South-East Asia and bordering China, the two countries are geographically close. Furthermore, the two countries are similar in their stage of economic development, culture, and customs. TCL believes that promoting its own brand in such a market will be relatively easier than elsewhere. In 1996, TCL acquired the Hong Kong-based company Luks Industrial, which had a television factory in Vietnam. TCL officially entered the Vietnam market when it set up a branch company there.

Then TCL began to set up branch companies in different countries and regions such as India, Hong Kong, the Philippines, Russia, Singapore, Indonesia, Thailand, Mexico, the Middle East, and Australia. TCL sells its own brand in these foreign markets. By 2004, TCL had set up 11 sales branches outside China.

Since 2002, TCL has gradually begun to target the markets in developed countries. North America, the EU, and Japan are the world's largest markets, so it made sense to try to gain some market share there. In order to achieve a great leap in development, TCL entered these developed country markets through acquisitions and joint-ventures. In 2002 TCL acquired the German company Schneider and the American company Govideo in 2003. In that year it merged with the French company Thomson's television division, establishing the world's largest television set manufacturing enterprise TTE (TCL–Thomson Electronics, of which TCL has 67 percent of the shares). TCL also set up joint-venture mobile phone companies with Alcatel. The founding of TTE, in particular, meant that TCL's television production business was truly global. The acquisition of Thomson's television manufacturing was based on the following strategic opportunities:

— To utilize the existing brand and distribution channel of Thomson's color television business to rapidly enter the European and the United States markets. In the United States for example, TCL's products are sold using the RCA brand; the Thomson brand is sold in Europe;
— To circumvent the EU and the United States' trade barriers;
— To employ Thomson's existing R&D ability and its patent technology;
— To realize a comprehensive cost advantage through expanding the scale of manufacturing and optimizing the allocation of resources;
— To internationalize TCL Corp's business operations and management team.

At present, TCL television's global marketing plan includes five main markets: the Chinese market and the emerging markets with TCL's own brand, the European market for the promotion of the Thomson brand, the US' market with the RCA brand, and the strategic OEM business market. TTE has 10 manufacturing bases globally, all of which are near its main markets. Five are located in China; the other five are located in France, Mexico, Poland, Thailand and Vietnam. In 2004, TCL's sales volume in the Chinese market was 8.87 million sets (about 18.4 percent of the total market share), 2.7 million sets in the European market (about 8.2 percent of the total market share), 2.87 million sets in the North American market (about 8.7 percent of the total market share), 3 million sets in the emerging market, and 2 million sets in the OEM business. By developing its multi-brand strategy TCL, had a global sales volume of 19 million sets in 2004.

2.4. Characteristics of Foreign Market Entry Strategies

The market choice and the market entry strategy of our three leading Chinese companies in the consumer electronics business have a number of common characteristics.

(1) These enterprises started to consider actively exploring overseas markets after having obtained a relatively stable market share in the domestic market and having acquired a clear competitive advantage. Haier's refrigerators had number one market share in the domestic market in the 1990s. Before TCL's entry into the Vietnam market in 1999, its color television market share was among the top two in the country. In 2001, when Bird set up its international department, its mobile phone market share was fourth in the domestic market, and number one among Chinese-made brands.

   Each company gained management ability and industrial strength during the competition in the domestic market, which laid good foundations for entry into foreign markets.

(2) When entering the overseas markets, these enterprises generally chose newly emerging markets as their entry point. Peripheral markets near China were often the first choice for overseas expansion because Chinese companies lacked international experience and ability, familiarity with the overseas market, and the necessary resources for international business. TCL's first choice was Vietnam. Haier's first attempt at foreign sales was in Indonesia. Bird's first overseas branch company was set up in Hong Kong. These countries and regions are close to China geographically with similar culture and customs. They represent the type of market that is psychologically close to the Chinese market. These enterprises then proceeded to enter the newly emerging markets in Asia, Africa, Latin America and Russia, etc. Basically, these emerging markets are in developing countries which were similar to China of a few years earlier in terms of their economic structures, consumption levels, and market demand. In addition, these markets have good growth potential. When entering these emerging markets, the three enterprises chose different entry methods. TCL mainly opted to set of branch companies. Haier's main method was through cooperation with local partners and the creation of joint-venture companies. Bird favored the utilization of local agencies to sell their products.

(3) The developed countries' markets also occupy an important position in these enterprises' internationalization strategies. After entering the overseas market, these enterprises began to target markets in developed countries. Developed countries are the world's largest markets with great market capacity. Being highly mature markets, competition is severe. The enterprises need to compete in developed countries' markets whether they are considering aspects like

expanding the enterprise's market share and creating a world famous brand, upgrading the enterprise's management and technology levels, or understanding the development trends of the industry and the market to cope with long-term competition.

The three enterprises chose different methods to enter developed markets. Haier's entered the American and European markets by establishing its own sales channels to promote its own brand. TCL entered by acquiring local brands. Bird decided on the OEM export mode.

(4) The OEM export mode occupies an important position in the internationalization process of these enterprises. In 2004, Bird's mobile phone exports through OEM to its strategic partner Sagem occupied 53 percent of its total exports (exports under its own brand were 47 percent). Similarly, in 2004 40 percent of TCL's total export volume was through OEM to strategic partners such as Philips (the other 60 percent were exported to emerging markets under its own brand name). By using the OEM exports, the enterprise can borrow its partner's brand and distribution channels to enter the developed countries' markets, thereby reducing distribution risk and achieving increased sales. Furthermore, OEM exports allow the enterprise to expand its manufacturing scale and reduce manufacturing costs, obtain technology and market information, learn about its partner's product design and manufacturing technology, and upgrade its own management capability. OEM exports can also promote strategic cooperation in other areas. They have enhanced Bird's cooperation with Sagem in areas such as research and development and purchasing, for instance. TCL cooperates with Philips in areas such as product development and sales in the Chinese market due to their relationship based on OEM exports.

(5) The speed of internationalization among these enterprises is very rapid. Starting from its 1999 entry into the Vietnamese market, it only took TCL five years to become a multinational enterprise. Bird launched its international department in 2001 and by 2004 their export volume reached 30 percent of its total sales. Haier built its first overseas factory in 1996 and had built 13 more by 2003.

3. International Marketing Strategies

3.1. *BIRD in India and in Europe*

Bird's international marketing strategy can be summarized in the words of Bird's General Manager, Xu Lihua: "Our key markets are the European market, including Russia; the Southeast Asian market, especially India; the South American market, especially Brazil; and in these key markets, generally speaking, we open up the markets by adopting the same kind of operational mode that we use in the domestic market. In the case of the European market and the US market, we mainly learn from Nokia, Motorola and Samsung's marketing methods, and sell our products through telecommunication operating companies, or adopt the OEM mode."

Bird in India

India's mobile phone market has grown rapidly. The number of mobile phone users has increased from 5.47 million in 2001 to 28 million in 2003. The main competitors in India's mobile phone market are internationally recognized brands such as Nokia, LG, Samsung, Motorola, Sony-Ericsson, and Panasonic. Their market share in 2003 was 33.3 percent, 23 percent, 16.7 percent, 13.3 percent, 4 percent and 2.7 percent, respectively. In 2003, Bird cooperated with India's local dealers and entered the Indian market by using their sales channels. The Indian market is the most important market for Bird's internationalization strategy.

In India, Bird used its own brand to enter the market. One reason being India's mobile phone market is not controlled by telecommunication operators, making it possible for Bird to sell its own brand. The second reason was that the Indian market is Bird's key overseas market. Establishing its own brand in the Indian market was necessary for Bird to continue its long-term business in India. The third reason was that the Indian market is mainly composed of new customers. Since new customers are unlikely to be loyal to certain brands, it was comparatively easier for new brands to enter the market. Bird's target clients in India were young users who are more accepting of new brands; they tend to act on their own, they like trendy and novel products, and they can afford to buy mobile phones. In keeping with these characteristics of young people, Bird's selling point in the Indian market was "Be Yourself" and "Dare to be different".

The principle Bird stuck to in international marketing was to design mobile phones based on local consumers' preferences which conformed to their habits and to environmental demands. The first mobile phone product Bird issued in India was its S288 mobile phone. This mobile phone was consistent in quality to that sold in China and it had sold well at home. There were two reasons for choosing a mature type and stable-quality mobile phone to be issued first in the Indian market. First, Bird had just entered the Indian market and had not yet set up its service system, therefore choosing a stable model which had been tested in the domestic market would make up for the lack of after-sales services. Second, Bird chose a well-tested model to establish its brand on entering a new market, because only products of consistent quality could help to establish a brand name. However, Indian consumers were complaining that the S288 speaker volume was too low. Many places were very noisy in India, so the speaker volume needed to be much louder than in China. Bird designers responded quickly and adjusted the speaker volume to a higher level to satisfy the specific requirement of the Indian market.

By the end of 2003, Bird had issued four mobile phone models in India, with prices ranging from 5000 Indian Rupees to 12,000 Indian Rupees (which is about

US$109 to US$261). The prices of the four models — S288, S1120, V10 and SC04 — were 5500 Indian Rupees, 7500 Indian Rupees, 2000 Indian Rupees and 12,000 Indian Rupees, respectively. Of these, the S288 and S1120 sold best. The SC04, called the women-star series in China, was aimed at young women. To cover both the low and medium end markets in India, Bird positioned its product was high performance at a relatively low price. Its bestseller's were the low end products.[3] This product positioning corresponded to consumer levels and the competitive situation in the Indian market. Bird's price range reflected its aim of selling high performance products at a lower price. Compared with Nokia, Motorola and Samsung products of the same type, Bird's mobile phone was 10–20 percent lower in price.

In order to control entry risks, and enter the new market rapidly and effectively, Bird chose dealers with local sales networks as its partners. On the basis of its marketing experience in China, Bird believed that a short sales channel was more advantageous in obtaining market information and responding quickly to the market, as well as making marketing support and control easier. Accordingly, Bird reduced the layers of sales channels by partnering with dealers who have their own retail stores.

Bird's first partner in India was a dealer selling telecommunications products. This enterprise, experienced in selling other international mobile phone brands, had 28 branch stores with at least one in every major Indian city. Of these branch stores, 10 are in India's capital, three in Bombay, 13 in India's more economically developed north, and two in southern India. Bird located one more company to act as its trader to complement the coverage by the first dealer and to increase market coverage in India. In 2004, Bird set up its own Indian branch office so that it could strengthen support for its dealers and have control over sales channels. Bird personnel in the branch office helped dealers design and produce posters and outdoor advertisements and gave guidance on launching a new product release, conducting a store promotion and displaying Bird products in-store. They also helped dealers build Bird brand shops. Through market research and customer visits, Bird personnel learned about the market situation, the percentage of Bird products in stores, and the number of service staff in mobile phone stores.

Bird redesigned its TV ads and billboards in respect for Indian cultural regulations. There are strict restrictions on exposing the female body; therefore, Bird's ads in India focused mainly on its mobile phone for the advertising image.

Bird in Europe

The European market is the world's second largest mobile phone market after the Asian market. It is also a relatively mature market with mobile phones becoming

---

[3] Interviews at Ningbo Bird Co, 28 April 2005.

rapidly popular, the European market focuses on mobile phone exchanges replacement.

The European mobile phone market is controlled by the telecommunication operators. As a result, Bird's entry strategy was to use the OEM mode, including manufacturing for international enterprises through OEM (for example, Bird's OEM orders from France's Sagem Company) or custom-made manufacturing for local operators (for example, manufacturing for Vodafone). Bird's most important OEM partner is France's Sagem Company. By making use of OEM exports, Bird sold its products in the European market using its partners' brand names and sales channels. Bird's clients were drawn to its advantages in design, quality, and cost. In 2004, Bird's mobile phone OEM exports reached 1.79 million sets, which accounted for 53 percent of the total export volume of 3.37 million sets.

Other open-style markets targeted by Bird were the Italian and Russian markets. In Italy, Bird's used its own brand and cooperated with local dealers. Bird's choice of dealers was determined by their sales channel coverage, their experience in selling telecommunications products, and their commitment to promoting and selling Bird products. In the rapidly growing Russian market, Bird began by adopting the Bird-fly mode, cooperating with local dealers and using their sales channels.

Bird's target consumers in the European market were young people who are more likely to be attracted by new brands. Bird positioned its newcomer mobile phone as a novel, trendy and high performing product at a low price. To reflect the character of its youthful market Bird's advertisements in the European market adopted the slogans: "Vanity is my favorite sin" and "Anatomy of art".

Bird's pricing policy in Italy and Russia was similar to its pricing policies in other markets. Prices were 10–20 percent lower than similar models of mobile phones from Nokia, Motorola and Samsung, a strategy from Bird's position; as a supplier of a high performance product at a low price.[4] Most of its sales volume in the Italian and Russian markets was filled by Bird's low- and medium-level products, a phenomenon related to the high-income of European consumers.

3.2. *Haier's Strategy in Developed Countries*

In the early stages of its internationalization, Haier decided to use its own brand to enter the markets of developed countries. Chinese enterprises that were relatively weak in funding and commercial strength faced great risk in entering these markets: almost all multinational enterprises were actively present, the competition was intense, and new brands had to break down entrenched brand loyalties. Nonetheless,

---

[4]Interviews at Ningbo Bird Co, 28 April 2005.

Haier believed that only by entering markets of developed countries' could it keep abreast of market trends and technology development. This is necessary of it were to create a world famous brand. Haier realized that "only by having its own world famous brand can the enterprise achieve extra profits in the international market and lay a solid foundation for the enterprise's international management and long-term development" (Wang Zhile, 2004). If consumers in developed countries accepted its brand and Haier became a famous brand, then it would be much easier to promote its brand in other countries. Accordingly, Haier decided to use its own brand to enter the markets of developed countries in the early stages of its internationalization.

Based on market research, Haier studied consumer specific needs and identified niche markets that were not currently served by leading international brands. Haier developed new products to serve these niches. Thus, Haier developed niche products targeted at young people who would readily adopt what is new (for example, the computer-desk mini-fridge for American college student apartments, and the "personal washing machine" for Japan's single women). Haier discovered that some Americans drink wine on a daily basis. With the wine stored in the kitchen refrigerator, which is inconvenient as the wine is drunk in the living room. Therefore, Haier designed a compact wine cellar for the living room. In the early stages of its entry into the markets of developed countries Haier adopted this kind of niche marketing strategy to avoid direct competition with the mainstream brands. By developing products to meet untapped demand, Haier gradually gained acceptance by local consumers and dealers. By 2003 Haier had accounted for 50 percent of market share in America's under 70 L refrigerator market;[5] the niche marketing strategy had worked. Then Haier gradually extended its target from the niche market to the mass market, and also extended its products from refrigerators to washing machines, etc. Thus Haier clinched 10 percent market share in the American large-sized 500 L mainstream refrigerator market. Following the success its refrigerator products, Haier put out other products, such as washing machines, air conditioners, color TVs, and other household appliances on the US market. This gradual entry into the market and gradual introduction of its products helped Haier to familianizer itself with the market, save costs, lower risks, and accumulate experience.

Haier insisted on good quality and good pricing. It did not, however, have customers with low prices or attempt to beat its competitors through price wars. These principles, which Haier commits to in the Chinese market, were also adopted in the international market in order to change the commonly held view that Chinese products are cheap. For instance, in Japan's professional electrical appliance retail stores, Haier's 5 kilo water-agitating washing machine is 19,800 Japanese Yen,

---

[5]In the first half of 2004, Haier earned US$0.53 billion through exports, exceeding the export volume of 2003. (www. people.com.cn. 13 July 2004).

which is cheaper than the Japanese brands and similarly priced as the Korean brands. Haier's 5 kilo drum washers with dryer features are 62,790 Japanese Yen, which is cheaper than the Japanese brands but more expensive than the Korean brands (which are priced at 57,500 Japanese Yen).[6]

The distribution industry in developed countries is mature, dominated by large-scale retail stores and the network of multinational retail enterprises such as Wal-Mart and Carrefour. Their networks stretch over not only the local market but also the global market. Only by tapping their sales channels can an enterprise achieve large scale sales. In 2003 Haier began its "big client, big orders" strategy, actively establishing and developing business relationships with major retail store enterprises in each country.

Since 2004, Haier products have tapped the networks of the top 10 chain stores in the USA, including Wal-Mart and consumer electronics retail chain Best Buy.

Across the Atlantic, Haier products are displayed in the top five large-scale chain stores and professional electric appliance stores in Europe's five main countries. In Japan, Haier products are sold by 10 major professional electrical appliances chain stores, such as Yamada-Electric. In addition to developing its own sales network in the Japanese market, Haier also cooperated with Japan's Sanyo Electric, using Sanyo's network in Japan to sell Haier products.

Haier adapted its sales promotion methods according to different market characteristics. Its advertising slogan in the US was "What the world comes home to", while in Europe it was "Haier and higher". Because TV advertising budgets are very expensive in the USA. Haier tried to look for low cost and effective marketing communication at the point of sale. For example, in contrast to the black and white packaging of other air-conditioning products, Haier used bright yellow and red colors in its packaging to attract US consumers. Haier also provided instructions, on how to choose the right amount of cooling power according to the size of a room. It played up the advantages of Haier air-conditioners, calculating for the consumer the savings from using its product in the context of the energy consumption standard in the USA. This promotional method helped to overcome the lack of sales promoters in America's large-scale chain stores. In another effort to communicate directly with consumers, Haier put up a neon sign in Japan's busiest business street in August 2003. That was the first advertising board in Tokyo's Ginza district set up by a Chinese enterprise.

Haier established the "locally-designed, locally-made, locally-sold" regional sales networks in both the North American and European markets, to better satisfy local consumers demand and to quickly respond to the market. In the US market, Haier set up its design center in Los Angeles, its manufacturing center in South Carolina (Haier's own factory built in 2000), and its marketing headquarters in

[6]Chen Yuming (2004). Why Japanese people take Haier as an example when talking about business? in *Beijing Youth*, 26 October.

New York. In the European market, Haier constructed design centers in Lyon, France and in Amsterdam, Holland. Its manufacturing center was started in Italy (the Meneghetti SpA refrigerator factory bought in 2001), and its marketing head-quarters founded in Milan. Besides these, Haier has four more sales centers in Europe — located in Spain, Britain, Holland and Italy — through which, Haier products are sold all over Europe. This "three-in-one" marketing system enables Haier to acquire the latest market information and understand local consumer demands in the quickest way. Haier can then produce suitable products for the local market, provide consumers with better services, achieve localized manufacturing, and make its products more competitive. Furthermore, this system makes it easier for Haier to learn about advanced technologies in the markets of developed countries and improve its product design and development ability. Haier is also able to obtain better components and equipment because the Italian factory is located in a region of Italy where the majority of top suppliers are located.

3.3. *TCL in Vietnam, India and the Global Market*

TCL in Vietnam

TCL's internationalization process began in Vietnam. TCL acquired Hong Kong-based Luk's, a television manufacturer, which also meant the acquisition of Luk's TV factory in Vietnam. Thus TCL (Vietnam) Co Ltd was created in 1999 to enter the Vietnamese market. TCL (Vietnam) Co Ltd has one factory (in the Bien Hoa Industrial Zone, Southern Dong Nai Province), and three sales branches (in Ho Chi Minh City, Hanoi and Danang). The company employs 15 Chinese and 420 Vietnamese employees.

Vietnam's economy is growing rapidly and has a fair market size and development potential. It is also geographically close to China with similar culture and customs. Nevertheless, when TCL entered the Vietnamese market in 1999 it found a difficult sales environment. Japanese televisions and Korean products had become bywords among Vietnamese consumers for high quality household electrical appliances. Japanese TVs occupied 60 percent, while Korean TVs occupied 30 percent of the market. Annual demand of the Vietnamese television market was 700,000 sets, but 11 multinational enterprises that manufactured household appliances had already set up factories in Vietnam with an annual output of 3 million color TVs. Since supply exceeded demand, the competition was intense. Also, during the vigorous, early stages of Sino-Vietnamese cross-border trade, a large quantity of products from China entered the Vietnamese market. These products were cheap but of poor quality, which gave Vietnamese consumers an unfavorable impression of the quality of Chinese products. Furthermore TCL was a newcomer to Vietnam so few people knew its brand. TCL lacked its own sales network in the market and it was unfamiliar with local policies, laws, environments and customs.[7]

With the characteristics of the Vietnamese market in mind, TCL focused on promoting its own brand while, at the same time, building its sales networks and perfecting its after-sales service system. Thus TCL expanded its market and established a competitive edge. TCL was committed to executing its marketing concept of "let[ting] ordinary customers in Vietnam enjoy a first-class world product and service at affordable prices" (Wang Zhile, 2004).

Thanks to their early entry into the market and their advantages in product technology and brand names, Japanese and Korean television producers generally orient themselves towards the medium- and high-priced markets in Vietnam. Their products are relatively more expensive, and are promoted on their famous brand names. TCL tries to avoid competing directly with them. TCL targets its markets in cities where its sales branches are located, before gradually expanding to peripheral medium and small-sized cities and rural areas. TCL focusses on the medium and low-priced on markets — which yield the majority of consumers — where it mainly promotes its 14-inch and 21-inch color TV series. At the same time, the 25-inch and 29-inch wide screen color TVs are also promoted to enhance the TCL brand. As Vietnam is prone to thunderstorms and TV reception is weak in the suburban and rural areas, TCL has developed television products that are lightning-proof and have good reception. Each TV set is also subjected to strict quality control inspections, and sold at a lower price than for the same type of TV by its Korean rivals, Samsung and LG. This has helped TCL to achieve a high cost-performance ratio.

During the initial stages of its entry into the Vietnamese market — when the TCL brand was unknown — TCL built its own dealer networks and strengthened its relationship with its dealers. Given the small scale of Vietnamese market, the senior managements of Japanese and Korean factories did not make it a-priority to communicate with local dealers. TCL, on the other hand, sent its branch managers and salesmen to visit its dealers. They brought for product demonstrations sample TCL TVs on their frequent visits to help dealers expand the retail network. They also visited retail shops to help the retailers sell more TCL products. TCL established a sales network that basically covered the whole Vietnamese market by cooperating with the dealers. TCL adopted a diverse after-sales service based on the management idea of "creating value for the customers". Generally speaking, free television maintenance is given for two years in Vietnam. TCL was the first to offer a service commitment of "three years' free repair, lifelong maintenance." It set up over 100 repair centers and developed an after-sales service system with a 24-hour hotline. Maintenance personnel would visit customers as soon as possible after receiving calls. A backup TV set is brought along for the customer's use if the

---

[7]Xia Yanglin (2005). From Vietnam to India: TCL'Overseas Strategy. *China Management*, 30 January.

problem cannot be fixed on the spot. TCL's competitors, on the other hand, require their customers to send their faulting TVs to assigned repair centers. TCL's service after-sales has greatly enhanced the Vietnamese consumer's reception of the TCL brand name.

TCL pays particular attention to establishing its image in the Vietnamese market. It works with the Vietnamese Youth Organization in setting up the Vietnamese Youth Foundation. For each TV set sold in Vietnam, TCL donates five Yuan to the foundation which gives financial assistance to outstanding young people to study and undertake research in China. In addition, TCL actively participates in local welfare activities, donating money to Vietnamese affected by natural disasters, the disabled, and the Vietnamese education system.

In 2002 TCL sold 100,000 televisions in Vietnam, giving it a 14 percent market share. The company was the third most successful TV producer in the country, behind LG and Samsung. TCL has become a mainstream brand name in Vietnam's television market. Now TCL's products in the Vietnamese market also include air-conditioners, mobile phones, VCRs, and DVD players (Wang Zhile, 2004).

TCL in India

In August 1999 TCL entered the Indian market through a joint-venture with an Indian dealer — Baron International Ltd. TCL and Baron International co-invested US$28 million to found TCL Baron Electronic Co. Ltd. The investment ratio was 51:49. TCL wanted to establish this joint-venture to promote the sale of its own brands in cooperating with Baron International and utilizing its sales network. Owing to TCL's lack of overseas management experience and its unfamiliarity with the Indian market at that time, the joint-venture's daily operations and marketing strategies were controlled by Baron International. Baron International's marketing strategy set a very low price for the products supported by lots of gifts and advertisements, regardless of the expenditure as its goal was to enter the market quickly. This strategy rapidly increased TCL's television market share but damaged TCL's brand image. In pursuing only sales volume, it also created huge debts. In August 2001 TCL had to dissolve the joint-venture keeping only a branch office. The debts had reached 250 million rupees.[8]

The Indian television market has huge potential. Investigations conducted by ACNielsen ORG-MARG — a leading market research company in India, showed that among the most wanted merchandise in India, a color TV is second only to a house. The Indian television market had a 15 percent annual growth rate; it was estimated that the size of the market would reach 10 million sets by 2006. TCL therefore saw India as a strategic overseas market. The company established

---

[8]Ye Nan (2005). TCL: An Indian Version of the Countryside Enveloping the City. *Global Entrepreneur,* 7 April.

TCL India Holding Pte Ltd in March 2004 to restart its large scale entry into the Indian market and set up its own sales network. In August of the same year, TCL India Holding bought a subsidiary of Indian Thomson Co and established its headquarters in India's economic center — Mumbai — with 30 Chinese and over 300 Indian employees.

The Indian television market is composed of two types of enterprises. The first is multinational enterprises such as Panasonic, Sony, LG and Samsung. The second type is composed of India's local enterprises such as BPL, Onida, and Videocon. Between them, LG and Samsung occupied 30 percent and 20 percent, respectively, of the total Indian TV market in 2004. Samsung competes mainly with LG in the high-end market in big cities. On the other hand, LG's low, medium and high-end products cover the whole Indian TV market, including towns and rural areas.

In the early stages, TCL targeted the medium and small-sized cities, as well as rural areas in establishing its own sales network. First, TCL conducted detailed market research in all of India's small and medium-sized cities and towns, as well as their peripheral rural areas with populations of about 100,000 people. They were researching into consumer behavior and qualified dealers. TCL discovered that consumers in India's small and medium-sized cities and rural areas were similar to consumers in China. Owing to their limited income, they were more willing to buy high performance products at relatively lower prices from dealers with whom they were familiar. Thus, TCL priced its high performance 29-inch color TV at 19,000 Rupees while the Indian-made BPL color TV cost 29,000 Rupees.[9] In addition, TCL chose qualified dealers to promote TCL sales. TCL personnel frequently visited dealers to ensure that they abided by TCL's sales policies and maintained stable sales channels and sufficient funds. At the same time, TCL cultivated good relationships with its dealers by supplying high quality products at competitive prices, maintaining open communication, and offering good after-sales services to customers. To educate Indian dealers about TCL and strengthen their relationship, TCL invited its 130 main dealers to visit its headquarters in China at the end of 2004. After this visit the Indian dealers' confidence in TCL products was considerably enhanced. By January 2005, TCL's Indian company had set up 20 branches in various places, formed a sales network comprising 2,700 distributors and dealers covering the entire Indian market. It had also built a mature after-sales network with 100 after-sales centers. To better satisfy its Indian consumers TCL also set up a research institution in India with 40 research engineers. The high import tariff duties prompted TCL to cooperate with seven local Indian television factories and import parts for TV sets to be assembled in India, thereby reducing costs. TCL also plans to build its own factory in India.

In 2005, TCL's business objective in India was to achieve one billion Yuan of sales income, to be among the top five market leaders in India's television market, and to become the leading brand name in the market within three years.

---

[9]Li Ke (2005). Discovering India. _Chinese Entrepreneurs_, 10 May.

TCL in the Global Market

TCL and the French company Thomson signed a joint-venture memorandum in November 2003 which led to the funding of the TTE joint-venture company (TCL-Thomson Electronics) in Shenzhen, China, in July 2004. TCL is the holding company, with 67 percent of the shares; Thomson holds 33 percent of the shares.[10] TCL saw the founding of TTE as an opportunity to start its global marketing activities. TTE's business model was to provide consumers with innovative, high-quality products that offer excellent value. This was to be accomplished by employing highly-efficient management and enthusiastic employees. The goal was to become the global leader in the color TV industry.[11]

TCL's global management concept saw the division of the global market into five large markets and five profit centers, namely China, Europe, North America, emerging markets, as well as an OEM profit center. Each profit center is responsible for meeting customer demand, product development and promotion, coordinating marketing activities, and managing cost accounting and profit assessment of its respective market.

TCL coordinated its global sales through a multi-brand strategy and achieved a global sales volume of 19 million sets in 2004.

In the Chinese market, TCL products are sold under the TCL brand as well as the ROWA brand. With these two brands, TCL has a broader consumer base. In 2004 the TCL brand sold nearly 8 million sets, occupying 18 percent of the Chinese color TV market. Medium and high-end color TVs (including LCD and PDP televisions) are sold under the TCL brand, while the ROWA brand focuses mainly on more basic televisions. In 2004, ROWA's sales volume was about 1 million sets. In the Chinese market, TCL set up five regional management centers in Beijing, Shanghai, Chengdu, Huizhou and Xi'an. The company also opened 27 sales branches and 168 management departments, covering the entire Chinese market with over 20,000 sales shops. Extensive sales channels and networks, good after-sales services, and a quick response to market demands have helped to guarantee TCL's success in the Chinese market.

In the European market, TCL products are sold under both the Thomson and the Schneider brands, but the focus is on promoting Thomson brand. Thomson is a famous brand name in Europe with a long history, occupying 8.2 percent of the market share in 2004. Thomson products are sold mainly through big retailers such as Media Mart, Carrefour, Euronics, Darty and Comet, and its retail network covers 80 percent of Europe's retailing business.

---

[10]In July 2005, TTE Co (TCL–Thomson joint-venture) bought Thomson's marketing rights in the North American and European markets. In August 2005, TCL acquired from Thomson 100 percent of the stocks of TTE.

[11]Interviews at TCL, 15 April 2005.

In the North American market, TCL products are sold under both the RCA and the Scenium brands, though the focus is on the RCA brands. RCA products are sold mainly through big retailers such as Wal-Mart, RadioShack, Best Buy, Circuit City, Target and The Home Depot. RCA has 220 dealers and 10,000 retail shops in North America. In 2005 TTE launched two specific campaigns to sell RCA brand products. The first campaign was aiming at making RCA products appear younger, using the theme of "science, technology, and affordability". In recent years liquid crystal, plasma, rear projection, and digital TVs have become trendy in the USA. However, RCA's image among American consumers tends to be conservative and old fashioned. To counter this image, TTE tried to link the RCA brand with youthful passion and focused on selling new types of trendy televisions. The second campaign undertaken to sell RCA goods was improving its sales network and intensifying the relationship with its customers. TTE focused its attention on its major clients, who accounted for 80 percent of its sales volume, and gave up some minor clients. TTE chairman Li Dongsheng says that "because 80 percent of TTE's sales volume is accomplished through these major clients, naturally we should serve them well first; giving up some minor clients may affect the total sales volume in North America, but it contributes to the total profit, because giving up minor clients ensures better service to the major clients; the reduction in sales volume can be recovered in the long run. And TTE will focus on serving well its top 25 major clients from now on."[12]

In the newly emerging markets, TCL focused on selling TCL brand TVs, using its experience in the Chinese market and its relative product superiorities to build a sales network and after-sales service system. In 2004 TCL occupied 16 percent of the TV market in Vietnam, 10 percent of market share in Malaysia and 10 percent in The Philippines.

In the OEM market, TCL utilized its advantage of scale and quality control ability to strengthen its strategic cooperation with multinational enterprises and use their brand names to improve its sales.[13]

To lower costs and enhance its competitiveness, TCL reorganized its operations on a global basis in three areas: manufacturing, purchasing, and research and development. TTE has 10 manufacturing bases globally, all of which are near its main markets. Five of them are in China, and the other five are located in France, Mexico, Poland, Thailand and Vietnam. Products manufactured in China are mainly for the domestic market, the emerging market, and the OEM market. The low-cost manufacturing methods adopted by the factories in China were introduced to its factories in Mexico. Products manufactured in its Mexican factories

---

[12]Wang Zhen, Sun Yanbiao (2005). Li Dongsheng Vows to Get Thomson's Color TV Sales Right in the European and American Markets. *Number One Finance and Economics Daily,* July 28.

[13]Interviews at TCL, 15 April 2005.

are mainly for the North American market. Those manufactured in Poland and France are mainly for the European market. Products manufactured in Thailand go to Southeast Asia, Europe, and America, while those manufactured in Vietnam are mainly for the Vietnamese and the Southeast Asian markets. Through this global organization of manufacturing resources and the creation of manufacturing bases near its main markets, TCL can respond quickly to the ever-changing demands of its global customers and can avoid the anti-dumping restrictions imposed on Chinese televisions by European and American countries. In terms of purchasing, TTE has built up a global purchasing platform, enlarged its scale of purchasing, standardized its parts and accessories, and reduced its number of suppliers in order to achieve economies in its purchasing costs. TTE cooperates with Thomson in research and development. TTE's five main research centers have stronger research and development ability, and can use the most advanced technology. By reorganizing its R&D, TCL has accelerated the introduction of new products on a global basis. This kind of global research and development capability facilitates the production of great varieties of TCL televisions. The company's products vary from the economical to the luxurious, from those with basic functions to the high-tech, from analog systems to digital systems.

3.4. *Characteristics of International Marketing Strategies*

In analyzing the international marketing strategies of these three consumer electronics manufacturing enterprises, we identified the following characteristics:

(1) The international marketing activities of the three enterprises are at different stages. Bird's international marketing activity is at the export stage, which is the initial stage of international marketing. Bird uses two approaches: indirect export through OEM and direct export under Bird's own Brand name in Europe and in emerging markets. The products are manufactured in China. In the process of exporting its own brand, to the emerging market Bird uses its experience of marketing in the domestic market as a reference, by extending its domestic marketing technique to the overseas market.

Haier builds an international marketing system of "locally designed, locally manufactured, locally sold" in the world's main markets. It is based on the polycentric marketing concept and aims to satisfy local consumers' demand and respond quickly to the market. Haier endeavors to design products according to the needs of the host countries' consumers, manufacturing in local factories and using local sales networks to sell its own brand name products. Haier mainly exports its own brand directly. Haier's international marketing activities have the characteristics of a "polycentric" organization in the sense of Permuter (1969).

TCL's international marketing activities are global. The joint-venture TTE, of which TCL is the holding company, gives TCL a global marketing perspective to regard the Chinese, North American, European, emerging markets as an integral whole. It builds its marketing networks on a global basis, optimizing the global deployment of its research and development and purchasing and manufacturing systems to coordinate global sales with a multi-brand names strategy. TCL's international marketing activities have the characteristics of "geocentric" marketing.

(2) In emerging markets, all three enterprises opted to promote their own brands, using their experience in the Chinese market for reference. There are many similarities between many of the emerging markets, such as those in India and Indonesia, and the Chinese market of some earlier years. Thus, an effective marketing strategy based on the Chinese model is appropriate. This includes promoting its own brand, setting up a sales network and service network, attaching importance to supporting its network members, and responding quickly to customers' demands. In emerging markets, Chinese enterprises have product and management advantages compared to local enterprises. Compared to multinational enterprises, Chinese enterprises have the advantage of high performance at a relatively low price, as well as the advantage of relying on distribution support and services. In the markets of developed countries all three enterprises have adopted different marketing strategies. Bird entered these markets by adopting the OEM mode, borrowing its partner's brand and sales channels. Haier's entry was accomplished by using its own brand and setting up its own sales channels. TCL used the joint-venture company and its status as main shareholder for entry, leveraging its partner's famous brand and original sales channels.

(3) When entering a new market, all three enterprises avoid direct competition with multinationals operating in the local market. They try to differentiate from their competitors. For example, when TCL entered the market in Vietnam, it chose mainly country and township markets, avoiding the big city markets occupied by multinationals. When entering the market in the United States, Haier mainly chose the niche markets ignored by leading companies. If they cannot avoid direct market competition with these multinational enterprises, the Chinese enterprises usually compete using marketing strategies such as a quick response to customers' demands, supplying high performance products at a lower price, paying attention to distribution support and services, etc. After gaining marketing experience in the country and cities, these enterprises start to expand from the rural markets to the cities, from the niche markets to the mainstream market, and from mono-product to a variety of product lines.

4. Conclusion

To sum up, Chinese consumer electronics enterprises have started the internationalization process but are still at an exploratory stage in terms of marketing entry. The results of their internationalization differ greatly. These enterprises adopt different strategies when entering the international market, including processing materials supplied by clients, exporting, strategic alliances, direct investment and acquisitions. The same enterprise will adopt different entry strategies when entering different markets. Due to their short internationalization, it is difficult to make a comprehensive and totally reliable judgment on the results obtained by adopting different market entry modes. Based on the limited statistics we have to date, we have reached the following conclusions:

— Export is the most common entry strategy; it minimizes risk, but the enterprise's control and influence over the overseas market is also minimal. It also has to face the problem of customs barriers. The major adjustment to customs duties made recently by the USA and the European Union (E.U.) has caused great difficulties for these enterprises. Over a short period of time, processing materials supplied by clients and exporting is a workable strategy to internationalize these enterprises. In the long run, however, this strategy is too vulnerable to changes in the foreign countries' import policies, and too full of uncertainty to be reliable.

— A strategic alliance is the main strategy adopted by these enterprises when marketing their own brands overseas. Generally, they manage their marketing and sell their products by cooperating or establishing a joint-venture with one or several dealers in the target market. There are two advantages to this strategy. For one, their partners are more familiar with the local market. Furthermore, the alliance partners have more extensive sales channels and networks. These two advantages help Chinese enterprises open up the market very quickly and create management experience and trademark conditions for Chinese enterprises' overseas direct investment. Although some strategic alliances end up in failure, most Chinese enterprises have successfully cooperated with their partners overseas.

— In recent years, Chinese enterprises have begun to enter the international market on a large scale through M&A. Owing to the short period of this trend, we can hardly judge its effectiveness. We can, however, anticipate that there are many challenges involved. The acquired enterprises usually have certain problems and one needs time and effort to meld different enterprise cultures together in order to be effective. Whether or not Chinese enterprises can solve these problems becomes the key factor for the success or failure of the merging strategy.

These enterprises mostly choose their target market from emerging markets and within that market they target the low and medium-end consumers. The marketing strategies that they adopt are mainly low prices and high quality services. By cooperating with their overseas network partners, these enterprises have all achieved some success and the market shares of some brands have grown. This indicates that, overall, these marketing strategies are suitable when applied in an emerging market. Direct marketing activities by these enterprises is relatively rare. Haier chose the niche products to begin its marketing in the USA and it achieved some success. TCL carried out its marketing in the markets of developed countries' through the acquisition strategy in order to obtain a brand and sales channel, but the outcome of this strategy is as yet unclear.

References

Douglas, S.P. and Craig C.S. (1995). *Global Marketing Strategy*. New York: McGraw-Hill.

Hu Zuohao (2002). Guoji ying xiao de liang ge liupai: biaozhunhua guandian dui shiying hua guandian" (Two Schools in International Marketing: Standardization Viewpoint Versus Accommodation Viewpoint). *nan kai guanli pinglun*, di 5 juan di 5 qi, 29–35 ye Nankai Business Review, Vol. 5, pp. 29–35.

Johanson, J. and Vahlne, J.E. (1977). The International Process of the Firm: A Model of Knowledge Development and Increasing Foreign Market Commitment. *Journal of International Business Studies*, 8 (1), 23–32.

Keegan, W.J. (1999). *Global Marketing Management*, 6th ed. New Jersey: Prentice-Hall.

Perlmutter, H.V. (1969). The Tortuous Evolution of the Multinational Corporation. *Columbia Journal of World Business*, 4 (1–2), 9–18.

Root F.R. (1994). *Entry Strategies for International Markets*. New York: Lexington Books.

Wang Zhile (ed.) (2004). *Zouxiang shijie de zhongguo kuaguogongsi* (Chinese Multinational Enterprises which Go Global). *Zhongguo shangye chubanshe*, Beijing: China Commercial Press.

Wang Yuanyue and Ji Jiangyue (2003). *Chaoyue zhongguo qiye chengzhang jixian de TCL* (TCL — An Enterprise Surpassing the Growth Limit of Chinese Enterprises). *Gongye daxue chubanshe*.

Zeng Zhonglu (ed.) (2003). *Zhongguo qiye kuaguo jingying* (Chinese Enterprises' Multinational Management: Policy Making, Management, and Case Analysis). *Guangdong jingji chubanshe*.

Sun Jian (2003). *Haier de qiye zhanlue* (Haier's Enterprise Strategy). *Qiyeguanli chubanshe*, Beijing: Enterprise Management Publishing House.

Chapter 6

TECHNOLOGY-BASED COMPETITION AND CHINESE MULTINATIONALS

Jean-Paul Larçon and Geneviève Barré

HEC Paris

1. The Chinese Science and Technology System

1.1. *The New China's Innovation System*

Science and technology programs have been promoted by the Chinese government since 1985 because they are key engines of economic growth based on high technology, economic transformation, and national independence. But, following the pace of economic reforms during a transition period of 30 years, the China Innovation System has evolved over time, aiming at different priorities and implemented through various programs and regulations.

Top Chinese leadership always kept a firm grip on the country's science and technology policy, which has been monitored mainly at two levels: the State Steering Committee of Science and Technology of the State Council and the Ministry of Science and Technology (MOST).

Since 1985, national policy was thus pursued systematically through a series of long-term science and technology programs such as:

— the "Key Technologies R&D Program" launched in 1983. It focused on agriculture, information technology, environment protection, and sustainable development. It identified enterprises as the major technological innovators,
— the "Spark Program" launched in 1986 to facilitate technology transfer to rural areas,

— the "863" Program — "National High Technology R&D Program", which was launched in 1986 in order to enhance China's international competitiveness and improve China's overall capability of R&D in high technology. It was followed by the "873" program in 1987.
— the "Torch Program" launched in 1988 supported high technology industry through the development of science parks and incubators, project financing, and human resource training.
— The "Innovation Fund for Small Technology Based Firms" launched in 1999 supported the establishment of new technology-based companies.

The "863 Program"

The origin of the "863 Program" (863 Ji Hua) lies in the initiative taken in March 1986 by four leading Chinese scientists: Wang Daheng, Wang Ganchang, Yang Jiachi and Chen Fangyun. They recommended major, focused investments in advanced fields of science and technology in order to narrow the gap between China and developed countries. This vision was personally approved by the Chinese leader Deng Xiaoping, which allowed the elaboration of specific objectives and detailed program.

The program covered eight key technology areas: biotechnology, space, information, laser, automation, energy, new materials and marine technology. It has been extended regularly in the framework of the five-year plans. From 1986 to 2001, the "863 Program" enjoyed state financing of RMB 11 billion and involved more than 20,000 researchers and administrative staff in more than 3,000 research institutions, universities and enterprises.

It contributed directly to some of China's major achievements in biotechnology, space industry, and information technologies such as sophisticated robots, new hybrid rice varieties, new drugs, and Chinese language operating system (OS).

Research institutes have always had a key role in the implementation of the program, even though in recent years the R&D projects conducted by enterprises receive increased funding. Two thirds of the projects aim at applied technical development and one third at more academic research objectives.

The "863 Program" has directly contributed to the innovative competitiveness of Chinese corporations thanks to the financial support it offers for the creation or adaptation of new products and processes. In addition, it helps companies put new technologies on the market more quickly.

In April 2001, the State Council approved continued implementation of the "863 Program" in the 10th Five-year Plan and confirmed the program's objective: to enhance China's innovative ability and competitiveness. The budget was increased substantially and the implementation process was co-managed by the MOST and the Commission of Science, Technology and Industry for National Defense.

The State Council put the program under co-management because the mid to long-term objectives included both civilian and military objectives.

China's Science and Technology (S&T) programs led to major achievements.

In 2003 the successful launch and safe return of China's Shenzhou V spacecraft meant that China had become the third nation in the world to successfully send a man into orbit. Foreign experts estimated China's annual spending on space programs at US$2 billion, approximately 20 percent of the NASA budget.

"Program 863" also focused on the development of high performance computing networks in China. The program led to the Legend Group's development of the supercomputer "DeepComp 6800" for the Chinese Academy of Sciences (CAS). It was also instrumental in the later development of "Dawning 4000A", the first Chinese supercomputer to be listed among the world's 10 fastest supercomputers. The Dawning 4000A is manufactured by Dawning Co. Ltd for the Shanghai Supercomputer Center (SSC) for the Ministry of Science and Technology (MOST).

Major High-Tech Projects 2006–2020

The 2006 "Medium to Long-Term Strategic Plan for the Development of Science & Technology" outlines China's high-tech priorities and policies such as financing, intellectual property rights, technological standards, and public procurement.

It covers seven major avenues:

— integrated circuits and software, which implies the creation of new R&D centers;
— new-generation networks such as the Internet, national digital TV network, and mobile phone network;
— advanced computer technology and information power grids;
— biotechnology and medicine, genetics, production of vaccines, traditional Chinese medicine;
— civilian aircraft, engines, and helicopters;
— satellite applications for meteorology, oceanography, telecommunications, etc;
— new materials, especially for information, biological, and aerospace industries.

China's R&D Intensity

Funding for these programs has grown rapidly over time. Between 1991 and 2002 the R&D effort increased on average by 15.2 percent annually in real terms. The Chinese R&D intensity (R&D expenditure as a percentage of GDP) has rapidly increased from 0.6 percent of GDP in 1995 to 1.34 percent in 2005.

China's R&D intensity is still lower than that in Japan (3.12 percent), the US (2.76 percent), and the EU-25 (1.93 percent). However, in absolute terms, China has been catching up very rapidly, especially since 1999. In 2001 China ranked number four globally in terms of domestic R&D-related expenditures with a total of

US$72 billion at purchasing power parity. This means that the country was behind the United States (US$285 billion), the EU (US$187 billion), and Japan (US$104 billion), but ahead of all other economies, including individual member states of the European Union.

The percentage of R&D expenditure financed by the Business Enterprise Sector in China was 57.6 percent in 2001, a percentage similar to the EU-25 situation (56 percent), but much lower than the percentage in the US (64.4 percent), and in Japan (73.9 percent). In fact, the share of direct government sector spending in China remained quite high, representing 29 percent of total R&D expenditures in 2001.

The Key Role of the Chinese Academy of Sciences

Founded in 1949, the Chinese Academy of Sciences (CAS) has a key role in China's innovation system.

The CAS has a total staff of over 58,000, of whom 39,000 are scientific personnel. It is the parent organization of 89 research institutes and the hub connecting 688 academicians and the country's most talented scientists. CAS researchers have developed the state's first atomic bomb, the first satellite, and they contributed to China's manned space mission.

Since 1994 the CAS has also developed specific tools to attract top Chinese researchers returning from abroad such as the "Hundred Talents Programme."

From 1998 to 2003, CAS researchers published 119 articles in *Nature* and *Science*, two leading scientific journals. This accounts for half of the total written by Chinese scientists.

Government agencies, universities, research institutes, and companies are competing for what is a scarce resource today: top researchers, scientists and engineers. To meet the growing demand for a scientific workforce, universities have had to increase the numbers of students in science and engineering, especially at the advanced research level and PhD programs.

In 2004 the Ministry of Education announced that it would almost quadruple the number of universities with world-class scientific capabilities from 10 to 38.

China Ministry of Science and Technology (MOST) put a systematic emphasis on the necessity to attract more talent from home and abroad in the high-tech sector. MOST also endeavors to develop specific policies which draw on the potential for the repatriation of talented Chinese scientists and engineers with overseas training and experience.

The CAS thus plays a major role in research and in education as well as in promoting the development of China's high and new technology industries.

In 2001 a first batch of 13 CAS related institutions were turned into companies. Twelve of them became limited liability companies, such as Legend Holdings Ltd which controls Lenovo, and is still under control of the CAS. The last one was merged with a state-owned enterprise.

Initiated in 1998, China's pilot project, called the Knowledge Innovation Program (KIP), became China's major incubator for the development of high-tech industries and the monitoring of the transfer of S&T innovation results.

As of 2005, China's innovation system was still managed from the top by a few key national decision-makers: the State Council, the MOST, and the CAS. However, this management involves a variety of actors including universities, state research institutes, state-owned or private enterprises, and the research community. Among other institutions, the National Natural Science Foundation of China (NSFC) supports basic research and some applied research, identifies and fosters talented researchers in the realm of science and technology.

In 2006 the innovation system was much more enterprise-centered than in the past and was managed more like a network of semi-independent units than a traditional hierarchy.

1.2. *China's High-Tech Clusters*

The selection of high-tech development zones in China was not only based on the existing network of research institutes and the specialized objectives of S&T programs, but also the ambition of balanced regional economic development.

Although the largest share of basic research is conducted in the Beijing region in state controlled institutes, China has to transform the heritage of its R&D investments made in such provinces as Sichuan and Shaanxi that had a key role in specific sectors during the cold war. Naturally coastal cities are also very active in R&D, especially applied research and development in companies with the support of government.

The latest generation of the "863 program" devotes special attention to local clusters and encourages local governments to focus on specific high-tech areas and build their own comparative advantages.

This adds a new element of competition and specialization to the development of high-tech clusters. The development is influenced by the central government, local authorities, and company initiatives.

However, the development of China's high-tech parks from 1988 to 1997 was planned mainly by top governmental officials who were clearly influenced by existing models such as Silicon Valley in the US, Tsukuba in Japan, or Hsinchu Science Park in Taiwan. The overall objective of China's science parks was to increase cooperation between research institutes, universities, and local corporations in order to accelerate the development of new technology-based private firms. Science parks targeted industrial development in areas such as: micro-electronics and electronic information services, space and avionics, optics, machinery and electronics, life science and biological engineering, new materials, new energy resources, ecological science and environmental protection, medical science, and bio-pharmaceutical technology.

Thus industry, government, and academic cooperation, which in the past had been strong in China, found a modern expression in the science parks with the emergence of the entrepreneurial dimension. Furthermore, this cooperation has manifested itself in recent years as an incubator and supporter of the financial market by offering venture capital.

China has developed up to 53 "high-tech industry development zones" which have contributed to the rapid growth of China's high-tech activities. Statistics from the Ministry of Science and Technology show that from 1991 to 2002, major economic indicators of 53 high-tech development zones in the country grew almost 50 percent on a year-to-year basis, with an increase of total turnover volume from 8.73 billion yuan (US$1.06 billion) to 1,532.64 billion yuan (US$186.9 billion). In the meantime, the number of workers employed in high-tech parks surged during that period from 140,000 in 1991 to 3.49 million — an increase of nearly 25-fold.

Beijing Zhongguancun Science Park

Beijing offered the best conditions to be the pioneer among high-tech industry development zones. The city offered a unique concentration of government decision-making centers, research institutes, and high tech corporations. Beijing is the home of the PRC's highest authorities, the State Council, the Ministry of Science and Technology, the Ministry of Defense, the Ministry of Education, as well as the Beijing municipal government. Beijing is the home of leading research centers such as the Chinese Academy of Sciences (CAS), the Chinese Academy of Engineering (CAE), the National Natural Science Foundation of China (NSFC), and two leading research and teaching institutions: Tsinghua University and Peking University.

Initiated by the State Council in 1988, Zhongguancun Science Park (ZSP) received a state-level status and has been the model for other high-tech parks in China. The development of science parks like ZSP was considered as important for China's technological competitive capabilities as the creation of Shenzhen Special Economic Zone in the 1980s and the opening-up of the Pudong District in Shanghai in the mid-1990s.

The park is located in Haidian District in northwest Beijing and has six additional subsidiary parks in other districts. ZSP research institutes can be credited with key Chinese technological ventures such as the nuclear weapons program, the missile and satellite programs, and the large computer program.

Covering an area of about 100 square kilometers, the park has a unique capacity to attract scientific and engineering talents. Some 400,000 highly educated teachers, researchers, engineers, scientists and support staff work in the science park. In 2005, some 14,000 high-tech companies were operating in the park, with major activities in software development, IT products and services, optical electro-mechanical integration technologies and products, bioengineering, pharmaceuticals, new materials, and environment protection technologies. The park is the largest software development and production centre in China.

Some leading Chinese companies were born in Beijing's high-tech cluster. For instance, the legendary Lenovo Group was founded in 1984 with seed money from the Computer Technology Institute of the CAS. Another example is Datang Telecom Technology (DTT), which was created in 1988 by the Chinese Academy of Telecom Technology. Tsinghua Unispendour Group (Thunis) was founded in 1993 by Tsinghua University and China's second largest notebook supplier. The Founder Group was started in 1996 by Peking University and the country's No. 2 PC manufacturer.

The relationship with foreign MNCs and the international R&D environment is a key element in the park's dynamics. Foreign companies cooperate with their Chinese counterparts and share in the training and development of the work force of scientists, engineers, and technicians. This pool of human resources has one of the highest mobility rates in China. Companies such as Nokia, Hewlett Packard, UTStarcom, Matsushita, Mitsubishi, Microsoft, Oracle, Novartis, Sharp Microelectronics (SMC), Ericsson, Sun Microsystems, Schlumberger, and Bell have subsidiaries, R&D labs, or offices in the park.

Government support for the Park has always been very strong, including a broad spectrum of incentives and special regulations like: research funding, preferential bank loans, tax breaks, easier access to land-use, simplified visa procedures, and support to returning overseas students.

The entrepreneur and finance sector are now competing with the more traditional governmental and scientific communities to be the major influence in park dynamics.

Since 2005, the Ministry of Science and Technology and the Beijing Municipal Government have been pushing for the park to play a more active role as incubator and training center for innovators. They also want the park to attract more venture capital, which was introduced in the Park in 2000 (see Box 6.1).

1.3. *China's Science-Driven Companies: Tsinghua Holdings*

Universities have a key role in China's innovation system and contribute directly not only to the development of new theories and technologies, but also to the transformation process of these new technologies from prototypes to new products and services on the market.

Beijing's Tsinghua University is one of the largest applicants for patents in China in six scientific disciplines. It has also been one of the leading contributors to the development of new businesses based on university research output. Starting in

Box 6.1:   Venture Capital in China and the High Tech Sector.

In 1985 the State Council created the first venture capital firm, China New Technology Venture Investment Company, as a tool to develop various high-technology industries.

In 1998 Shenzhen was chosen by the Chinese government to experiment with new regulations on venture capital because of the combination of the high-tech sector and a well-developed financial system.

In 2000 Zhongguancun Science Park (ZSP) authorities created the first VC companies aiming at supporting medium- and small-sized high-tech companies established by research institutes and helping them grow and be more competitive.

In 2005 80 percent of China's venture capital focused on the development of small- and mid-size technology enterprises. A total of US$6 billion was invested in 2,000 projects.

The Chinese Ministry of Science and Technology recognized that venture capital plays an irreplaceable role in the development of the high-tech industry. This led the way to less governmental influence and new legislation, including adaptation of VC practice of the China's Company Law.

A key element in the reform would be to raise the maximum percentage of shares that could be traded for technology and intellectual property.

Since 1999 the opening of a Growth Enterprise Market (GEM) has provided the first alternative channel for emerging companies to raise funds for business development in Hong Kong. Later in 2007 the China Security Regulatory Commission (CSRC) announced the launching in 2008 of the Shenzhen Growth Enterprise Market (GEM). Companies listing on the Shenzhen GEM would be required to have total equity of at least RMB 30 million.

In 2007 the Chinese government also set up a special fund of 100 million yuan (about 12.8 million US dollars) to encourage venture capital companies to invest in technology-based small- and medium-sized enterprises (SMEs).

Furthermore, the National Development and Reform Commission (NDRC) and the Ministry of Finance jointly issued guidelines for government-backed venture capital investment in order to support high-tech industries like: integrated circuit manufacturing, software outsourcing, telecom technology, digital video and audio development, auto electronics, and new material development. The government-backed fund would take controlling stakes in the companies receiving the investment.

1988, it developed a portfolio of companies called Tsinghua University Enterprise Group. This group was restructured in 2003 to constitute Tsinghua Holdings Co., Ltd. a limited liability company wholly owned by Tsinghua University.

The portfolio of Tsinghua Holdings includes at least seven listed companies such as Tsinghua Unisplendour Group (Thunis), Chengzhi Shareholding, and Tsinghua Tongfang (see Box 6.2).

Tsinghua Tongfang Co., Ltd. (THTF) is run by scientists. The founder of the company, Lu Zhicheng, is a graduate of the university. He was a faculty member at Tsinghua University from 1977 to 1997, during which he taught and

Box 6.2: Tsinghua Science Park and High Tech Ventures.

Tsinghua Science Park

Tsinghua Science Park was founded by Tsinghua University in 1994 to foster innovation and commercialization of university research projects.

Tsinghua Science Park occupies 25 hectares of land in the heart of Beijing Zhongguancun Science Park.

It promotes a culture of "techno-entrepreneurs" and has acted as an incubator since 2001 to promote high-tech start-ups. The incubator is an important part of the Park; it helps develop both technological achievements and high-tech enterprises. The R&D Center of the International Enterprise Center welcomes international companies such as P&G, Sun, Schlumberger, and NEC.

Tsinghua Science Park has established branches all over China: in Nanchang (Jiangxi Province), Kunshan (Jiangsu Province), Xi'an and Xianyang (Shanxi Province), Langfang (Hebei Province), and Zhuhai (Guangdong Province).

Beijing's government offers preferential conditions for graduates returned from overseas to develop new high-tech activities.

Tsinghua Holdings Co., Ltd.

Tsinghua Holdings Co., Ltd. was founded in 2003 with a registered capital of RMB 2 billion following a restructuring of the former Tsinghua University Enterprise Group. It is a limited liability company wholly-owned by Tsinghua University and an exclusive university platform for its science and technology development, corporate financing, research commercialization, startup incubation, and international cooperation.

Tsinghua Holdings is the founder and largest shareholder of seven listed companies including:

— Tsinghua Tongfang, listed in 1997 in Shanghai, China's third largest PC vendor.
— Tsinghua Unisplendour, listed in 1999 in Shenzhen, specializing in information technology and communications.
— Chengzhi Shareholding, listed in 2000, specializing in pharmaceuticals and biotechnology.

Tsinghua Holdings also has minority interests in over 30 other companies such as Solar, Capital Biochip, Venture Capital, and Yuanxing Bio-Pharm.

Tsinghua enterprises' total revenues went from 773 million RMB in 1995 to RMB 19 billion in 2005.

Among the A-Share companies, "Tsinghua Cluster" represents 1 percent of the entire A-Share market value and 40 percent of the "University cluster."

---

conducted research on computer-controlled artificial environments. In 1989, Lu Zhicheng created the first company project in the field of artificial environment engineering. He founded Tsinghua Tongfang in 1997 by merging different business units developed by the University. THTF is controlled by Tsinghua Holdings which has a 50.4 percent share, and is listed on the Shanghai Stock Exchange.

Lu Zhicheng's vision was that Tsinghua Tongfang would make scientists multimillionaires because they would be able to exchange their IPR for company stock options.

Tsinghua Tongfang Software Co., one of the subsidiaries of Tsinghua Tongfang created in 2000, was one of the first companies in Beijing to allow its staff to buy shares of the company. Eight percent of the 50 million Yuan (US$6.02 million) of the company's capital was controlled by the research staff in the form of intangible assets. The new company was based at Tsinghua University's software technology center, China's first ever center to export software. The center focused on the development and marketing of software for e-commerce, education, enterprise information management, and digital appliances.

The Chairman of the Company, Sun Jiaguan, is also a former faculty member of the university and a member of the Chinese Academy of Engineering. He is the inventor of a computer auxiliary design system which has exclusive intellectual property rights in China.

From 1997 to 2003, Tsinghua Tongfang diversified its activities and grew rapidly. Revenues increased from US$47 million to US$812 million.

Tsinghua Tongfang (THTF) runs the world's most comprehensive database of Chinese scientific journals. This database, named the China Knowledge Infrastructure (CNKI), is based on a collection of 18.7 million research papers published in 7,200 Chinese journals and magazines over the last three decades, more than 200,000 master theses and doctoral dissertations in the past five years, and 3 million other documents.

In 2004, the project generated 200 million Yuan (US$24 million) in revenues and 23 million Yuan (US$2.78 million) in profits.

Tsinghua Tongfang has also become the leader of the integrated circuit (IC) card business in China. It has its own capability in IC card design, card reader design, and industrial application development. THTF controlled 40 percent of China's smart ID card market in 2004 and has begun to develop its international activities. It is already the major supplier to the world's top smart card companies, such as Gemplus.

Tsinghua Tongfang is China's third largest PC vendor, behind top vender Lenovo and second ranked Founder. THTF's new plant, opened in 2005 with a capacity of 3 million, is the largest PC factory in China. It also develops application software, offers value-added contents, and provides a variety of computer network and system integration services.

Government sponsored technological projects are at the origin of most Tsinghua Holdings enterprises. In 1995 the Chinese government gave Tsinghua University the "Large Container Inspection System" development project. The research was conducted by the nuclear research departments of the university and led to very positive results. Thus the decision was made to move to a phase of industrialization; a new company was born: Nuctech.

The company developed large fixed and mobile x-ray inspection equipment (THSCAN) used by customs offices to check the contents of shipping containers. Nuctech inspection systems have also been applied in other areas such as aviation security inspection, industrial manufacturing, medical devices, environmental protection and food processing.

By 2005 — 10 years after the beginning of the research program — Nuctech proprietary x-ray inspection system had been exported to 30 countries and held about 60 percent of the international market of container inspection systems.

Without neglecting emerging markets and clients from Asia, Africa, the Middle East, Central Europe, Nuctech had targeted specifically the most demanding potential international clients such as Australian and Hong Kong customs departments, or the Israel-Palestinian Authority for the container inspection systems at the crossing between Israel and the Gaza Strip.

Nuctech's next targets were evidently North America, Western Europe, or the Japanese market, all of which were still controlled by Western and Japanese competitors. Nuctech was demonstrating an impressive combination of capabilities including technology development, entrepreneurial spirit, international vision, and capacity of implementation. New Chinese high-tech ventures demonstrate a very unusual capacity to learn and move very quickly.

2. Business Strategies and Technological Capabilities

2.1. *Technological Innovation Capabilities: Qingdao Hisense Electronics*

Founded in 1969, Hisense is among China's top 10 electronic manufacturers; it employs more than 10,000 people and its revenues hit 22.1 billion Yuan ($2.67 billion) in 2004. Hisense has been listed on the Shanghai Stock Exchange since 1997 but is still a government-controlled company, with 58.72 percent of its shares belonging to Qindao Municipal Government and state-owned entities (see Box 6.3 and Annex A.6).

Hisense Group is diversified into four major businesses: household appliances (television, air conditioners, refrigerators), IT (computer, software and network security products), telecommunications (CDMA mobile phone, etc), and services.

Hisense's Technology Roots

Technological innovation is at the center of the company's culture and policies. Hisense spends 4 percent of its sales on R&D and Hisense Technical Park, founded in 1993, is the major source of new products for the company. It focuses on the

Box 6.3: Government Support to Technology-Oriented Companies: Qingdao Municipal Government.

Qindao Municipal Government, in close relationship with the provincial government and the State Council at the national level, has a key implementation role in economic development and supporting the growth and transformation of local champions.

In the 1980s and 1990s it helped state-owned enterprises such as the Haier Group, Hisense, Tsingtao Beer, Double Star — a shoe manufacturer — and Aucma (freezers & refrigerators) with tax breaks, economic incentives and support in M&A and corporate restructuring.

The local government is active in attracting foreign direct investment and opening space for economic development in specialized areas such as the Qingdao Economic & Technical Development Zone (QDZ), one of the first 14 national-level economic zones approved by the State Council in 1984.

Qingdao is one of China's major electronics and home appliance centers. In 2007, sales of electrical home appliances in Qingdao are expected to reach 180 billion yuan (US$22 billion), with 40 percent of parts produced locally. The IT sector is also emerging with the production of integrated circuits and mobile handsets with Hisense, LG and Lucent Technologies.

A series of key industries is represented both by national champions and the foreign multinationals present, with 1,852 approved foreign-funded projects from 53 countries and regions. The industries and their companies include:

— household appliances, electronic & IT industries: Aucma, Haier, Hisense, Hitachi, Mitsumi, OTC, Sanyo, Sindo-Ricoh.
— automobile, container & shipbuilding industries: American Standard, CIMC, Clarke, CNOC, CSIC, Federal Mogul, Kamatsu, SAIC-General Motors, Takeuchi.
— new materials: Almatis, BaoSteel, Hyosung, Kiswire, Posco, Saint-Gobain, Sekisui.
— port & logistics industry: Maersk, P&O, BAX GLOBAL, DP World, Yitochu, MSC, ZIM, COSCO, CMST, Sinotrans, China Shipping, Panama shipping, Ocean & Great Asia Logistics, Lions Container, Pacific Container, Pros Logistics, Dragon Logistics, Kerry Logistics, Hanjin Logistics, HK Merchants Group, etc.
— petrochemical industry: Air Liquide, Dragon Air, GS, Kohap, LG, PetroChina, Praxair, Rhodia, Sinopec, SK, SOMO.
— bio-pharmaceutical industry: Shanghai Pharmaceuticals.

Production costs in Qingdao are one-eighth those of Korea and Japan and one-fifth those of Europe and the US, according to the CCPIT Qingdao Sub-Council of China.

Qingdao has also actively developed its infrastructure to host the sailing competitions of the 2008 Olympics with a planned annual budget of US$200 million.

application of digital and internet technologies, intelligent technology, and chip development.

The R&D centre employs more than 1,500 staff and teams of post-doctoral researchers. It benefits from the support of government R&D programs and is commissioned to implement state-level research projects and be an industrial base for China's "863 Program."

In 2005 Hisense announced the successful development of a new processing chip for color TV named 'Hiview'. It was the first industrial digital TV chip with independent intellectual property rights in China's audio and video field. The new chip adds capacity and new functions at a lower cost and will reduce China dependence on foreign technology, a key objective of the Ministry of Information Industry (MII) which funded the project.

Hisense's strategy aims at competing on domestic and international markets with superior quality and design based on in-house technology.

In its television business Hisense switched very rapidly from color TVs to LCD (liquid crystal display) and high-end plasma display panel (PDP) flat screen TVs.

Thus, Hisense's direct competitors are both Chinese giants like Haier and foreign multinationals such as Matsushita, LG, and Samsung, all of which have a strong presence in China and in international markets in terms of sales and manufacturing.

Hisense is therefore obliged to fight on three fronts: technology to develop higher quality products, operations to reduce cost and improve marketing, and distribution to increase volume.

Hisense, which has already the largest color TV production base in Northern China and an annual production of 6 million units, plans to grow a step further and to "go global", in order to increase the scale of production, to increase bargaining power with suppliers, and to firmly establish its brand and reputation domestically and internationally.

Hisense's Internationalization Process

Hisense Import & Export Co., Ltd. was created in 1991 and is responsible for the export of televisions, air conditioners, refrigerator, DVDs, computers, CDMA mobile phones, cordless telephones. They also import supporting parts and accessories. Hisense's exports are growing extremely rapidly, covering some 50 foreign markets and representing revenue of US$400 million in 2004.

However, in 2004 the company decided to accelerate its internationalization process by manufacturing abroad and cooperating in the long term with foreign partners to secure distribution, sales, and service.

Hisense had its first experience in manufacturing abroad in South Africa, a country which it entered in 1994 and where it developed a successful sales and service network.

In 2001 Hisense seized the opportunity to acquire a former Daewoo plant and developed it into the largest color TV production base in the country. In 2005 Hisense South Africa Development Enterprise had an annual output capacity of 300,000 units and a 15 percent market share.

Nevertheless, the key targets were the developed markets of Japan, the US, and the European Union, where it was necessary to get around the difficulty of current or potential protective barriers.

In 2002, Hisense created a 50–50 joint-venture with Sumitomo, the leading Japanese trading company. The JV "Summit Hisense" opened Sumitomo's distribution channels in Japan and abroad to Hisense consumer electronics products. Similarly, Hisense will open its distribution network in China to Japanese high-end electric appliances to be sold in rich coastal cities.

In the USA, Chinese TV makers faced very serious anti-dumping measures in 2003, with the US Department of Commerce imposing duties of 28–46 percent on TV sets exported by four Chinese TV makers — Sichuan Changhong Electric Co., Xiamen Overseas Chinese Electronic Co (Xoceco), Konka Group, and TCL.

Hisense looked for niche strategies, investments, and partnership in order to keep the door open. In 2005 it signed a cooperation agreement with US Digital Television Inc (USDTV) to supply digital high-definition TV sets to the US market.

USDTV will market the digital TV products and services via Wal-Mart. A shareholder in USDTV and Hisense would charge hardware costs plus a percentage based on subscription fees paid to USDTV.

In Europe Hisense had to face many difficulties.

The first one was brand recognition. The Bosch–Siemens Household Appliance Group (BSH), which controlled 25 percent of the German appliance market, had registered in 1999 the trademark "HiSense" in Germany and the European Union. The trademark differed from the name of the Chinese manufacturer's brand only by the use of a capital "S".

This led to an acrimonious legal battle between the two companies and six years of negotiations on the trademark issue; Bosch–Siemens originally asked 10 million Euros (US$13.07 million) for the trademark, which Hisense did not accept.

Taking into consideration the long-term interests of Bosch–Siemens in the Chinese market, a settlement was reached in 2005 with the offices of China's Ministry of Commerce.

Bosch agreed to transfer the use of the "HiSense" trademark to the Hisense Group for 500,000 Euros (US$670,000) and Hisense agreed to withdraw its application for the Bosch trademark in China.

After the lawsuit, Hisense started registering trademarks in more than 100 countries. For the Chinese government and Chinese companies like Hisense exporting electronic and high-tech products, Intellectual Property Rights was becoming a major issue because of their strong impact on market penetration, brand recognition, and profits.

A second series of difficulties was linked to import duties and quota limitations. At the end of the nineties Chinese television manufacturers had to support import duties of up to 40 percent . This made it impossible for Hisense to compete against leading European brands such as Siemens or Philips; Hisense sold only 2,500 televisions across Europe in 2002.

So in 2003 Hisense started investigating manufacturing opportunities in new EU member states such as Hungary, Poland, and the Czech Republic. All three countries had relatively cheap and skilled labor and a central location in the new enlarged Europe.

Hisense chose Hungary and the industrial park of Sárvár, run by Flextronics — the Singapore-based provider of design and manufacturing services — to produce its television sets for the EU market. With up to 60 percent of the value of the parts and labor used coming from Europe, the products qualify for the designation "EU-made." The other 40 percent of parts and labor comes from China, allowing Hisense to partly capitalize on its low cost base. Production started in 2004, with French retailer Carrefour among the first clients with a planned output of 300,000 units for 2005.

At this stage of development, Hisense — like other multinational companies — had to reorganize its value chain by creating manufacturing hubs abroad and allocating more resources downward in marketing, distribution, service, branding, IPR, and localization of activity.

2.2. *China's Industrial Standards: China 3G*

In order to reduce its dependence on foreign standards, foreign technology, and foreign Intellectual Property Rights, China is actively developing its own standards and its active participation in international agencies in charge of developing international standards.

This is made possible by the size of China's domestic market, the large presence of foreign MNCs in the domestic market, and the close cooperation between the Chinese government, R&D institutes, and companies.

China is the world's largest mobile phone market and the Chinese government wants to lessen its dependence on foreign companies and technology in this area.

Since 1985 the International Telecommunications Union had been conducting an evaluation process and promoting convergence for the third-generation of mobile telecommunication systems (3G mobile standard).

China's Ministry of Information Industry (MII) took a very active role in the process and was able to submit in 1999 the proposal of a Chinese standard: TD-SCDMA (time-division synchronous code-division multiple access).

After much discussion and debate, the Chinese standard TD-SCDMA was accepted together with European standard WCDMA — the 3G version of Europe's

GSM — sold by Nokia, Ericsson and Siemens, and the American standard CDMA 2000 — the 3G version of CDMA — developed by Qualcomm Corp.

TD-SCDMA marked a milestone for the Chinese telecommunications industry, as it was the very first telecommunication standard proposed by China to be internationally accepted. The government did not want to see the third-generation system dominated by European and US systems, as it was in the past.

The project had been planned carefully and well-financed. Chinese research institutes had been mobilized through China's "863 Program" to work on 3G and beyond. TD-SCDMA had been developed in secret by the China Academy of Telecommunication Technology (CATT), the Datang Group, and a foreign partner, Siemens. It is believed that the Academy and its partners have invested billions of Yuan in TD-SCDMA technology. The cooperation between Chinese and foreign enterprises with Chinese government support worked perfectly. Telecom operators have been asked to follow the move.

In 2000 seven Chinese and foreign telecom operators and equipment manufacturers formed the "TD-SCDMA Technology Forum" to promote the global standardization, manufacturing, and marketing of this third-generation (3G) mobile technology. These organizations were: Datang Telecom Group, Siemens AG, China Mobile Group, China Unicom Group, Huawei Technologies, Motorola and Nortel Networks.

This has been a clear victory for China's telecommunications industry. Two North American mobile phone makers joined the club and supported a Chinese wireless technology competing with European and US standards.

However, the implementation process was less successful. In 2005 WCDMA and CDMA 2000 were introduced in Europe, Japan, and the Republic of Korea. TD-SCDMA, on the other hand, was not yet implemented in China. A new scheme then emerged with key players proposing 3G networks that would bundle WCDMA and TD-SCDMA, or use TD-SCDMA as a complementary technology.

At that stage the Chinese government had the sense to delay issuing licenses in order to give TD-SCDMA time to catch up to the other standards or negotiating a compromise. China's government had won the battle of international acceptance of its national standard, but a de facto standard in China would result from the competition between two actors: Chinese firms and their foreign partners which are actively developing their R&D facilities to be ready to operate with one standard or another once a political decision is made.

2.3. China's Telecom Industry: Foreign Competitors and National Champions

China's telecom market has developed enormously in the past 20 years. Phone penetration jumped from 0.4 percent in 1980 to 13 percent in 1999, with the number of fixed line subscribers moving up from 4.1 million to 108.8 million. China imported its first mobile phone telecommunication facilities in 1987, and it took a decade for the number of subscribers to reach 10 million.

At the end of 2004 the country had more than 310 million fixed line subscribers, 330 million mobile phone users, and 95 million internet users.

This represented a massive investment by China in telecom infrastructure. The Ministry of Information Industry (MII) had the delicate task of balancing different objectives: quickly building a modern infrastructure by leapfrogging over outmoded technologies with foreign technology, while also protecting and nurturing domestic manufacturers.

Foreign equipment vendors were invited to the country but were restricted by complex regulations and felt considerable pressure to transfer technology, create local content, and offer equity stakes in joint-ventures.

Alcatel Shanghai Bell

When the first joint-venture for switching equipment — Shanghai Bell — was established in China in 1984, the Chinese government defined in very clear terms what should be transferred to the Chinese side by the foreign partner and in what manner. In 1998, more than 74 percent of Shanghai Bell's hardware and 90 percent of its software products were developed and made in China. The government also allocated quotas to this joint-venture, which defined the maximum that Shanghai Bell could sell to the domestic market and thus the export objectives of the JV.

In 2002, Alcatel — which had inherited its participation in Shanghai Bell from ITT Belgium — consolidated its presence in a partnership with the Ministry of Information Industry by incorporating 12 of Alcatel's joint-ventures. Alcatel and the Chinese government established Alcatel Shanghai Bell, an entirely Chinese company in which Alcatel effectively holds 50 percent plus one share. As part of the deal, Alcatel agreed to make its worldwide technology base and research and development programs available to Alcatel Shanghai Bell.

Alcatel Shanghai Bell has 5,800 employees and currently employs more than 2,000 R&D staff. The company maintains a research and innovation center in Shanghai that develops next generation communications solutions such as 4G and optical transmission technologies.

In Alcatel we see the foreign partner transformed into, if not a purely domestic company, at least a local player contributing R&D directly into China's long-term objectives and policy for telecom equipment.

Meanwhile, strong domestic contenders had emerged such as Datang Telecommunication, Great Dragon Telecommunication Group (GDT), Huawei Technologies, and ZTE. Chinese operators China Telecom and Unicom were encouraged to buy Chinese products by the Ministry of Information Industries (MII), a national preference similar to Canada's support for Nortel, US support for Lucent, or German support for Siemens.

Local champions were also encouraged to enter the international market, increase their technological capabilities, and build their international reputation.

National Champions

The two largest Chinese telecom equipment manufacturers, both founded in the late 80's and headquartered in Shenzhen, Guangdong Province, Southeastern China, were Zhongxing Telecom (ZTE) and Huawei Technologies Co., Ltd. They were competing in the domestic market but also had aggressive plans for overseas expansion.

ZTE was founded in 1985 by a handful of state-owned companies affiliated with the Ministry of Aerospace Industry. It has been listed on the A-Share market of the Shenzhen Stock Exchange since 1997 (A-shares are reserved for Chinese investors). In 2004 it was very successfully listed on the main board of the Stock Exchange in Hong Kong, becoming the first Chinese company to issue both A-shares in China and H-shares in Hong Kong. ZTE's largest shareholder is Zhongxing Telecom Equipment Ltd., one of 520 key state-owned enterprises identified by the State Council, which holds 44.1 percent of the shares.

In 2004, ZTE had 21,000 employees and sales contracts worth approximately US\$4,111 million (RMB 34 billion). It invested nearly 10 percent of its annual sales income into R&D. ZTE benefited from national research funding, such as China's 863 "Program" and the "Torch Program", which was developed in 1988 by the Ministry of Science and Technology (MOST) and particularly focuses on Information Technology.

Huawei Technologies was founded in 1988. It is a private "people-owned" company. The ownership structure lacks transparency and is quite complicated. It includes the founder Ren Zhengfei who eventually amassed up to 5 percent of the shares, but it also includes joint-ventures or subsidiaries of Huawei, provincial telecom operators, and the employees of the company either collectively and individually, with the labor union being the largest shareholder. From the very beginning, Huawei has issued shares to employees who bought them with their annual bonus.

Among other elements, this might explain the fact that Huawei has not yet gone public, even if rumors of such a move have circulated since 2002. From 2002 to 2007, company officials indicated regularly that Huawei would be listed sooner or later; however, based on the company's financial situation, there was no urgency of an IPO. Huawei might also have chosen to invest massively in new technologies such as 3G or international markets before going public.

Thus, Huawei's strategy is currently less dependant on the financial market than even ZTE, a state-owned enterprise. However, if ZTE's links with Chinese government bodies are more formal, both companies can be perceived as effectively differentiated partners of Chinese telecom policy at the national and international level.

Unlike most high-tech operations in China, Huawei has not used joint-ventures with foreign partners as a major source of technology and knowledge. Huawei bet mainly on its own research potential and the recruitment and development of local talent.

Each year Huawei hires 2000 to 3000 graduates from China's top universities. Forty percent of its 16,000 staff is dedicated to R&D. Huawei Technologies is following a very proactive patent strategy. For example, they applied in 2003 for more than 3,700 patents with cross-certification with foreign multinationals; 85 percent of these were invention patents.

Finally, even if there is still a lot to accomplish, China's telecom policy has already reached major goals: rapid development of the infrastructure, easy access to advanced technology, and emergence of national champions.

2.4. *The China–India Information Technology Link*

The software industry in China has been growing rapidly during the past few decades and has played a significant role in the economy. Both government policies and corporate competitive strategies are shaping China's competitiveness in the sector.

India, however, has an edge over China in the software business. Chinese high-tech companies have been closely following the Indian model in that area and exploring opportunities of fruitful exchange between the two countries.

Such exchanges go both ways. Indian software giants like Tata Consultancy Services (TCS), Infosys Technologies, Satyam Computer Services, and Wipro are very active in China. They are, for example, specializing in software for the finance, securities, insurance, and telecommunication business in Shanghai's Pudong District.

NIIT, a leading Indian IT training company founded in 1981 in Delhi, has been active in China since 1998 and has over 100 education centers in 25 provinces through partnerships with universities, software technology parks, and other IT companies.

In 2005 the Shenzhen government asked Indian software company Zensar Technologies to train 1,000 Chinese software students in India for global software project management. The objective is to turn Shenzhen into the leading Chinese outsourcing destination.

Huawei Technologies had started with recruiting Indian engineers — some of whom still work at Shenzhen headquarters — but made a bolder move in 1999 when it opened a development center in Bangalore with around 70 people.

In 2000 Huawei announced the development of its Bangalore hub and the creation in India of the second largest software development base after China, expanding its existing R&D facilities and its potential for a strategic partnership with Indian software services companies. "We are leveraging Indian software development skills and complementing it with the Chinese expertise in system design and system architecture," said Huawei Technologies India's Chief Operating Officer at that time.

Huawei Technologies invested US$80 million to set up its R&D centre in Bangalore. In 2005, Huawei Technologies opened an 800-strong software R&D lab in Bangalore. The centre works on 3G, wireless, and optical transmission solutions. The company has also outsourced work to Wipro, Infosys, and Mphasis. Huawei has made investments of US$100 million in India and planned to have a total workforce of 2,000 by 2007.

Huawei's presence in India is also linked to the steady growth of the Indian market, and the Bangalore R&D center is a good way to serve local demand.

In 2005 both Huawei and ZTE were in competition with Siemens, Nokia, Ericsson, Alcatel, Motorola, and Nortel for a Bharat Sanchar Nigam Ltd's (BSNL) GSM network expansion project. BSNL is the largest telecommunications company and second-largest GSM service operator in India.

2.5. *China's Telecom Vendors, ZTE,*
and Huawei's Go Global Strategy

Huawei and ZTE's first steps abroad were in emerging markets. Chinese telecom equipment manufacturers had a strong price advantage: their products are usually 20 percent –30 percent cheaper than those of foreign rivals.

ZTE's first move overseas was in Pakistan in 1998 with a turnkey networking project involving 266,000 ports.

ZTE Corporation has undertaken the construction of Africa's biggest mobile telecom network, which cost US$90 million. In Brazil, Chinese companies ZTE and Huawei offer prices of up to 50 percent lower than their competitors in Brazil by importing equipment manufactured in China.

In 2003, the CDMA mobile phone, a new source of revenue for ZTE, was successfully put on the international market. ZTE won a US$100 million mobile phone order from VIVO (a Brazil telecom carrier) in May 2004. This was the most valuable mobile phone contract ever won by a Chinese mobile phone manufacturer to date.

In 2004 ZTE's new leadership defined the three major growth sources for the company: overseas expansion, mobile phones, and 3G.

Moving from emerging markets to developed economies was a real challenge; how sustainable would the competitive advantage of Chinese vendors be? Cost would still be an advantage, but technology, adaptation to client needs, and good service would be much more important to compete in the home market of leading western MNCs. ZTE planned to use the financing proceeds from its Hong Kong listing to expand its international sales network in Europe and the USA, establish production overseas, and beef up its research and development spending.

Huawei has been also very active on the global scene. It won contracts in emerging Asian, African, Eastern European and Latin American countries.

Huawei broke into the Brazilian market in 2001. After courting the Brazilian telecommunications company Telemar for two years, it was rewarded with a contract to provide internet equipment for home use, edging out Alcatel. In 2004 Huawei entered into a significant next-generation networks (NGN) contract with Embratel, the first telecom provider in Brazil.

In 2003, it beat out seven bidders, including Siemens AG and Alcatel, to upgrade the network of Etissalat, the United Arab Emirates' carrier.

In Russia it spent three years constructing more than 3,000 kilometers of optical cables for Russia Rostelecom, the leading fixed-line telecom operator.

Nonetheless, Huawei progressively shifted its efforts from Asia, Africa, and South America to build a presence in the European market, the world's second-largest third-generation (3G) mobile phone market after Japan.

In 2005 Huawei employed 1,300 people in Europe, 75 percent of whom were locals. Regional headquarters are in Britain, but 26 satellite offices contribute to increasing localization, partnering with local corporate customers and a quick response to local markets demands.

Huawei beat Ericsson in 2004 to win a contract from Dutch carrier Telfort to build a 3G mobile communications network in the Netherlands. In 2005, the company announced that it signed a European frame agreement with alternative Sweden-based carrier Tele2.

At that time, British Telecom was planning to build its next generation networks, the "21st Century Network", which was a project worth US$20 billion. This was a good opportunity for Huawei, which invested a lot in securing the contract. BT initially considered a large number of candidates among telecom equipment vendors, and Huawei had to go through a series of audits and tests conducted by BT. This screening ranged from product environment certification to working conditions within Huawei factories and even within plants of its subcontractors in China. Finally, in 2005 Huawei was shortlisted along with Fujitsu, Alcatel, Ericsson, Cisco, Lucent, Siemens, and Ciena.

Huawei's low cost but high quality products were gaining increasing recognition in Europe and challenging the western establishment.

North America would be Huawei's next target.

Huawei, which had already been working for North American companies on an original equipment manufacturer basis, created in 2001 a wholly-owned subsidiary later called "FutureWei" in order to do business in the US. The headquarters are in Plano, Texas, three miles from the Telecom Corridor and 10 miles from the Dallas Corridor. Huawei also has two small US R&D labs in San Diego and Santa Clara. The objective of these implantations was to provide telecommunications and enterprise networking equipment to the U.S. and Canadian markets, with a focus on research and development, design, direct sales networks, OEM, and ODM relations with US companies. However, development in the USA was not as successful as in Europe. It was not easy commercially and it was not easy to staff local talent, even if Huawei recruited from leading giant local telecom companies like Nortel Networks Corp. and Cisco. It probably was not easy because of distrust of products "Made in China".

In 2003, Huawei had to face a legal battle in the USA: Cisco Systems, the world's top producer of internet switches and routers, began to sue Huawei and its subsidiary in the USA for infringement on its intellectual property rights. Cisco and Huawei compete in selling routers that direct traffic on the internet. After more than one year, Huawei and Cisco reached a settlement and Huawei agreed to change its source code, manuals, on-screen help system, and command line interface, the text-based system through which users can configure Huawei's products.

Meanwhile, Huawei entered a global partnership with 3Com in 2003 to develop computer-networking equipment. 3Com owned 49 percent of the new joint-venture Huawei-3Com Co., Ltd. (H3C), a company employing 2,600 engineers with headquarters in Hong Kong and R&D centers in China (Beijing, Hangzhou and Shenzhen) and India (Bangalore). Huawei-3Com opened representative offices in Latin America, Asia-Pacific, Hong Kong, Japan, and Russia.

However, in the competition with Cisco, Huawei and 3Com were still in a very inferior position. Cisco's total sales amounted to US$22 billion in 2004 with a net profit of US$5.3 billion, compared to Huawei and 3Com's total sales of CNY 31.7 billion and profit of US$1 billion. In 2006 the JV Huawei-3Com was taken over by 3Com which accelerated the financial problems of 3Com, which was later acquired by the asset management firm Bain Capital Partners with Huawei as a minority partner.

In 2007 Huawei international revenues exceeded domestic sales. Even if the company has difficulties penetrating the very competitive US market, the international revenue is an extraordinary achievement which cannot be explained exclusively by cost advantage. On the contrary, it is a demonstration of the company's capacity to develop advanced technology solutions both through massive internal R&D efforts, partnerships, and the ability to transform this technology according to client needs on the Chinese market and the international scene. It also means Chinese competitors such as ZTE and Huawei are replacing weaker western competitors on the list of global competitors.

3. Conclusion

Technology-based competition is vital for Chinese multinationals to carve their niche in world markets. They benefit from a very favorable environment which includes strong government support, a sophisticated network of university-based institutions, and a large pool of well-trained researchers and engineers.

Their strategy includes development of in-house R&D capabilities, R&D partnership in China and abroad, and technology-based acquisitions.

However, the financing of such an adventure is quite specific to China and the current governance of Chinese MNCs. Most of them are listed on the stock exchange as direct or indirect emanations of state-owned entities; or like Huawei they are not yet listed. Thus, financing the technology investment is linked both to cash flows generated by the companies, research budgets financed by government, and loans from state-owned banks and financial institutions.

With the domestic market being more competitive, Chinese firms competing on price, and the step-by-step transformation of the banking system, these conditions might change in the future. Meanwhile Chinese multinationals are taking advantage of the situation, betting on innovation and quickly upgrading their processes, products, and services.

References

Dahlman, C. and Aubert, J.E (2001). *China and the Knowledge Economy: Seizing the 21st Century*. Washington DC: World Bank Institute.

Fischer, W.A. and von Zedtwitz, M. (2004). Chinese R&D: Naissance, Renaissance or Mirage? *R&D Management*, 34(4), 349–365.

Fisher, W.A. and Alii (2003). Alcatel in China: Business as an Adventure. *Case Study IMD Lausanne.*

Huang and Alii (2004). Organization, Programme and Structure: An Analysis of the Chinese Innovation Policy Framework. *R&D Management*, 34(4), 367–387.

Larçon, J.P. (2003). Research on Strategic and International Management in China: An International Perspective. Xi'an Jiaotong University, Proceedings of China–Europe Strategic Management Seminar.

Liu, X. (2005). China's Development Model: An Alternative Strategy for Technological Catching-Up. Research Institute of Economy, Trade and Industry (RIETI), BBL Seminar 2005/03/22.

Low, B. (2005). The Evolution of China's Telecommunications Equipment Market: A Contextual, Analytical Framework. *Journal of Business & Industrial Marketing*, 20(2), 99–108.

OECD (2007). *Reviews of Innovation Policy China Synthesis Report*, Paris: OECD.

Rong Xianping (2004). Research on China's Small and Medium-Sized Enterprises' Cluster Development Model. *The Chinese Economy*, 37(5), 7–18.

UNCTAD (2005). *World Investment Report Transnational Corporations and the Internationalization of R&D*. Geneva & New York: United Nations.

Xie W. (2004). Technological Learning in China's Color TV (CTV) Industry. *Technovation*, 24(6), 499–512.

Xie, W. and White, S. (2004). Sequential Learning in a Chinese Spin-off: The Case of Lenovo Group Limited. *R & D Management*, 34(4), 407–422.

Yam, R. and Alii (2004). An Audit of Technological Innovation Capabilities in Chinese Firms: Some Empirical Findings in Beijing, China. *Research Policy*, 33(8), 1123–1140.

Chapter 7

INNOVATION & KNOWLEDGE TRANSFER IN CHINESE MULTINATIONALS

Li Donghong

Tsinghua School of Economics and Management

During the last five years, more and more Chinese enterprises have invested overseas in manufacturing, research or marketing activities. Their internationalization process is closely related to the pursuit of innovation and knowledge transfer at a global level. This process includes characteristics which are common to all multinationals, but there are also dimensions that are specific to China. Chinese multinationals are actively looking for the best way to develop their innovation capabilities through knowledge transfer at the international level.

In 2000, the Haier Group invested US\$ 30 million in its factory in Camden, South Carolina, USA, to produce refrigerators for the local market, transferring its technology and some of its management practice from China to the USA. In 2002, Shanghai Automobile Industry Corporation (SAIC) participated as a minority partner in the restructuring of GM Daewoo along with General Motors and Susuki in order to increase its international experience. In 2004, TCL entered a partnership with French Alcatel to build on its experience in mobile phone technology.

Innovation and knowledge transfer are key dimensions in Chinese companies' internationalization process. An increasing number of Chinese companies are accumulating technology and knowledge through their international experience, then transferring it to China and to their own international operations in order to grow, build their competitive advantage, and increase profitability.

151

1. The Knowledge Transfer Imperative

For nearly 25 years, Chinese enterprises have invested abroad to expand their markets, find low cost production bases, control key resources, earn more profit, and increase their competitive advantage by diffusing knowledge or integrating global resources. Jincheng (Motorcycle) Group invested in Africa and South Asia to enter new large emerging markets and increase profitability.

China National Petroleum Corporation (CNPC) and the China Petroleum & Chemical Corporation (SINOPEC) invested in Kazakhstan and Venezuela to control oil resources.

TCL has built factories in Vietnam and India for at least four motives: finding new markets, lowering the cost of production, increasing the return on investment, and transferring abroad knowledge and technology. Many Chinese companies have set up offices in the Silicon Valley, USA to keep up with the latest technological developments.

Although all these motives always play a part in the internationalization process, the emphasis on each motivation changes during the transformation process of the national economy and the stages of enterprise development. Generally speaking, for multinationals based in developed economies, primary motives for internationalization are market expansion, profitability, and building advantages over competitors. But for multinationals based in emerging markets, the primary motive can be technology and knowledge transfer to improve the capacity of innovation. It is especially true for Chinese enterprises due to the specific conditions of their business environment.

To most Chinese enterprises, the Chinese market is still more attractive than foreign markets and for quite a period of time to come, the main battlefield.

Growth Opportunities

The Chinese market will continue its fast growth in the medium-term and will play an increasing role in the global economy. First, many products in China are at their first stage of development and offer a great market potential. For instance, the total number of planes and automobiles in China is far lower than that in developed countries, and it will increase quite rapidly in the coming 10 years. Second, although the market for many products is very large, it is still small in terms of the consumption per capita, thus there remains a large area for growth. In 2006 China had the world's largest mobile subscriber base of 450 million, but a mobile phone penetration rate of slightly more than 34 percent, lower than the in USA, the Republic of Korea, or Singapore. The same is true for other goods such as coals, iron and steel: China is among top producers, but has a rather low consumption per capita.

Competition

In some industries, competition in China is less intense than in developed economies such as the USA and Europe: the market is less saturated, it is growing faster, and fewer competitors are present on the market. Some industries such as the military, petroleum, chemical, and electronic industries, as well as the automobile, telecommunications, banking and insurance, wholesale and retail, cosmetics, education and adult training sectors also benefit from strong and effective government protection. Chinese companies have thus great opportunities for growth and profit in these areas that are less open to competition.

Localization Advantage

Chinese enterprises have the advantage of greater familiarity with the local market. The Chinese market is more complex than the market of mature economies because of market size and diversity, the great regional differences in terms of economic development, the changes and uncertainties linked to the progressive shift from planned to market economy, the importance of social networks, and the specificity of China's cultures.

Thus, Chinese enterprises which are based in this complex market have learned from experience how to develop their activities, manage their operations and compete effectively.

For most Chinese enterprises, however a key motivation to enter international markets lies less in market orientation than in seeking technology, management skills, and human resources.

Technology

Technology in Chinese enterprises in most cases is not at the highest level. Chinese companies producing television sets, computers, mobile phones, washing machines, air-conditioners, and program-controlled communication systems have developed very fast in recent years, but do not own the core technology in these industries or the most advanced, new, related technologies. Up to 80 percent of DVD players are made in China, but Chinese manufacturers have to pay high license fees to Japanese or other companies that control the technology. In the textile industry, China has a very large production capacity but still imports the more innovative high-tech textiles.

Management Skills

The quality of managerial skills in Chinese enterprises is weak compared to companies based in developed economies. Business administration lacks rigor in terms of systems and procedures, and companies sometimes have outdated or an over-simplified vision of good management practice.

The productivity of a company like Shanghai Baosteel Group Corporation, which is among the best Chinese companies in terms of quality of management, is still lower than its foreign counterparts Japanese Nippon Steel Corporation or Korean Posco (formerly Pohang Iron & Steel).

The Quest for Technology

Technology and management are the two major weaknesses of Chinese companies both on the domestic and international markets. Thus, Chinese companies' priority to survive and grow is to develop their knowledge base, innovativeness, and core technology.

Knowledge assets are a major source of strength and competitive advantage (Teece, 1998). Foreign multinationals such as ABB, GE, or Philips develop profitable operations based on their technological superiority in China's domestic market, while their main Chinese local competitors compete on price, make little profit, and are sometimes eliminated. Most Chinese enterprises have realized the necessity of developing advanced knowledge and technology to compete in the home market with leading international competitors, build a sufficiently stable market share, and increase profitability.

In the international market, leading multinationals do not have to worry about anti-dumping measures and they make more of their profits with high-tech or -value added products. On the other hand, Chinese companies compete on price and sometimes sell below cost. This leaves very little profit for Chinese companies and opens the way to anti-dumping procedures by foreign governments, as illustrated by the penalties imposed upon Chinese color TV sets by European and North American countries in the last 10 years, and the quotas imposed on Chinese textile products by the United States and the European Union in 2005.

Chinese companies have the market potential and low cost advantage, but to succeed locally and internationally they have to significantly increase their technology and knowledge assets. So their main problem is to decide how to do it and eventually to use the internationalization process not as an objective per se, but as a means to acquire or build these assets.

The purchase of IBM's PC business by Lenovo Group Ltd. has greatly expanded its market, increased its sales, and changed Lenovo from a local Chinese enterprise into a multinational. However, a key element in the decision was the acquisition of proprietary technology in the field of personal computers, as well as management and marketing know-how in the industry.

In 2004, when TCL developed its partnership with Alcatel in the mobile phone business, the main objective of TCL Chairman Li Dongsheng was clearly techno-logical transfer and joint product innovation and development.

"It is a straightforward project. Our counterpart has no factory but two research centers with a small number of employees. The cooperation is not aiming at large-scaled operations ...what is most appealing to us is its technology".[1]

2. Chinese Companies' Knowledge Transfer System

2.1. *The Knowledge Transfer Process*

Foreign Multinationals in China

In a multinational corporation, the flow of knowledge can go from the headquarters to the subsidiaries — a forward transfer of knowledge — or from the subsidiaries to headquarters — a reverse knowledge transfer (Ambos and alii, 2006).

With the forward transfer, technology, product development, and product and process innovation are managed at the headquarters' level. International subsidiaries and units are mainly responsible for purchasing, production, marketing, and sales, and have a very limited role in terms of innovation. The flow of knowledge and innovation goes from the headquarters to the international units.

With the reverse knowledge transfer, knowledge and innovation are generated at the level of subsidiaries and are scattered around the world. The subsidiaries are mainly responsible for innovation and R&D; resources are limited to the top.

Of course, in a dynamic and fast changing environment, knowledge is created at different levels in all parts of the organization and has to be disseminated in a process of intra-company knowledge sharing.

With the intra-company knowledge sharing process, knowledge and technology are generated both at the top and the periphery, where subsidiaries are responsible for specific missions. The knowledge and technology sharing process is based on cooperation between departments within the company and joint initiatives.

In the eighties, the focus for innovation in multinational companies based in developed markets was mainly at the headquarters level, and the process was managed with a top-down approach. These companies were successful in their domestic market where they had built up a unique knowledge and technology base. They were transferring this accumulated knowledge to their subsidiaries in the form of products, equipment, technology and personnel, as well as in terms of rules and procedures introduced in the foreign offices, joint-ventures, or wholly-owned subsidiaries. This was the typical approach during the first stage of the internationalization of western multinationals in emerging markets. Then these

---

[1]He Yuxin (2005), TCL and Alcatel: Divorce or Separation? *Finance*, No. 5.

companies started reorganizing their innovation process on a global basis, developing a worldwide network of R&D centers.

In China, Microsoft has set up a Microsoft Research Center and Microsoft Asian Technology Center in Shanghai. IBM has established an IBM Software Development Center, IBM Information Technology Centers in Beijing, Guangzhou and Shanghai and the IBM China Research Center in Beijing. Intel has created the Intel China Research Center (ICRC).

As the innovation process naturally takes place also in the manufacturing and sales departments of foreign subsidiaries, the knowledge and innovation transfer takes place from the center to the periphery, with the headquarters mainly playing the role of mutual feeding agency.

Chinese Multinationals Abroad

Chinese multinationals differ strongly from their counterparts in developed economies. At the beginning of China's "opening up" policy, there was a lack of financing, technology, and trained personnel; the function of their internationalization process was through exports to get the foreign currency to buy the necessary equipment, technology and material.

Chinese government and companies were also sending their staff abroad to develop their knowledge and skills. The objective at that time was to acquire the knowledge and technology and to introduce it in China through imports, FDI, and international cooperation.

Simultaneously, foreign multinationals were also transferring technology to China through their offices, joint-ventures, or wholly-owned subsidiaries, as well as in importing equipment and proprietary technology into China. Many Chinese companies developed innovation capabilities through their partnership with foreign multinationals to increase their competitive advantage in the domestic market. With the capacity to quickly increase their international experience through all possible mechanisms: imports, exports, international offices, OEM, production under license, cross-border M&A, strategic alliances, and wholly-owned foreign subsidiaries, Chinese multinationals were then born.

How did they manage the knowledge and innovation transfer?

The forward knowledge transfer model

Chinese companies facing very severe competition in the domestic market started to prioritize investing in emerging markets, such as those of Asia or Africa. The target countries were at the same level of development and living standard as China, or even lower, as in Pakistan, India, Vietnam and Nigeria. This expansion was similar to that of western multinationals investing in emerging markets. Chinese enterprises have set up offices, issued production licenses, and organized joint-ventures or wholly-owned Chinese subsidiaries. They transferred their accumulated knowledge of technology, management, and marketing to these units in order to develop their sales and increase profits.

The reverse knowledge transfer model

The situation was different when the most advanced Chinese companies started investing in the US, Europe, Japan, and in Korea. Similarly, Chinese companies had to acquire equipment and proprietary technology and to train personnel, but they also invested directly in activities of research, development, and knowledge creation.

The learning process and transfer of knowledge from less developed countries was minimal, while through investments in developed economies, Chinese companies' foreign subsidiaries could feed their parent company with advanced technology and advanced management practice.

This approach will continue to have a key role in the knowledge acquisition process for years to come, until the Chinese economy has reached the middle-income level in the middle of the 21st century, according to the Chinese government's economic forecast.

The intra-company knowledge sharing model

At that point, Chinese multinationals will have to manage a process of knowledge sharing, knowledge dissemination, and enrichment throughout their organization.

One can expect that Chinese companies will also create relatively independent R&D centers in emerging economies that will contribute to this sharing of the knowledge flow between the center and the subsidiaries in order to strengthen their overall managerial and operational capabilities.

2.2. *The Focus on Developed Economies*

Chinese companies clearly understand that they will find the most sophisticated technologies and equipment, management techniques and skills, trends in consumer demand and marketing strategies, innovative staff, the freest environment for innovation, as well as the finest tradition of innovation in developed countries and in a few advanced developing economies.

However, knowledge derived by Chinese companies from exports or production under license for foreign multinationals is very limited because it does not give them direct contact with the final client in the foreign market. Chinese enterprises are in contact with intermediaries giving them limited feedback on the evolution of demand in foreign markets.

To develop their technology and managerial skills, Chinese companies have two approach: cooperating with foreign partners in the Chinese market or investing abroad.

Cooperating with foreign multinationals is interesting, but usually limited to outdated or mainstream technology because, in order to secure their technological advantage and bargaining power, foreign partners do their best to control the diffusion of their technology.

If exchanges are limited to joint activities in China, Chinese managers and experts would not necessarily come in contact with numerous and outstanding foreign experts and managers. Therefore, Chinese companies have to invest directly in developed countries or the most advanced emerging economies in order to nurture and gradually develop their innovation capabilities, accelerate the knowledge transfer, and develop the technological assets necessary to compete at a global level.

This process, however, has to follow a step-by-step approach:

— setting up international offices to learn more about the political and legal environment of the target country, the culture, purchasing power, consumer habits, market structure;
— investing directly in local operations in order to accumulate the knowledge of organization, human resource management, local government relations, society, marketing, and sales;
— opening local R&D centers with local engineers and technicians to keep up with the latest scientific developments and pioneering technology projects in order to transfer opportunities with strong business potential to headquarters and global level development;
— building partnerships locally with pioneering enterprises;
— disseminating a significant share of the information to other subsidiaries to accelerate the development of their innovation capabilities by the application and perfection of the knowledge and technology.

2.3. *Key Processes for Knowledge Transfer*

Companies have three major ways to acquire knowledge and technology through their internationalization process.

Strategic Integration

Through integration and acquisition, multinationals take full immediate control of the resources of acquired companies, which not only add to their capacity of innovation, but also facilitate the transfer and diffusion of knowledge inside the organization. Lenovo's acquisition of IBM's PC business is quite similar to Whirlpool's full takeover of Philips' household appliances business, or Sony's acquisition of Ericsson's mobile phone business.

Alliances and Other Cooperative Agreements

Multinational companies set up a joint-venture with a foreign partner or enter into a long-term contract of cooperation as a means to increase their innovation capabilities from the knowledge transfer of doing business together or developing a joint project. A company can directly absorb the knowledge and technology from its partner through the implementation process, learn from the collaboration with the staff of the partner, acquire knowledge from the parent company of the partner, or learn from its social network.

Examples of such cooperation can be found in the Motorola, Alcatel, and Nokia agreement to jointly develop a common GSM standard at the industry level, the GM-Toyota cooperative relationship in advanced technologies, or of the Renault–Nissan alliance and synergies in purchasing, manufacturing, R&D.

Independent Subsidiaries

A multinational can create a rather independent unit or a wholly-owned subsidiary in order to fully control the flow of knowledge in both directions. Haier America Refrigerator Corp. Ltd. in the USA is run rather independently from the rest the organization, for example. During their internationalization process, Wal-Mart and Citigroup experienced a similar situation with some of their international outlets or offices.

During their internationalization in emerging markets, Chinese companies have a variety of options to promote innovation and knowledge dissemination. They can start with an independent wholly-owned subsidiary in order to control the speed and scope of knowledge transfer and then enter joint-ventures only if it is necessary according to the local legal environment. They would go for strategic integration only if they want to absorb the local knowledge or technology.

On the other hand, in developed economies or middle-income economies, Chinese companies might bet on joint-ventures in order to have easier access to knowledge and technology possessed by foreign multinationals. This can help them attract personnel and top professionals that they would have difficulties recruiting in a wholly-owned independent unit, thus closing the innovation capability gap with leading multinationals more quickly.

Through M&A, Chinese enterprises have access not only to current innovations of the company, but also to the personnel and management process behind the innovation. But their limited financial resources, however, prevent them their from acquiring very large companies or business units which are leaders in innovation and management performance. Thus, their possible targets are either successful small and medium-sized enterprises (SMEs) possessing a technological or managerial advantage, or large companies with a strong knowledge or technology base but weak financial results.

Another key element for Chinese multinationals is to build close relationship not only with leading companies, but also with leading research and academic institutions. However, while Chinese companies' main objective is to have access to the most advanced technologies, the objective of their foreign partners is to have access to the Chinese market.

A major way for Chinese companies to learn is through joint-ventures with leading local companies. Research has shown that equity joint-ventures are a more effective means of knowledge transfer than the contractual cooperation (Mowery *et al.*, 1996). And international joint-ventures abroad have great advantages for Chinese companies:

— JVs provide more long-term benefits in knowledge and technology to Chinese companies while contractually-based agreements bring more short-term financial results.
— Working with leading international partners, Chinese companies can massively increase their innovation capabilities. If the JV is managed in a rather independent manner, it is responsible for its financial performance and has to conduct its own innovations and product development. The same advantages can be derived from JVs with more than two parent companies.
— Chinese companies have access to a broad variety of knowledge which can help them build a larger portfolio of capabilities in comparison with contracts where each partner concentrates on one dimension of the value chain or one type of capability, such as development, production, marketing, or management.
— International JVs are an excellent platform for companies to learn from each other (Kogut, 1988; Grant, 1996). Chinese companies benefit from the knowledge and technology brought by the partner, the autonomous innovation base developed inside the JV, and the learning experience of Chinese staff working on a daily basis with foreign colleagues on joint research and development assignments.

Thus, by setting up joint-ventures overseas with foreign companies, Chinese enterprises encourage autonomous innovation, knowledge accumulation, and diffusion through multiple centers of innovation and multiple routes of knowledge transfer at the same time (Figure 7.1):

— Innovation is generated at three levels: the level of the JV, but also at the level of parent companies.
— The flow of knowledge includes multiple routes: knowledge flow to and from the JV, knowledge flow between the parent companies.

3. Managing Risks

For many years, Chinese enterprises have tried to learn from their international experiences how to keep up with the latest developments in technology and management and to generate innovations through newly acquired and digested knowledge and technology. However, it has not been easy. In 1993, the 999 Group failed in its planned acquisition of a drug factory in Malaysia because of their lack

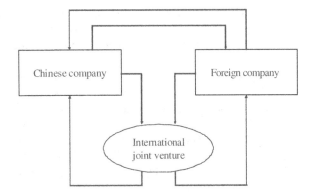

Figure 7.1:   Innovation and knowledge transfer through international joint-ventures.

of knowledge and underestimation of the key role of Muslim organizations in the production and sales of pharmaceutical products in the country.

Overall, the results are limited, even for those leading Chinese enterprises that have successfully entered the internationalization process.

Chinese enterprises face relatively high risks in this quest for technology due to their relatively weak power, their limited information on foreign markets and competitors, the rapid changes on the global scene, and the policy of foreign multi-nationals regarding technology transfer.

3.1. *Major Risks Faced by Chinese Companies*

Learning Cost

Technology transfer between countries and organizations has a price. Even after 25 years of economic development, Chinese companies do not yet have sufficient international experience. In many cases they have paid a high price to acquire knowledge or technology but, due to many uncertainties, did not get the expected results.

TCL's international expansion into Vietnam and India, and globally through partnership with French companies has been, in fact, quite costly.

In 1999 TCL Chairman Li Dongsheng considered that it would be relatively easy to develop TCL in Vietnam due to the limited cultural and political differences between the two countries. To enter Vietnam, TCL acquired Hong Kong-based Luks Industrial's Vietnamese television factory and made a detailed marketing plan. However, sales were almost non-existent the first year in Vietnam. TCL realized the necessity of a specific policy to build its brand image in Vietnam and the company quickly implemented measures for improvement. TCL's top management spent a lot of time motivating the commercial network, promoting the brand, and working with the local community through Vietnam Youth Foundation. TCL turned a profit 18 months after entering Vietnam, after a loss of RMB1.8 billion. Then TCL's market share grew rapidly, reaching 18–20 percent at the end of 2005; the No. 2 position after Sony.

In 2000, TCL entered the Indian market through a 51:49 joint-venture with Baron International Ltd. and invested US$20 million. TCL's market share in the television business was 2.7 percent in 2000 and 5 percent in 2001. Then the conflicts between the two JV partners, especially in marketing strategy, led to TCL's withdrawal from the Indian market. For TCL, it was a second painful lesson in internationalization. To come back to India in 2004, TCL had to create its own organization, called TCL India Holding Pte. Ltd., which achieved a 3–4 percent share in the national color TV market in 2006.

TCL's partnership experiences with French companies Thomson and Alcatel have also been very costly.

The TCL–Thomson JV — named TTE and created in 2004 with the goal of acquiring marketing knowledge and advance television technology from the French partner, lost US$77 million in its fist year and the value of its shares collapsed rapidly. The JV was close to breakeven in America, but it was a disaster in Europe, where most operations shrank or closed. TTE saw losses in 2005 and 2006 and Thomson's shares in the JV had to be taken over by TCL Group's specialized subsidiary, TCL Multimedia Technology Holdings Limited.

The TCL–Alcatel joint-venture — called TCL & Alcatel Mobile Phones Limited (TAMP) and created in August 2004 to take over Alcatel's mobile phone global business including its Intellectual Property Rights (IPR), generated a considerable deficit within eight months and had to be taken over by TCL in May 2005.

The losses at the international level made a very negative impact on the value of the shares on the stock exchange: TCL Corp. in Shenzhen, TCL Multimedia, and TCL Communication in Hong Kong.

Chinese companies, which in some cases are smaller and less profitable than their foreign counterparts, are very vulnerable in case of a major drawback in international acquisitions or partnership. The value of their shares can be seriously impacted which might endanger their capacity to finance growth.

Knowledge Loss and Boundary Dilemma

Knowledge transfer between organizations implies interaction and thus accepting a relative loss of knowledge. Companies cannot strictly control the flow of information either way. The loss depends on the nature of the information, the way it is disseminated, and the type of knowledge involved. This problem is especially serious in joint-ventures. When JV partners invest in a common high technology project, both have to contribute to technology or knowledge, both have to share the information related to the common project, and both want to learn from the other side. Quintas calls this situation the boundary paradox (Quintas *et al.*, 1997).

When a company opens its boundaries to receive information and knowledge from outside, through formal or informal mechanisms, it faces the difficulty of protecting its own knowledge base, technology, and other elements of its intellectual capital. Knowledge loss is for both partners. Chinese companies invest abroad and participate actively in international economic organization; they will transfer products, equipment, proprietary technology, management systems, trained personnel, and will also suffer from knowledge loss.

Brain Drain

Qualified personnel are a key source of knowledge, technology, and innovation. To implement their internationalization strategies, Chinese companies, especially when entering a joint-venture or creating a wholly-owned subsidiary, send experienced managers and top specialists abroad. They usually send their best people, recruit local managers and train them all in view of their international assignments. Some of them leave, finding better job opportunities in the international market.

This is especially true for Chinese enterprises that have developed R&D centers abroad looking for knowledge, technology, and innovation. After a certain period of time, these Chinese expatriates can be attracted by the local way of life, the working environment, or higher salaries offered by competitors. Chinese companies then serve as a bridge for specialists aiming at studying and working abroad. Some Chinese companies have lost 70 percent of their staff abroad after two years (Deng, 2005).

The overseas offices of many enterprises also become the bridge for some staff to study and work in other countries. In addition, the personnel hired overseas are also likely to leave after acquiring some knowledge and skills. The loss of personnel not only disrupts the capacity for future development, but also leads to the loss of some technology accumulated by the enterprise.

Conflicts inside the Organization

Conflicts can arise frequently inside Chinese companies because of the differences in culture, legal framework, business environment, purchasing power, and salaries between countries and regions.

A first dilemma is linked to the salary differences among people working in China and those working for foreign subsidiaries, those working in emerging markets, and those working in developed economies. Top executives based in China might have much lower salaries than executives working abroad, including Chairmen and CEOs who are paid less than the managers of subsidiaries based in rich countries. In terms of evaluation and rewards, the employee outside of China is also in a better position than his colleagues working in China.

Other difficulties come from the different perceptions between headquarters and subsidiaries regarding objectives, information, innovative and important projects, and the amount of investment or price to be paid for knowledge transfer.

3.2. *Facilitators of Knowledge Transfer*

Chinese companies can increase their knowledge base, paying more attention to the following elements:

Innovation Should be Treated as a Priority

The internationalization process is not an objective per se, it is a means to increase Chinese companies' competitiveness. So, in order to increase their capacity for innovation, they should focus on the acquisition of knowledge and technology and its diffusion inside the organization. In too many cases, developing an international presence has been seen as a fashionable trend and not sufficiently as a means to increase the company's competitive advantage.

Evaluating and Managing the Risks

In many cases, international investments have generated little benefit in innovation and technology compared to the investment amount. This is due to an inadequate evaluation of the risks prior to the investment, as well as an under-estimation of the difficulties of internationalization. Typically, foreign multinationals try to limit the transfer of knowledge or technology to companies based in emerging markets, if it cannot bring considerable profits. So in order to increase their ability to innovate, Chinese enterprises have to carefully consider the expectation of both parties, the areas of uncertainty, and potential losses, especially in their overseas ventures with foreign partners.

Focusing on Specific Knowledge and Technology Needs

Too many Chinese companies believe that cooperation with foreign companies automatically generates an easy knowledge and technology transfer. The opposite is true. The knowledge base of a foreign partner might exist but not be relevant to the Chinese partner's current development. The knowledge might be there but difficult to transfer. The foreign partner might have a very strong reputation in the industry and mastery of specific technologies, but be weak in others. So Chinese companies have to precisely identify their innovation and technology needs when they consider development and collaboration, then check the feasibility of transfer from their foreign counterpart. This would limit the danger of acting more on perception than reality.

Combining Two Sources of Leaning

Chinese companies have to combine the learning process based on imitation and the one based on autonomous innovation. In most cases Chinese companies are far behind leading global companies in innovation capabilities, accumulated knowledge, and technology. Thus, learning step-by-step and continuous imitation is still a reasonable approach for a rather long period. This approach can help Chinese companies keep track of the most recent developments, reduce the distance with their counterparts, and create more realistic and rational approaches to decision-making. However, it cannot lead to a real competitive advantage in innovation and technology, and in some cases it might result in approaches that are not adapted to Chinese companies. Therefore, Chinese companies have to build their autonomous innovation capabilities and develop their own technologies and managerial approach at the same time.

Working with international institutions

Chinese companies could reduce the risks, save time in their internationalization process, and lower the cost of knowledge and innovation transfer by working more with intermediate international organizations. They have a good knowledge of international cooperation and good relationships with leading global corporations.

4. Conclusion

The flow of international investments from Chinese companies has grown continuously in recent years and generated a wave of emerging Chinese multinationals with their parent company based in mainland China. The phenomenon of innovation and knowledge transfer, which in the past was dominated by western multinationals, now applies to China-based multinationals.

Outdated technology and management practice have been serious handicaps for Chinese enterprises. During the past 20 years Chinese companies have improved their technology and management through cooperation with foreign companies in the domestic market. A key dimension for Chinese companies' investments abroad is also to contribute to technology and management progress. Foreign subsidiaries of Chinese companies are a primary source of information and markets, technologies, and management, even if they also transfer their own knowledge and technology abroad.

From this point of view, although the majority of Chinese companies' international investment is oriented towards developing economies, the investments in developed economies are crucial to China's innovation process. The development of subsidiaries and joint-ventures in these markets is necessary for the acquisition of knowledge, development of competencies, and training personnel. Without these inputs, further steps in the internationalization process of Chinese companies could face even greater risks and higher costs.

References

Ambos, T.C., Ambos B. and Schlegelmilch, B.D. (2006). Learning from Foreign Subsidiaries: An Empirical Investigation of Headquarters' Benefits from Reverse Knowledge Transfers. *International Business Review*, 15(3), 294–312.

Deng Yangge (2005). Qi cheng haiwai yuan gong liushi zhi tong ,ruhe guanli wai pai jingli (Loss of 70 percent Overseas Work Force: How to Direct Managers Sent Abroad). *zhong wai guanli, nian di 5 qi (Management in and Outside China*, No. 5.).

Grant, R.M. (1996). Prospering in Dynamically Competitive Environments: Organizational Capability as Knowledge Integration. *Organization Science*, 7(4), 375–388.

Kogut, B. (1988). Joint-Ventures: Theoretical and Empirical Perspectives. *Strategic Management Journal*, 9, 319–322.

Mowery, D.C., Oxley, J.E. and Silverman, B.S. (1996). Strategic Alliances and Interfirm Knowledge Transfer. *Strategic Management Journal*, Vol. 17, Special Issue, Winter, pp. 77–92.

Quintas, P., Lefere, P. and Jones, G. (1997). Knowledge Management: A Strategic Agenda. *Long Range Planning*, 30(3), 385–391.

Teece, D.J. (1998). Capturing Value from Knowledge Assets: The New Economy, Markets for Know-how, and Intangible Assets. *California Management Review*, 40(3), 55–79.

Wang Xinchuan (2002). Zhongguo qiye zouchu qu de kunjing (The Dilemma of Going Abroad for Chinese Enterprises). *jingji yue kan, nian di 7qi (The Monthly Journal of Economy*, No. 7.)

Chapter 8

CORPORATE CULTURE AND ORGANIZATION OF CHINESE MULTINATIONALS

Wang Yihua

Tsinghua School of Economics and Management

The internationalization of Chinese enterprises started in the eighties on the Chinese mainland at the beginning of the period of "reform and opening up." For nearly two decades the main challenge faced by Chinese companies was the "internationalization of domestic competition and internalization of international competition." Joint-ventures and other collaborative agreements were key elements of the transformation of the Chinese economy; technology was imported, and Chinese exports were driven by foreign investors. China's market became a hot spot for cutthroat competition among international enterprises. At the same time Chinese enterprises were entering the stage of direct overseas investment and internationalization of their organization.

In 2004, the acquisition of the IBM Personal Computer Division by the Lenovo Group and the acquisition of Thomson of France by TCL started to catch the attention of western countries.

What is the nature of the international management of Chinese enterprises? How are they preparing, and implementing, their international strategies? What is the impact of their international organization on economic performance?

Most Chinese companies are still at a very early stage of development from the point of view of internationalization and have not had the time or the opportunity to be fully prepared for this phase of development. However, for Chinese companies as well as for their western counterparts, the success of the internationalization process appears to be strongly dependent on the choice of an international organization finely tuned to strategy.

This chapter focuses on two questions:

— What are the prerequisites for Chinese companies before embarking on the internationalization process?
— What organizational structures have Chinese companies developed to implement their international strategies?

1. Organizational Capabilities, Property Rights, and Corporate Culture

During our survey, we were deeply aware of the pressure, dynamism, benefits, and hardships that these enterprises experience in the internationalization process. The majority of these enterprises have a relatively strong consciousness of risk. However, only a few have met the organizational conditions to "go global." For Chinese enterprises, especially traditional ones, it is very difficult to enter the internationalization process for five reasons: firstly, they are faced with language and cultural obstacles; secondly, they are quite unfamiliar with the economic rules, social structure, legal environment, and mode of management in western countries; thirdly, they suffer low enterprise brand recognition; fourthly, they do not master always the necessary core competencies; and fifthly, their quality of management is still relatively low.

Without enormous courage, enthusiasm, and dynamism, and without powerful organizational conditions, it would have been almost impossible for Chinese companies to internationalize.

Two variables might explain the behavioral differences of Chinese companies regarding internationalization: the degree of strategic priority given to internationalization and the organizational capabilities necessary for successful internationalization (Figure 8.1).

A small first group of companies like Haier, Huawei, Lenovo, or Wanxiang has both defined internationalization as a leading priority and developed a strong organization able to support this strategy. This combination has led to successful breakthrough strategies.

A second category, which includes the vast majority of companies, is already aware of the necessity to internationalize not only to increase foreign market share but also for survival on the Chinese market. However, companies in the second category have not yet developed the appropriate organization structure or processes. They are stuck in the middle.

A third category comprises companies that have a good managerial organization, and great potential on the domestic market, and, even if it is not their first strategic priority, have been successfully exploring opportunities on the global market place. Among these "active explorers" is Nuctech, one of the subsidiaries of Tsinghua Tongfang Co.

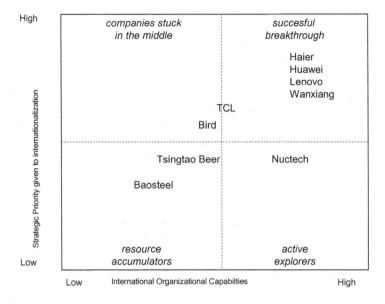

Figure 8.1:   International organizational capabilities and strategic priorities.

Finally, a fourth category comprises companies that are successful on the domestic market but do not perceive internationalization as a necessity, or at least not as the first priority. Thus, these companies have not yet transformed their organization accordingly. That said, they have the capacity to accumulate the appropriate resources to internationalize, and may be latecomers on the international scene.

Shanghai Baosteel belonged to this category, but since the Mittal–Arcelor merger in 2006 its priorities may change and the company could be obliged to accelerate its development both on the domestic and the international markets.

Tsingtao Beer is in a similar situation and has shifted priority to consolidation in the domestic market. For this reason, the strategic alliance with Anheuser–Busch in 2002 can be interpreted as a good solution for Tsingtao Beer to protect its long-term potential on the international market and accumulate the international know-how from its partner.

1.1. *Tsingtao Beer: International Capabilities and Strategic Alliance*

China's beer industry is at a stage of industrial concentration. There is rapid growth in demand and strong rivalry between the top three producers: Tsingtao Brewery

Group, China Resources Breweries Co. Ltd. (Snow Beer), and Yanjing Beer Co. Ltd. (Qufu Sankong Beer).

The extent of competition in the industry requires continuous optimization of performance, with production and sales volume being the highest in the world for three consecutive years.

Tsingtao Beer was founded in 1903. As an enterprise with over 100 years of history, Tsingtao Beer inherited the refined and meticulous quality management system of the Germans and engaged in continuous research and development in order to consolidate the unique taste of hop and malt sweetness that was developed in the 1950s. In the late 1990s, Tsingtao Beer had the opportunity to restructure and acquire or set up 48 subsidiary enterprises in 18 provinces and regions around the country. Through stringent management of its subsidiary companies with regard to production, market operations, equipment utilization, production quality, and taste, Tsingtao Beer established a uniform product line and its production, sales volumes, and brand value have continually been listed as No. 1 in the beer industry nationwide. In 2004, its sales volume reached 3.72 million kiloliters, and was ranked eighth internationally in terms of quantity. Tsingtao Beer formally put forward a plan to achieve "three transformations": from being production-oriented to being market-oriented; moving from product management to brand management; and from expansion of the scale of production to improvement in service ability in order to enhance its domestic competitiveness in the lead-up to becoming an internationalized company.

Tsingtao Beer's export volume accounted for more than 70 percent of China's beer exports and it is becoming the No. 1 brand in Asia's beer export market, with remarkable achievements also in areas such as Europe, America, Taiwan and Macao. Tsingtao Beer was, nevertheless, in no hurry to engage in large-scale transnational investment to establish overseas production bases and marketing channels.

Tsingtao Beer managers believed that China's market had already become an important part of the international beer market and that the company would certainly become the world's third largest beer company in the Chinese market with its annual 20 percent growth in demand. Moreover, in its comprehensive survey of the consolidation of the international beer industry, Tsingtao Beer found that world leaders have been able to develop a profitable international presence only after having consolidated their domestic positions.

Therefore, the internationalization process of Tsingtao Beer followed two stages: the first stage had to do with winning the battle against international competitors within the domestic market, and the second was actually going international.

The company waited to have sufficient market power in China before embarking on the internationalization process, which was reflected in their strategic priorities.

The company first developed its capabilities up to an international standard through consolidation of its presence in China and learning through international alliances. These alliances minimized the risks linked to international expansion.

In the view of Li Guirong, Chairman of the Group: (international expansion) ... "requires international resources and capabilities that the group would be too slow to acquire if it relied only on itself. While waiting for the accumulation of resources to be completed, the market would have already been eaten up by others. Large international companies master a series of skills and best practices adapted to the market economy. If we are to become international, we need first to learn from our competitors, and face these gaps squarely."

In October 2002, Tsingtao Beer and Anheuser–Busch formally signed a strategic alliance agreement. According to the agreement, Tsingbao Brewery Co. Ltd. issued three convertible bonds which required conversion into Tsingtao equity within seven years, representing a total investment of US$182 million. By April 2005, after the bond conversion, Anheuser–Busch's economic ownership interest in Tsingtao Beer reached 27 percent, becoming the second largest shareholder after Qingdao State-owned Assets Supervision and Administration Commission of the State Council (Qingdao SASAC).

As far as Tsingtao Beer is concerned, the strategic alliance with Anheuser–Busch had the following significance. First of all, it released the pressure on capital requirements. Tsingtao Beer had encountered profitability and capital requirements problems after the period of rapid expansion and acquisitions.

Secondly, Anheuser–Busch provided Tsingtao Beer with technology and management know-how, which laid a solid foundation for the supply chain interface, opened up the knowledge base, improved management efficiency, and effectively reduced the deviations in technical and taste indicators. Thirdly, Tsingtao Beer and Anheuser–Busch established an exchange of best practices. Tsingtao Beer sent batches of finance, marketing, and management personnel to Anheuser–Busch to learn its management methods. Directors and supervisors assigned by Anheuser–Busch will join the sub-committees of the board of directors of Tsingtao Beer to ensure more uniform technical standards and international business practice.

To maintain the freshness of beer products, the best market radius for a production enterprise is 300 kilometers. Therefore, to seize the overseas market, Tsingtao Beer had to establish local production and local distribution. In July 2005, a joint-venture called Tsingtao Beer (Thailand) Marketing Co. Ltd., was registered and established in Bangkok, Thailand (with a total registered capital of 15 million baht, Tsingtao Beer holding 30 percent, while its Thai partner held 70 percent). Tsingtao Beer had, therefore, chosen a beer manufacturer in Thailand to produce Tsingtao brand on an exclusive basis. It could be said that this constitutes a substantial change in the internationalization strategy of the

Tsingtao Brewery Corporation. Tsingtao Beer started with exports, but soon produced locally, exporting Tsingtao Beer brand, technology and standards. Finally, the strategic alliance with Anheuser–Busch is a major source of development for Tsingtao Beer's managerial capabilities, helping the company to fight on two fronts: consolidation on the domestic front, and starting the internationalization process in excellent managerial and organizational conditions.

1.2. *Wanxiang's "Human-Centered" Corporate Culture*

In the turbulent environment of "reform and opening up" in China, many Chinese enterprises have, for a time, been busy maintaining their daily operations and have neglected planning for their long-term development. They attached great importance to acquiring resource materials and had a low opinion of employee creativity and initiative. They relied on external support and gave up self-determination in favor of development. They blindly took the path of diversification and lacked the patience and courage of dedication. They cared for their own interests only and neglected creditworthiness and sincerity, the two qualities that are most important to their partners.

Our research findings indicate that the most successful international organizations share the following cultural characteristics: ambitious goals, sustained autonomy and control of initiative, patience and dedication, respect for employees, and finally pursuit of a win-win situation.

Under the leadership of Lu Guanqiu, the president of the Group, Wanxiang followed that path.

In the 1990s, during the 25th anniversary of its founding, Wanxiang put forward a clear objective: Wanxiang would become one of the 100 strongest enterprises in China and one of the 1000 strongest enterprises in the world. The philosophy of Wanxiang was "to create value for clients, to create benefits for shareholders, to create a future for employees, and to create prosperity for society." Wanxiang's management objectives were: "each can make the best use of his resources, make the best use of everything, make the best value of capital, and each can do his best according to his abilities."

When Lu Guanqiu founded the Wanxiang Company with six other peasants in 1969, it was a sole proprietary enterprise. In the early 1970s, it became a "collectively owned" enterprise.

Lu Guanqiu has always been people-oriented. He implemented an innovative property rights and distribution system and fully mobilized the enthusiasm of its cadres and employees. He believed that, "a good system can mobilize the enthusiasm of employees, and create productivity."

The Progressive Reforms of the Property Rights System

During the first stage (1978–1983) the emphasis was on establishing individual contracts and responsibilities — starting from the factory director's level — clearly defining the incentive mechanism for employees and ensuring favorable treatment of the frontline workers.

During the second stage (1984–1989) the objective was to introduce employee participation in equity ownership. Lu Guanqiu had been the first to implement a full complete reform of the shareholding system and of the corporate structure. At that time, 50 percent of Wanxiang's ownership belonged to the Township and Village Government (TVG) and 50 percent to the enterprise. Of the latter, 50 percent belonged to Lu Guanqiu, 25 percent to Wanxiang management, and the remaining 25 percent to employees. The shares held by the TVG were gradually acquired by Wanxiang later on.

During the third stage (1990–1994) the Wanxiang Group was reorganized and Wanxiang Qianchao Co. Ltd. ("Qiancho") was listed on the Shenzhen Stock Exchange.

In the fourth stage (1995 onwards) Wanxiang followed new guidelines for corporate strategy, management control, and investment policy.

The "corporate strategy guidelines" covered the strategic decision-making process, competition analysis, long-term objectives, elaboration of sustainable competitive advantage, collaborative strategies, and synergies between businesses.

The "management control guidelines" focused on the business units' responsibilities for strategy implementation, responsibilities of profit centers, and their participation in the profit-sharing scheme.

The "investment policy guidelines" referred to the long-term and short-term financial performance of the group, client satisfaction, management potential, and innovative learning from subsidiaries. They helped employees to reach final decisions regarding investment in new projects and renewal investments.

For complicated historical reasons, some of the parent company's property rights were ambiguous as they fell under "collective ownership." Lu Guanqiu believed that it is very hard to be fair when "sharing the past" because of the difficulties of working out an equitable distribution *vis-à-vis* individual contribution. "Sharing the past" is not as good as "sharing the future." Employees of the Wanxiang Group have two layers of income: the current year's salary, and an annual bonus. Today, each employee of the Group is entitled to invest 80 percent of his annual income in the parent company and become a shareholder of the parent company. The number of employees' shares have increased with development of the company. Accordingly, the percentage of the "collective ownership" will increasingly become smaller, whereas the percentage of individual ownership will increasingly become bigger thereby avoiding disputes over the historical contribution and helping employees to work towards the group's future development.

As all subsidiary companies controlled by the Wanxiang Group are joint-stock enterprises with a clear definition of ownership rights, employees will not own any of the subsidiary companies shares.

This reform has laid a solid foundation for the internationalization of the Wanxiang Group, allowing it to adapt to global competition and consolidate its competitive advantage.

Rewarding Individual Performance

Based on the requirements of the various stages for corporate development, Lu Guanqiu stipulated that the annual income of outstanding employees in key management positions should be commensurate with the daily profit of the company.

In the 1970s, Lu Guanqiu became the first to introduce the "bonus" system to his company. When daily profits of the company reached RMB10,000, the first batch of employees who received a RMB10,000 annual bonus were the most outstanding employees.

In the 1980s, Lu Guanqiu implemented his "remuneration calculation linked to profit" practice. When daily profits of the company reached RMB100,000, the first batch of employees who received an annual income of RMB100,000 were the outstanding salesmen of the company.

In the 1990s, Lu Guanqiu put into practice his "multi-layered distribution" system, which ensured that when daily profits of the company reached RMB1 million, the first batch of employees who received an annual income of RMB1 million were the outstanding managers.

In 2004, when daily profits of Wanxiang reached RMB5 million, the first batch of employees who received an annual income of RMB5 million were professional managers.

In 2010, when the daily profit of Wanxiang will reach RMB10 million, the maximum annual income of its core staff will also be RMB10 million.

Wanxiang's remuneration system embodies Lu Guanqiu's philosophy that gives equal attention to corporate development, shareholder interests, and employee remuneration. Based on the requirements of the various stages of corporate development, Lu Guanqiu linked remuneration of the employees in key posts to the business performance of the company. This has considerably mobilized the enthusiasm and creativity of both management and employees of the Group.

Wanxiang "Dynamic Employment" Management

In the Wanxiang Group, there are five forms of employment, namely: permanent employees, regular workers, contractual workers, workers on probation, and temporary workers. Each group benefits from an incentive mechanism which manages promotion or demotion. This facilitates the continuous improvement of employee behaviour and performance, thereby ensuring organizational vitality.

Wanxiang also established a personnel notation system that achieves internal, cross-regional, cross-cultural, and cross-posting staff movement. The system not only allows internal human resource sharing, but also effectively prevents external loss of personnel. It satisfies both corporate needs and employees' desire for development.

Wanxiang moulds and guides its employees' behavior through timely and effective measures of reward and punishment. Lu Guanqiu believes that these measures make clear the values that he advocates for all employees and is key to the system: "tangible values are limited, while intangible values are unlimited." It took him 30 years of effort to build such a practical and open business culture.

Philosophy of Employment

Lu advocates the evaluation of contributions and values based on "accomplishments." He demands that employees in their respective posts "handle and finish one practical thing a day, a new thing a month, a big thing a year, and a meaningful thing [in] a life." He encourages executives to "speak the truth, do practical things," and states that "everyone has a field of activity, and all should strive to be the first in command." The philosophy of Wanxiang is to offer financial and intellectual benefits to its employees. Financial benefits — "pocket rewards" — refer to respecting the value of labor and determining the amount of remuneration in strict accordance with employees contributions. Intellectual benefits — "head rewards" — refer to educating employees to love their country and their community by working for common prosperity. Only when the state is rich and prosperous, when the enterprise is generating large profits from hard working individuals, can each employee become rich. At the same time, "head rewards" means encouraging employees to continually learn new technology and acquire new knowledge. Wanxiang puts those employees with both integrity and professional competence in very important positions. Those with integrity but lacking professional competence have less important positions, while those with neither integrity nor professional competence will not be entertained. One must be on guard against those with professional competence but without personal integrity. Wanxiang encourages acts that "sacrifice one's own interests for the sake of others," permits acts that "put the public interest ahead of private gains," criticizes acts that "put private gains ahead of the public interest," and prohibits acts that "use a public office for private gain." These principles have ensured the integrity and competitiveness of the Wanxiang team.

Principle of Autonomy and Self-determination

Having worked, their way up Wanxiang workers understand that "there is no pie in the sky, there is no such thing as a free lunch, and everything has to be created by man himself." They strived for all kinds of support and resources, but never relied either upon the state or their partners. In 1989, Wanxiang rejected outright Zeller's request to undertake its export business on an exclusive basis. In the latter part of the 1990s, it also turned down the bid by the American company — General Motors — to take over its subsidiary Wanxiang America. Wanxiang refused to "follow the fashion, play forms, tell lies"; rather, it walks its own way, and fulfills its own dream.

Conservative Investment Policy

Before making any investment, Wanxiang would meticulously studied development trends to understand the actual situation of the enterprise and weighing its own abilities before seize the opportunities for investment. It would prefer to lose an investment opportunity rather than choose the wrong investment project. In the words of Lu Guanqiu: "The government wants sales revenue, we want profits." Thus, Wanxiang will not touch what it does not understand. It always acts according to its abilities, and never goes beyond its capacity to minimize any risk. By remaining in the auto parts and components industry, it has developed technology, processes and continuity of its market from spare parts to components, from components to system, and from system to modules. In China, where the auto industry has sustained continuous development, the profit margin of auto parts and components production is far lower than that of whole-car production. Nevertheless, Wanxiang is not deterred, as it tenaciously strategies for growth and development in its professional field. Never impulsive the company has never made an investment mistake, resulting in 36 years of sustained development and continuous profit.

Cooperation and Win-Win Strategies

Lu Guanqiu advocates "benefiting others for co-existence, joint creativity, and common sharing." He also believes that, between countries, regions, enterprises, and even peoples, one's own existence can facilitate another's long-term development only through cooperation and alliances. Moreover, only through benefiting others can one benefit oneself and achieve mutual promotion for common improvement, thereby opening up opportunities for survival and development. Wanxiang holds that every investment is never to plunder but to sow a seed. As such, investors should respect local government, business partners, project rules and regulations, and stick to the principles of good faith and mutual respect.

1.3. *The "Basic Law" of Huawei Technologies*

Property rights reform is an unavoidable problem in Chinese enterprises' internationalization process. The problem of assets ownership can be solved only with a clear and explicit definition of property rights, thereby encouraging international talents, integration with the international capital market, and the management of international risks. In other words, clear property rights are the precondition for Chinese enterprises to engage in multinational management.

At the present stage of development of the Chinese market economy, the majority of enterprises are faced with various sorts of property rights and distribution problems. Such problems include: the property rights owner is absent, the property rights relationship is complicated, or the property rights are over-concentrated or cannot be distributed according to key resources and practical contributions. This issue results in potential mistakes in the strategic decision-making process, confused routine management, low enterprise vitality, and poor methods of execution, thereby rendering it difficult for these enterprises to achieve a healthy growth in their domestic market, let alone to engage in international business.

Our research findings convinced us that through reform of property rights and the distribution system, the most successful enterprises can create enormous dynamism, enthusiasm, creativity and initiative among key employees, thereby creating organizational conditions for internationalization.

Since Huawei's development of the C&C08 Digital SPC Switching System in 1994, Ren Zhengfei, president of the Huawei Group, recognized that the company had the opportunity to become a global supplier in the field of telecommunications equipment.

In 1996, he invited a batch of college and university teachers to join him in drafting the "Basic Law of the Huawei Group," which was based on wide discussion within the Group. The basic law summarized the first 10 years of Huawei's undertakings and pointed out the developmental path and the core criteria underpricing it for the next 10 years.

Knowledge and talent are the key company resource in Huawei's Basic Law. In Chapter 1, dedicated to the objectives of the company, the statement on the values of the Huawei Group are as follows:

Article 16: We believe that labor, knowledge, entrepreneurs, and capital create all the values of the Company.

Article 17: By means of conversion to capital, we represent and recompense the accumulative contributions of labor, knowledge and management and risks of the entrepreneurs; by making use of our stock ownership arrangement, we establish the fundamental forces of the company and retain effective corporate control to ensure its sustainable growth. Knowledge, capitalization and our dynamic property rights system, which adapts to technological and social changes, are the direction of our continuous exploration. We implement an employee shareholding system to benefit model employees who identify themselves with Huawei, to form a company and a community of destiny on the one hand, and continually promote the most accountable and capable employees to become the backbone of the company on the other.

Article 18:   The basis of stock ownership distribution: sustainable contribution, outstanding talent, moral character and the undertaking of risks. Stock ownership distribution will be inclined towards the core layer, and the stock ownership structure will support dynamism and reasonableness.

Until 2004, Huawei had opted for the status of a limited liability company and did not seek market listing. The company said that this decision was made to allow the company to achieve its long-term objectives and avoid the influence of the near-term return and short-term behavior of stock investors. Huawei's leadership firmly believed that fundraising was not the major difficulty. They considered talents to be the source of Huawei Technologies' creativity, force of market expansion, strength of resource integration, and the most important and active production element.

In April 2004, Huawei completed its most extensive and thorough restructuring since its establishment and straightened out its complicated internal stock ownership composition. The Group was reorganized with Huawei Holdings (Shenzhen Huawei Holding Co., Ltd) as the parent company of a series of subsidiaries, including Huawei Technologies, Huawei Mobile, Huawei Software, Huawei Holdings, Huawei University, Huawei Services, and Huawei Property.

In 2004 the shareholder composition of Huawei Holdings was thus: Ren Zhengfei, 0.97 percent (RMB35 million) and the Labor Union Committee of Shenzhen Municipal Huawei Investment Holdings Co., Ltd. 99.03 percent (RMB3,581 milion). That is why Huawei is said to be 100 percent owned by its employees. As stated earlier, internal shares are allocated to employees according to their contribution to the company.

After this restructuring the company would be in a better position to begin its internationalization process. In 2007 Huawei had not yet gone public, and many experts were predicting that it would be listed on either the Hong Kong or US stock market in time.

Ren Zhengfei, Huawei's founder and president, owns very little of the company's stock which clearly underlines his unbiased strategic authority. The transparency and democratization of Huawei Holdings Ltd. stock ownership has in fact mobilized enormous enthusiasm, creativity, and cohesion among Huawei workers. There is a "wolf" culture at Huawei: although the managers of each department have specific missions, they have learned to cooperate, to engage in group warfare, to be quick and accurate, and to keep at reaching their commercial goals.

The property rights system and the internal allocation of company worth are integral seperated the strategic vision of Ren Zhengfei.

Since its establishment, Huawei has been making efforts to provide a higher level of compensation for its employees than the industry average. Towards the end of the 1990s, the level of compensation at Huawei was the highest within the telecommunication industry in China.

In the Huawei Basic Law, the statement on worth allocation is as follows:

Article 5:   Huawei advocates forming a community of interest between clients, employees and its partners, and endeavors to explore its internal dynamic mechanism according to the distribution of the production means. We will never let Lei Feng (any selfless and hard working employees) be in a disadvantaged situation, as contributors should certainly receive a reasonable return.

Article 18: The worth that Huawei may allocate is mainly in respect of rights of organization and economic benefits; the forms of allocation are: positions and opportunities, salaries, rewards, bonus, retirement pension, medical assurance, stock ownership, dividends, and other personnel benefits. Huawei implements a form of allocation which integrates both work performance and seniority.

Article 19: Priority of efficiency, attention to impartiality, and sustainable development, are the basic principles of our value distribution. The basis of distribution according to work is: ability, responsibility, contribution, and attitude towards work. Distribution according to work should be drawn apart with full difference, and the curve of distribution should maintain its direction and there should be no inflection point [...]. Distribution according to work and distribution according to seniority should be adequately proportional to each other, and any increase or decrease in the proportion for distribution should be based on the principle of sustainable corporate development.

Article 20: [...] the ultimate standard for measurement of the reasonableness of value distribution shall be corporate competitiveness and achievement, as well as the morale of all employees, and their sense of belonging to the Company.

The worth allocation system, the business culture, and the momentum for development at Huawei have attracted the participation of an impressive batch of graduates trained in telecommunications and other specialties, so much so that it once reached a point of "talent monopoly." With its youthful spirit, its team of employees have helped to create the "Huawei miracle."

Contrary to the "eagerness for quick success and instant benefits" that is prevalent in financial circles, the standard for the industrial comprises is "effort in 10 years."

With their lofty ambition, broad vision, and 10 years' of effort, the leadership of both Wanxiang and Huawei have developed their cultures, molded their teams, built up their organizations, and equipped themselves with the organizational ability to withstand the risks of internationalization and compete on a global scale.

2. Globalization and Organizational Structures

2.1. *Stages of Organizational Development of Chinese Emerging Multinationals*

Many Chinese companies are still at an early stage of their internationalization process.

Shanghai Baosteel, for example, only started its internationalization process quite recently and its percentage of international activities is still relatively small.

Baosteel entered into international trade in 1988 by exporting 10 percent of its production. The main objectives were to test product quality, to learn about the international market, and to ensure a balance of foreign exchange. Then, in 2001–2003, at a time when the international mineral resources market was in recession, Baosteel established joint-ventures with Australian mining companies to ensure mining resource stability and cost advantages. Later in 2004 Baosteel invested in Brazilian mining companies. However, Baosteel's main battlefields are still in the domestic market.

Baosteel's business development department has a key role in the coordination of activities between organizational units:

— it cooperates with the strategic planning department in order to formulate the strategic plan at the corporate level, and to follow up on its implementation.
— it is responsible for the preliminary feasibility studies and the follow-up on the implementation of all overseas investment projects.
— it supervises the foreign subsidiaries and representative offices (Bao–he, Bao–mei, Bao–ou, Bao–xin, and Bao–ba engaging in steel products trade, Bao–dao [Hong Kong] in raw materials trade, Bao–yun and Bao–jin in shipping transport, and Bao–ao and Bao–huarui in mining operations) and coordinates the activities of foreign subsidiaries and their relationship with headquarters.

The marketing and sales of carbon steel products in international markets is managed by the sales department — Baoshan Iron & Steel Co. Ltd. — in a manner similar to that of sales on the domestic market. The department oversees five regional divisions: Asia and Australia, America and Europe, and Africa. Foreign subsidiaries are mainly sales organizations, with a relatively high degree of independence. They are managed like their regional counterpart within the Chinese domestic market.

The organizational characteristics of Baosteel and of other Chinese companies in their early stages of internationalization fit well with the label "international" given by Bartlett and Ghoshal (1991) in their typology (Table 8.1).

The distinction made by Howard Perlmutter (1969) between the ethnocentric, polycentric, region-centric, and geocentric orientation of the firm might also yield

Table 8.1:   Organizational Characteristics of Transnational Companies.

Organizational characteristics	Multinational	Global	International	Transnational
Configuration of assets and capabilities	Decentralized and nationally self-sufficient	Centralized and globally scaled	Sources of core competencies centralized, others decentralized	Dispersed, interdependent, and specialized
Role of overseas operations	Sensing and exploiting local opportunities	Implementing parent company strategies	Adapting and leveraging parent company competencies	Differentiated contributions by national units to integrated worldwide operations
Development and diffusion of knowledge	Knowledge developed and retained within each unit	Knowledge developed and retained at the center	Knowledge developed at the center and transferred to overseas units with minimal adaptation	Knowledge developed jointly and shared worldwide

Source: Adapted from Bartlett and Ghoshal (1991).

clues about the path followed by Chinese companies in terms of international strategy and organization: each degree of international orientation corresponds to a type of organizational structure (Rugman and Hodgetts, 2000).

However, the Chinese experience demonstrates specific features and some shortcuts to the most advanced stages of global development.

2.2. *Wanxiang's Acquisition and Integration Policy*

The objectives of Wanxiang international strategy have been twofold: on the one hand, mastering technology and brands, and, on the other hand, conquering the international auto parts market. The strategy is characterized by a series of acquisitions and a strong emphasis on the US market. In 2000 Wanxiang acquired Zeller, among the top three auto parts suppliers in America. In 2001 Wanxiang took control

of Universal Automotive Industries, Inc. (UAI), the largest American brake component supplier, and in 2003 it acquired 33.5 percent of Rockford Powertrain Inc.
the largest American supplier of wing-type drive shafts (See Box 8.1).

Taking Over Zeller

In 1995, Wanxiang learned that Zeller, a client of Wanxiang in the US, was expe-
riencing a downturn in revenue. As Lu Guanqiu wanted to know more about the
situation, he delegated Ni Pin, his son-in-law and General Manager of Wanxiang
USA, to visit the headquarters of Zeller in Ohio. Zeller managers welcomed Ni
Pin but did not say a single word about their production and market share. Ni Pin
was not allowed to visit Zeller and had a weeklong hide-and-seek style negotiation.
Upon his departure, Max and Kelvin Zeller, the owners of the company, handed Ni
Pin an envelope expressing their willingness to sell off Zeller at an initial price of
US$19.36 million. Since Ni Pin understood that there were many bad assets that
needed to be disposed of the deal was not completed. In 1998, Zeller suffered a
severe loss, while the sales volume of Wanxiang US had reached US$30 million,
nearly 10 times that of 1994, since its establishment. This was a primetime for
acquisition.

At that time another US company was also considering acquiring Zeller but they
did not want the intangible assets, such as its brand and patents. Ni Pin contacted
the company and suggested that, "You may take away what you want from Zeller,
and I, mine, and then we jointly expand our market; or, we may join hands with
Zeller and re-seize the market." Accordingly, an agreement was soon concluded
and Wanxiang took over Zeller's brand, technology patents, specialized equipment
and global distribution network for only US$420,000 in cash. The direct effect of
Wanxiang's acquisition of Zeller was an annual sales increase of Wanxiang branded
products in the US market alone of US$5 million. This localization strategy enabled
Wanxiang to almost instantly become a US operator.

Taking Over Universal Automotive
Industries (UAI)

At the end of September 2001, Wanxiang took control of UAI, a company founded
in 1981 and specialized in the manufacturing and distribution of brake components.
Fifty percent or so of its products were sold under its own brand UBP. In 1994, UAI
was listed on NASDAQ, and became the leader of the brake maintenance market
in the United States. In 2001, UAI started to experience a downturn because of
severe competition in the US market, high production costs, hazardous overseas
acquisitions, and poor management. UAI shares dropped by 90 percent.

Ni Pin had been in contact with UAI since 1996. Wanxiang was interested
in working with UAI because it could bring four benefits to Wanxiang: first,

Box 8.1: Lu Guanqiu's Vision and Wanxiang's International Development.

The Wanxiang Group is a leading actor in the Chinese automobile components industry. However, its predecessor was a mere Township and Village Enterprise (TVE) founded in 1969, in the Zhejiang province. In the age of the planned economy, with a dream of changing their fate, Lu Guanqiu decided to lead his Wanxiang people to seek success amidst niche openings in the market. Starting with farm machinery, and after having endured many setbacks, Wanxiang finally entered the auto parts and components industry. Several accomplishments led to the success of Wangxiang, including: overcoming the peasant attitude that "a small fortune keeps a mind at peace" and overcoming their "clumsiness and carelessness" endurance and hard work, constantly endeavoring to becoming stronger, not blaming anyone or anything, with acute market insight and striving for development opportunities. After passing a rigorous examination for reliable, quality products, the firm finally became one of the three designated universal joint production enterprises of the Ministry of Machinery Industry in China in the early 1980s and was eventually incorporated into the national plan.

With courage, patience, and concentration, Wanxiang has successfully expanded its products over the past two decades to include bearings, shock absorbers, brake gears, etc., and has achieved a leap from parts to components, and from components to systems. The domestic market share of its leading products grew over 70 percent during this period. After 1994, Wanxiang started to export its products and, after 1997, its products entered the suppliers' network of the world's first-class main automotive plants, such as GE and Ford. After 2000, Wanxiang subsequently successfully acquired a number of American companies specialized in the field of automobile maintenance, parts, and components. At present, Wanxiang manages a network of 31 companies in eight countries, including the United States, the United Kingdom, Germany, Canada, and Australia. Eighteen of these companies are sole proprietary or share controlled enterprises. With the aim of "multiplying tenfold both of its daily profit and annual income of its employees for every 10 years of enterprise struggle *(fen dou shi nian tian ge ling)*," Wanxiang achieved 36 years of continuous growth, sustained profit, and stable development after starting with merely RMB4,000 yuan in capital. Today, Wanxiang has a total of RMB8 billion in high-quality assets.

Stage One: Selling Apples (1982)

The Quest for Autonomy

In 1982, Wanxiang started to manufacture domestically auto parts and components (universal joints) that had previously been imported. Given its products' high-quality, Wanxiang received its first order from Zeller, an automobile maintenance company in the United States. Afterwards, it signed a contract with Zeller to export 200,000 sets of universal joints each year for the next five years. However, in 1987 Zeller requested the exclusivity of sales of Wanxiang's products, a demand that was

(Continued)

rejected outright by Lu Guanqiu, General Manager of Wanxiang Group. Cooperation between the two companies therefore came to a deadlock. As a result, Zeller reduced its order by 50 percent that year, which resulted in overstocking of finished Wanxiang products and difficulties in funding turnover. This, in turn, lead to losses. The people at Wanxiang had braced themselves and, through concerted efforts, were able to develop 60 new product varieties and enter 18 new national markets in the same year including Italy, Japan, and Germany. In subsequent developments, as Zeller could not find more suitable products with a better price-performance ratio, it restored its cooperative relations with Wanxiang. This prompted Wanxiang to set up independent marketing channels and build up its own brands in the United States.

Balancing the Risks

In the early 1990s, Wanxiang started to supply universal joints for state-owned auto plants. However, several instances of industrial policy adjustment by the planned economic system of China made Wanxiang realize that it should not put all its eggs in one basket. To lessen domestic market risks, Wanxiang needed to create a balanced portfolio of activities: one third domestic maintenance, one third domestic component supply, and one third international maintenance.

Stage Two: Opening-Up the Apple Garden (1992)

Wanxiang management realized that without a brand, patents, and a foundation in their hands, it would only become a target for others and it would be very hard to find a foothold in the international market. Exporting products is no different from "selling apples." Wanxiang was not satisfied with just "selling products" to the United States, for it had determined to develop its own market and open up an "apple garden" in that country. Therefore, Wanxiang dispatched its personnel to the United States to find clients, to study how to organize Wanxiang marketing, and to build up the reputation of its QC brand.

One can imagine the difficulties and problems that a Township and Village Enterprise (TVE) would face in pursuing independent development in the United States. But Wanxiang had taken this step with determination. Lu Guanqiu discovered a talented and capable young man, Ni Pin, a graduate of Zhejiang University, and appointed him to a key position and assigned him important tasks. Through hard work and after having overcome all sorts of difficulties, Ni Pin was able to meet the expectations of the Wanxiang management and finally open up the United States market.

Stage Three: Expanding the Apple Garden (1994)

With approval of the then Ministry of Foreign Trade and Economic Cooperation, Wanxiang officially established its 100 percent holding company Wanxiang America Corporation in Chicago. The company was committed to establishing a universal

(*Continued*)

Box 8.1: (*Continued*)

joint auto parts and components distribution network covering both the European and the American continents and building up further the reputation of the "QC" brand. It subsequently set up sales companies in countries such as the United States, the United Kingdom, Mexico, Venezuela, Brazil, and Canada. However, Wanxiang clearly understood that, as a newcomer, it is very difficult to expand into an auto parts and components market that has already been carved up. To achieve greater development, Wanxiang America needed more resources: brands, technology, clients, capital, and *guanxi*, or relations. They therefore started to closely monitor and track the business and strategies of the main auto parts manufacturers in the United States.

Stage Four: Integrating the Apple Garden (2000)

In 1995, Wanxiang noticed that Zeller, which was established in 1923, had problems owing to poor management and intended to sell the enterprise. After repeated negotiations, Wanxiang successfully acquired Zeller in 2000. From that time, Wanxiang began to "act as a boss of foreigners, use the capital of foreigners, acquire the enterprises of foreigners, and make money out of foreigners." After Zeller, Wanxiang acquired UAI, Rockford and other companies. Wanxiang was assisted by leading financial institutions such as Citibank and Merrill Lynch. The company was acquiring the international brands, technology, markets, and sources of financing that were urgently needed. To date, Wanxiang has set up 30 facilities in eight countries, built up an international marketing network covering more than 40 countries and regions, and has been selling parts to leading automobile companies like GE and Ford.

The successful international strategy has ensured a more balanced portfolio of activities. Wanxiang's objective is to have two thirds of its activity in the Chinese domestic market, and one third on the international maintenance market.

For Lu Guanqiu, Wanxiang's successful presence in international markets is not based primarily on advanced technology. Other companies are offering top quality products. It is also not based on low cost since some Chinese competitors might even have lower costs. Wanxiang's president considers that the steady and rapid development of the company is based on the integration of resources from both domestic and international markets, the management of synergies between domestic and international activities, the leveraging of international resources, and the ability of its organization to support the internationalization process.

expanding Wanxiang's exports; second, creating an interface platform in America; third, introducing the UAI brand into China; and fourth, use of UAI's distribution in the United States. Finally, the acquisition of UAI would be a great source of value creation for Wanxiang and a major opportunity to continue the internationalization process, international financing, technology sharing, and opportunities for Wanxiang employees. Ni Pin started approaching UAI in 2000 but had to be patient. The opportunity came with the fall of UAI shares and the fact that the company was facing the danger of being excluded from Nasdaq. Ni Pin re-adjusted the bottom line of his negotiating position and further reduced the price of acquisition by 31.86 percent, based on the average stock transaction price of the company over the preceding year. Ni Pin stressed: "What we can offer is not just capital; even more, we can also offer the capacity for resource allocation, the backing of our powerful Group, and the extensive Chinese market." UAI also clearly understood that, for the next 10 years or even longer, there would not be another country like China that could provide enormous market opportunities. On 28 July 2001, Lu Guanqiu gave the formal greenlight for Wanxiang to become UAI's No. 1 shareholder. Ni Pin reached an agreement with UAI's general manager, Arvin Scott. With a 21 percent share of UAI stock, plus options, securities, bonds, and other contractual agreements, Wanxiang owned a total of 58.8 percent of the voting power. Wanxiang could start building on strong synergies between the "Made in China" and "Made in the United States" trademarks.

Taking Over Rockford Powertrain

In 2003, Wanxiang US successfully acquired the century-old Rockford — inventor of the winged joint coupling shaft and the world's largest first-class supplier.

Rockford was founded in 1890. It accounts for 70 percent or so of the chassis market. Aside from heavy-duty drive shafts, Rockford also manufactures mechanical and hydraulic clutches and power steering gears used by heavy-duty non-expressway vehicles.

Wanxiang began its relationship with Rockford in 1995, when Rockford was literally at its height. During the period of the Gulf War, Rockford became the main supplier for the United States Department of Defense, which added further luster to its reputation. However, by 1998, Rockford was experiencing, a deficit. The relationship between Wanxiang and Rockford evolved from ordinary client to that of potential strategic partners.

In 2000, Wanxiang began negotiations with Rockford for acquisition and cooperation. Meanwhile, there were one American and two European companies which were potentially interested. These companies had the same objectives as Wanxiang.

Wanxiang could help Rockford overcome its problems of scale, lack of stable ownership, and limitations of product development. Rockford agreed to make Wanxiang its new leading shareholder and investor.

Wanxiang America has had a key role in Wanxiang's internationalization process. The company includes 30 subsidiaries and employs 1000 local employees, of which only six are Chinese dispatched by Wanxiang headquarters. The company benefits from the support, financial resources, and the manufacturing cost advantages of the Wanxiang Group.

In 2000, Wanxiang America was chosen to be Wanxiang's major internationalization vehicle and was thus entitled to buy back the shares of its parent company.

When Wanxiang America exceeds the planned profit rate of growth agreed to by the Group, it may use 50 percent of its excess profits to buy back the shares of its parent company, with 40 percent of the Group's stock ownership as the upper limit.

No doubt, this plays a powerful role in inspiring the ambitious manager of the US subsidiary of Wanxiang. The company has demonstrated its capacity to acquire the assets it needs on the international market and to integrate them at a corporate level.

2.3. *Huawei Technologies' Transnational Capabilities*

Huawei Internationalization Process and Organization

Founded by Ren Zhengfei in Shenzhen in 1988, Huawei long ago established its objective of "becoming a world first-class equipment supplier."

The company is slowly but surely building its global presence. It boasts a global marketing and service network, quickly providing clients with quality services. In 2006, 31 of the world's top 50 telecommunications operators, including Vodafone, BT, Telefonica, FT/Orange, and China Mobile had selected Huawei as their supplier. This means that Huawei provides services to more than 1 billion users around the world. In 2006, Huawei's overseas sales revenue accounted for over 50 percent of its total sales revenue. In the overseas market, Huawei focuses on overall cost leadership and regional differentiation.

In 1996 when Huawei started its internationalization process, its dominant organizational form was that of an international company.

Huawei followed the strategy of "the easy way first," that is investing first in emerging markets of Russia, Latin America, Southeast Asia, Middle East and Africa. Then Huawei started focusing on developed markets. After five years of extensive organizational restructuring, Huawei successfully passed scrutiny and assessment by the Western European telecommunications operators and won clients in Germany, France, Spain, the United Kingdom, and the Netherlands.

In 1997, Huawei invited leading international consulting companies to help it quickly bridge the gap in management. IBM, Towers Perrin, The Hay Group, Pricewaterhouse Coopers (PWC) and Fraunhofer-Gesellschaft (FhG), became Huawei's consultants in the areas of process transformation, employee stock option plans, human resource management, financial management and quality control. In 2002 and 2003, Huawei successfully passed internationally-recognized quality standards accreditation procedures.

Through organizational structure and process transformation, Huawei not only won an entry ticket to the telecommunications markets of developed countries, but also increased its organizational capabilities and capacity manage by coordinating and controlling an international network.

Since 1998 the internationalization process of the company also includes the creation of a series of R&D centers overseas in India (Bangalore), the United States (Dallas and the Silicon Valley), Europe (Stockholm), and Russia (Moscow). Their mission is to rigorously track leading edge technology and the characteristics of market demand in various countries. They would quickly feed back the information to the research institutes in mainland China to ensure the local responsiveness of Huawei products and services to the needs of different international markets.

The international strategy of Huawei is thus highly flexible. The strategic moves and the necessity of offering highly differentiated products and services in international markets have strongly influenced the organization. The company has built real transnational capabilities. However, in 2007 the company still displayed a tendency towards ethnocentrism: in order to reduce costs, the center of gravity of R&D, marketing, and production of Huawei Technologies is still in China.

Managing Talents

Ren Zhengfei, President of Huawei, believes that, to be worthy of its name, international talents are key to becoming a transnational company. Such a company should cultivate internal talent on the one hand, and attract international talent on the other. Huawei corporate university was officially registered in 2005 and offers technology, management, and corporate culture training for its clients, managers, and employees.

At the same time, Ren Zhengfei decided to recruit more than 1000 CPAs from Hong Kong in order to develop a global standard financial and accounting system.

The remuneration, bonuses, and participation in the stock ownership plan of Huawei employees, including the marketing staff employed in foreign subsidiaries, are based on quarterly performance assessments.

A Client-Centered Strategy

"Client service is the only reason for Huawei's existence; client demand is the only motive power of Huawei's development." Therefore, Huawei's mission is to focus on challenges and the pressure of client attention, to strive for competitive communication solutions and services, and to continually create the maximum value for clients. This core concept and basic strategy formed in its China market has been extended to its international market. To ensure end-to-end delivery of superior quality, excellent service, and low price, Huauwei has established eight regional headquarters, 85 representative offices, and technical service centers across five continents. It has also formed a three-layered client service system integrating the general headquarters, regional headquarters, and representative offices, and has established close cooperation with its various related companies and R&D centers. For instance, in 2005, Huawei's department of research and development met the special requirements of Telfort of Holland for UMTS network equipment in time and at little cost, saving considerable running cost for the client and winning high recognition.

International Strategic Alliances

Huawei has established competitive and cooperative relations with both upstream and downstream business partners. Since 1997, Huawei has set up 10 joint R&D laboratories with Texas Instruments, Motorola, IBM, Intel, Agere Systems, Sun Microsystems, Altera, Qualcomm, Infineon and Microsoft. In 2003, Huawei established a JV with 3Com to manufacture enterprise digital network equipment. In 2004, Huawei established a JV with Siemens to develop the TD-SCDMA mobile communication technology for the Chinese market. In 2005, Huawei signed a strategic cooperation agreement with Telefónica to carry on operational innovation in the 3G and broadband fields, and agreed to jointly develop and expand the Latin American market. The same year, Huawei signed a mutual assistance commodity consignment agreement with Marconi in the United Kingdom. According to this agreement, Marconi would use its exclusive Marconi brand to re-distribute Huawei's telecommunications digital communication products to telecommunications operators, while Huawei will re-distribute Marconi microwave equipment in its wireless network projects, including the next generation of microwave equipment and its related network services. In addition, Huawei has also signed a global procurement framework agreement with Vodafone Group PLC, and has officially become the preferred telecommunications equipment supplier for the Vodafone Group's global supply chain.

Huawei's overall international performance is a success. Huawei is present in more than 90 countries and regions, including developed economies. Although from 2001 to 2002 the global investment in telecommunications infrastructure dropped by 50 percent, the value of Huawei's international sales still grew by 68 percent, up from US$328 million in 2001 to US$552 million in 2002.

In 2000, international sales accounted for about 10 percent of Huawei's total revenue, while in 2006 65 percent of contract sales were from the international market.

Huawei's organization follows its flexible strategy. It stills exhibits characteristics of the international type, including its ethnocentric vision, but also characteristics of the transnational model, like its network dimension and geocentric vision.

References

Andersson, S. (2000). "The Internationalization of the Firm From an Entrepreneurship Perspective. *International Studies of Management and Organization*, 30(1).

Barkema, H.G., Bell, J.H.J. and Pennings, J.M. (1996). Foreign Entry, Cultural Barriers, and Learning. *Strategic Management Journal*, 17(2).

Bartlett, A.C. and Ghoshal, S. (1991). *Managing Across Borders: The Transnational Solution*. Boston, Mass: Harvard Business School Press.

Chen Fosong (2001). *Shije Wenhua Shi Gaiyao* (Summary of World Cultural History). *Hua zhong keji daxue chubanshe*, Huazhong University of Science and Technology Press.

Cullen, J.B. (2002). *Multinational Management: A Strategic Approach*. Cincinnati, Ohio: South-Western Thomson Learning.

Dunning, J.H. and Bansal, S. (1997). The Cultural Sensitivity of the Eclectic Paradigm. *Multinational Business Review*, 5(1).

Gomez-Mejia, L.R. and Palich, L. E. (1998). Cultural Diversity and the Performance of Multinational Firms. *Journal of International Business Studies*, 28(2).

Grosse, R. and Trevino, L.J. (1996). Foreign Direct Investment in the United States: An analysis by Country of Origin. *Journal of International Business Studies*, 27(1).

He Zhiyi (2002). Haier, Lianxiang, TCL qiye wenhua jianshe de fenxi yu bijiao (Analysis and comparison of Haier, Lenovo and TCL business culture construction). *Qiye huoli di 12 qi, Enterprise Vitality*, Issue 12.

Hofstede, G. (1980). *Culture's Consequences: International Differences in Work-Related Values*, London: Sage.

Knickerbocker, T.F. (1973). *Oligopolistic Reaction and the Multinational Enterprise*. Boston: Harvard University Press.

Knight, G. (2000). Entrepreneurship and Marketing Strategy: The SME Under Globalization. *Journal of International Marketing*, 8(2).

Medina Walker, D., Walker T. and Schmitz J. (2003). *Doing Business Internationally: The Guide to Cross-Culture Success*. New York: McGraw-Hill.

Morosini, P., Shane, S. and Singh, H. (1998). National Cultural Distance and Cross-Border Acquisition Performance. *Journal of International Business Studies*, 29(1).

Oliver, C. (1997). Sustainable Competitive Advantage: Combining Institutional and Resource-Based Views. *Strategic Management Journal*, 18(9).

Palich, L.E. and Gomez-Mejia, L.R. (1997). Cultural Diversity and the Performance of International Firms. *Journal of International Business Studies,* 28(2).

Porter, M.E. (1991). Towards a Dynamic Theory of Strategy. *Strategic Management Journal*, 12(8).

Roth, K. and O'Donnell, S. (1996). Foreign Subsidiary Compensation Strategy: An Agency Theory Perspective. *Academy of Management*, 39(3).

Rugman, A.M. and Hodgetts, R.M. (2000). *International Business: A Strategic Management Approach*. New York: Financial Times/Prentice Hall.

Schwartz, S. J. (1999). A Theory of Cultural Values and Some Implications for Work. *Applied Psychology: An International Review*, 48(1).

Terpstra, V. and David, K. (1991). *The Cultural Environment of International Business*. Cincinnati, Ohio: South-Western Publishing.

Xi Xudong (2004). *Kua Wenhua Gailun*. Methodologies on Cross-Cultural Management. Zhonghuao jingji chubanshe, Beijing: China Economy Publishing House.

Zhang Rende and Huo Hongxi (2001). *Qiye wenhua gailun* (Introduction to Business Culture). *Nai kai daxue chubanshe*, Nankai University Press.

Zhao Changwen and Mao Daowei (2000). *Zhongguo Daxing gongye qiye guojihua jingying guanli shije* (External Expansion Strategy of Transnational Industrial Companies and International Business Management of Chinese Large-Scale Industrial Enterprises). *Guanli Shije* di 2 qi, *Management World*, Issue 2.

Chapter 9

CHINESE MULTINATIONALS AND GLOBAL VALUE CHAINS

LENOVO — A NEW GLOBAL LEADER IN THE PC INDUSTRY

François Duhamel

Universidad de Las Americas, Puebla, Mexico

1. Introduction

The reconfiguration of value chains, resulting from Western firms' willingness to focus on core activities, creates acquisition opportunities that some Chinese MNCs have been eager to seize in order to sustain their recent internationalization efforts. We illustrate this phenomenon through the example of Lenovo, which now ranks as the 3rd largest company in the world in the PC market, after the acquisition of IBM's PC Division in 2004.

Chinese groups such as Lenovo, TCL, SAIC, CNPC, Hisense, Chunlan Group Corporation, Galanz Group, or Techtronic Industries Company, to quote a few examples, may belong to different industries and address different markets and sales channels, but they all share a common objective: to become global players, rapidly (Zeng and Williamson, 2003). Whether they chose to develop initially as subcontractors for Western firms, or built their own brands from the start, they now wish to expand abroad on their own initiative, acquiring supposedly better performing international brands and climbing up the technnological ladder.

Some of these companies have privileged acquisitions as a way to grow quickly. The *China Daily* reports (*China Daily*, 5 September 2006) that China's overseas investments, so far considered of little to no significance, amounted to around $12.3 billion in 2005's. Mergers and Acquisitions (M&A) accounted for half of 2005's outward direct investment flows. The question we address in this chapter deals with the specific triggers that prompted the process of international expansion for Chinese firms. We identify Western firms refocusing efforts on their core businesses, leaving entire business units "up for grabs" for other companies, as an essential trigger for Chinese firms eager to develop internationally through acquisitions. In this context, the question remains: how could Chinese companies ever succeed, especially when they target foreign firms suffering from already falling margins, declining market shares, and ailing brands?

In the first part we will focus on Chinese firms' strategic advantages and limitations. In the second part of this chapter we will study the impact of Western firms refocusing efforts on Chinese firms' internationalization strategies, illustrating this phenomenon with the example of the sale of IBM's PC Division to Lenovo Group Limited, which stands as the leading computer firm in China, and ranks nowadays as the 3rd PC maker worldwide after this acquisition in May 2005. In the third part, we will assess the implications of such a strategy for the firms involved and their future perspectives.

2. Chinese Firms' Strategic Advantages and Limitations

Some major Chinese companies have developed efficient manufacturing bases and extensive, relatively affordable sales forces networks in a context of massive foreign investment and intense competition at home. The emergence of these powerful Chinese companies has traditionally come mainly from a cost advantage, but also from the development of reliable products and recognition of their place in the world market. In industries such as domestic appliances, electronic equipment, chemicals, oil, or steel, domestic firms in China have gained a relatively beneficial position within their own country, and over time have accumulated many valuable resources, partly through government protection.

The more successful Chinese firms tend to internationalize more and more, due to national and regional policies aimed at fostering the development of firms outside their borders (Zweig, 2002), but also as a consequence of the intense competitive pressures and looming over-capacities that now prevail in China in many industries and reduce margins (Gao *et al.*, 2003). The saturation of their domestic markets may have prompted the internationalization of those companies as they acknowledge their weakening position in their domestic turf in the long run.

However, the factors that brought the success of those Chinese firms in their home markets, such as preferential government contracts, privileged networks, easy access to capital or assets, and high tariffs, are not likely to be replicated abroad. Brands coming from developing countries are still associated with low costs and low levels of quality, even if the quality of "Made in China" products, particularly, may be up to international standards nowadays.

In many ways Chinese MNCs resemble their counterparts in other emerging countries. Even if they may profit from a "latecomer advantage" (Cho *et al.*, 1998) by taking the latest technological developments without incurring the underlying costs and by using the newest technologies without being burdened by the legacy of old systems, more traditional products, or conflicting sales channels, they tend to suffer from the same difficulties. These difficulties include: narrow product lines preventing them from sharing resources in a cost-effective way across multiple products, lack of international experience, and, above all, poor resource bases (Aulakh *et al.*, 2000).

Those companies, particularly, still lack numerous resources, which may severely hinder their foreign expansion efforts. Chinese MNCs need to develop strategies to compensate for their relative lack of resources and their reputation of inferior quality. The larger Chinese firms now have the ability to provide high quality products at a lower cost than their Western counterparts. Competing abroad requires larger R&D investments, stronger marketing programs, more extensive sales organizations and sophisticated supply chain systems, as well as careful public relations (Deng, 2004). The biggest difficulty for Chinese firms investing abroad is to determine who is going to own the commercial networks, how to develop efficient distribution schemes and successful brands, and how to master human resource policies in countries unfamiliar to them.

To sustain their internationalization efforts, Chinese MNCs may try to build the necessary skills demanded by foreign markets through organic growth in a step-by-step approach, through alliances, or through the acquisition of selected foreign companies. Companies such as Haier and Huawei decided to build their own brands, which shows that, however difficult it may be, organic growth is not totally out of reach for Chinese MNCs. "Link-type" alliances are often seen as a more efficient way to get rapid access to foreign markets, whereas acquisitions to strengthen presence in foreign markets gave poor results (Garette and Dussauge, 2000). Thus, choosing acquisitions represent a paradox in this context. Normally Chinese companies trying to enter foreign markets should consider alliances or joint-ventures because of their relative lack of knowledge of the markets they aim at (Belen and Villalonga, 2005).

2.1. *The Lenovo's Example*

Lenovo is a unique success story in China's corporate world.

To understand the company's particular trajectory, resources, and strategy, we will first highlight some key aspects of the evolution of its business.

The company now known as Lenovo Group Limited was established in 1984 as a spin-off from a government-funded research institute, the Institute of Computing Technology (ICT), which was dependant on the Chinese Academy of Sciences. Liu Chuánzhì and 10 of his fellow researchers from the ICT invested RMB 200,000 in the venture, which was later established as the "Lianxiang" Group (in Chinese) and "Legend" Group (in English). This was the predecessor of Lenovo Group (Annex 2–Annex 11).

The architect of Lenovo's strategy, Liu Chuanzhi, is a graduate from the Xidian University, the founder and Chairman of the Board of Legend Holdings Limited — the parent company of Lenovo Group — the "Godfather" of China's information industries, and the leading personality of Zhongguancun Science Park.

In the early days, Lenovo could use ICT facilities free of charge, as well as ICT's name and reputation. ICT provided engineering services and also provided personnel for implementation at the production stage. It also provided legitimacy and political connections, which were so important to develop a business in China in the eighties (Xie and White, 2004). Nowadays, Lenovo[1] benefits from a 27 percent market share in PCs in China, with an iron grip on government and education markets. It also ranks first in the Asia-Pacific region (excluding Japan), with a 12.2 percent market share in 2004, according to IDC. Sales reached about US$3 billion in 2004, from US$460 million in 1994.

From its early days when they started to assemble PCs in 1991, Lenovo has been a differentiator and a specialized company.[2] The Company is not considered as a low-cost provider in the Chinese market, as it gained an image as a fast and technology-intensive producer (*Business Week*, 1999). They pursued a differentiation strategy in China, as it developed specific applications and operating systems designed for the Chinese market, improving user-friendly home entertainment devices. They also differentiated their products for the local corporate markets (Gold *et al.*, 2001; Xie and White, 2004). They also developed extensive sales networks, enabling them to go to smaller cities in China that Dell, for instance, which concentrated on larger cities, had difficulties reaching. Legend, as it was called initially, based its success on the ability to provide its customers with PCs equipped with the latest processors, at a time when foreign counterparts would only offer inferior versions to the Chinese market.

Legend was not designated by the Ministry of Electronic Industries to be among the leaders of China's PC manufacturing industry. This relative absence of support may have pushed Legend to develop different systems creating stronger pressures

---

[1]The Company's name changed to Lenovo in 2003, in order not to hinder future international expansion, since the name Legend was already registered in several countries by other companies.

[2]Lenovo is now a company focused on a more narrow range of products, including desktop computers, notebook computers, mobile handsets, servers and peripherals. The Company ended its venture in IT services in 2004, selling the activity to AsiaInfo for US$36.3 million. It sold 50 percent of its motherboard activity to Ramaxel Company. A joint-venture with AOL Time Warner to develop an Internet portal, FM365, closed in 2004. Lenovo is still fighting in the mobile handset business, in an intensely competitive Chinese market.

on performance, as compared to the more classical state-owned companies which relied on traditional distribution schemes (Xie and White, 2004).

Lenovo now faces very strong competitive pressures in its home market from firms such as Dell and Hewlett-Packard, but also Chinese competitors such as Founder and Tongfang (and even TCL). Due to the saturation of the home market and falling margins, remaining a local player is not a long-term option for Lenovo. To be able to gain all the benefits derived from being in a global industry, where size and geographical coverage matter, they need to expand overseas in both developed and emerging markets. This means finding sources of competitive advantage and going up against Dell and HP.

3. The Impact of Western Firms Refocusing Efforts

3.1. *Reconfiguration of Global Value Chains*

A large scale reconfiguration of value chains on a global basis is taking place, as large Western firms tend to focus their activities on core, more profit-yielding markets in order to avoid the low margin commodity businesses (Gereffi *et al.*, 2005). Generally speaking, those companies would concentrate only on the profitable parts of the value chains upon which they can exert a vertical control. The consequence is that they will try to dispose of the activities they consider as dead weight, or manage through external contracts what they previously managed in-house.

This creates a major window of opportunity for Chinese companies eager to grow through acquisitions. They can compensate for their lack of resources and valuable brand names by appropriating those chunks of value chains that other companies wish to divest. Chinese firms now find opportunities to increase their knowledge about how to do business in advanced economies, as well as increase access to brands and sales channels. This phenomenon creates major and historically unique opportunities for the internationalization of Chinese firms choosing acquisitions to enter world markets. They can take possession of the parts of the global value chains relinquished by Western companies.

Such a reconfiguration happened in the PC industry, which is now entering into its maturity stage. Market entry is easy because intellectual property and technical barriers are low (Curry and Kenney, 1999). In the PC industry, the sources of competitive advantage exhaust progressively, possibilities of differentiating oneself from competitors become thinner. Margins erode, products become commoditized. Claims of technical superiority are more and more difficult to prove, due to product commoditization. Most innovations can be rapidly copied, and, therefore, the value of any innovation is hard to sustain.

PC assemblers, whether they address the corporate or the consumer markets, must ensure reliable and tested systems configurations, efficient services and technical support, advertising and, most of all, efficient supply chain management in a context of rapid technical changes in components (mainly semi-conductors and hard disk drives) to avoid inventory depreciation (Curry and Kenney, 1999). PC marketers have basically two ways to improve their performance: provision of ancillary services (pre-packaged software, links with internet providers) and original just-in-time logistic services may differentiate competitors in this sector (Curry and Kenney, 1999: 15). Economies of scale are likely to be less significant. In the PC industry, as is now well known, the value has migrated from the hardware to the services, software, and microprocessors; as Sun's president and chief operating officer says, we are "moving from the old world, in which one buys a PC and cares a great deal about its comparative hardware features, to one in which the hardware is nearly identical, and the value's moved to services available through the device and over the network."

3.2. *Complementarities of Value Chains*

In 2003, IBM's sales turnover for the PC division was US$9.56 billion dollars, with a net loss of US$258 million. This loss was due to a US$586 million expenditure on product maintenance. In the same year, Lenovo reached a turnover of US$2.97 billion, with a net profit of US$135 million. Acquisition of IBM's PC Division was possible because IBM was refocusing efforts on services, software development, and servers.[3] IBM was disposing of any activity that did not bring differentiation and margins. IBM sold its router equipment facilities to Cisco and its hard disk division to Hitachi Data Systems. For the PC business, IBM's first plans may have been to sell the division to a Japanese company, such as Toshiba, or to a Korean Company, such as LG, or even to an equity fund. The crucial point for them is to gain access to markets in China. IBM hoped to piggyback on Lenovo's influence and sales force as it targeted Chinese banks, manufacturing companies, and government agencies.

In the same way, but in the domain of consumer electronics, Thomson Group, after generating nearly all of its revenues from television manufacturing five or

---

[3]"Today, computing and its uses are again changing radically — to what we've been describing as on demand business. This is opening up tremendous opportunities for IBM, and it's why we have invested billions of dollars in recent years to strengthen our capabilities in hardware, software, services and core technologies focused on transforming the enterprise. At the same time, the PC business is rapidly taking on characteristics of the home and consumer electronics industry, which favors economies of scale, pricing power and a focus on individual users and buyers. These are very different business and economic models, and they will diverge even further in the years ahead."

six years ago, shed its consumer electronics operations, selling parts of its TV tube manufacturing interests to a Chinese Group, TCL. Shortly afterwards TCL also acquired Alcatel mobile phone production facilities. In the process, Thomson tried to reinvent itself as "a professional media services provider specializing in post-production, physical media-creation and distribution, professional broadcast equipment, and supply of set-top boxes and home gateways to network operators." The company also reorganized its divisions accordingly.

3.3. *The Acquisition of the IBM PC Division by Lenovo*

The deal with IBM was closed on 1 May 2005, after a first announcement early in December 2004 and an official approval from US authorities. Lenovo acquired IBM's PC Division for US$1.25 billion in cash and shares, and took over US$500 million in debt. The deal gave Lenovo control over a business that generates estimated annual sales of US$12 billion to US$14 billion and has an 8 percent world market share. The acquisition represents a major change for Lenovo. In 2003, Lenovo's sales outside China accounted for less than 2 percent of its revenue. Following the acquisition, these sales represent more than two-thirds of Lenovo's turnover. Lenovo hired 10,000 IBM PC employees, including about 2,300 in the United States — mostly product designers, marketers and sales specialists. The remaining 7,700 people came from the Great Wall venture.[4] Dell still holds the No. 1 position in PC sales with 16 percent, followed by HP with 14 percent, and IBM/Lenovo with 8 percent in 2004, according to Gartner.

Under the acquisition agreement several transition periods were set up, particularly in terms of branding. IBM transferred the "Think" brand family to Lenovo and granted the right to use the IBM logo, with some restrictive conditions, under a five-year royalty-free licensing agreement (See Box 9.1).

For communications, Lenovo was supposed to use IBM's sales channel and online website for a period of five years. In addition, Lenovo is supposed to be the preferred supplier of PCs to IBM Global Services.

What Lenovo hopes to find through the acquisition of IBM's PC Division is expertise in managing the PC Business in the more advanced markets. Lenovo is

---

[4]As for servers, one week after the announcement of the sale of its PC division to Lenovo, IBM signed an agreement with another Chinese Company, China Great Wall Computer Group. It created a joint-venture, with an 80 percent stake from IBM. International System Technology Company (ISTC), will be based in Shenzhen, and will produce servers for Asian firms. Due to the acquisition of IBM PC division by Lenovo, the joint-venture with Great Wall reduced its scope in servers. The JV, named ISTC (International Systems Technological Company) is based in Shenzhen, and will manufacture IBM eServer X series and P series for the Asia-Pacific market.

Box 9.1: The IBM Lenovo Agreement: Selected Transition Services Agreements.

Services	Years	Annual limit	Payment	Contents and observations
Marketing Support	5	US$150 millions	Lenovo to IBM	Client team support, Information technology, Fixed assets accounting (for EMEA and Asia Pacific). Customer fulfillment services, Sales center services, Ledger support services (for EMEA and Asia Pacific), Incentives and commissions services (EMEA and Asia Pacific), Transitional tax services (in EMEA and Asia Pacific)
Customer Financing	5	US$9 millions	IBM to Lenovo	Provision of leasing and financing services to end-user customers by IBM
Excess surplus disposition	5	US$60 millions	IBM purchases	IBM has exclusive right of first offer for all the PCs manufactured by or on behalf of Lenovo returned to Lenovo by remarketers and cannot be resold as new
Distribution channels financing	5	US$88 millions	Lenovo fee to IBM	IBM will finance remarketers purchases of inventory from Lenovo IBM responsible to take up credit, funding and operational risks and related liabilities associated
Warranty and maintenance	5	US$220 millions	Lenovo fee to IBM Global Services	Base warranty services, post-warranty and warranty upgrade 95 percent of all maintenance and warranty services in a prescribed territory will be offered to IBM (outside PRC) IBM shall pay to Lenovo a sale referral fee equal to 5 percent of IBM's revenues from sales to Lenovo's customers of IBM's technology deployment services and related branding services
Internal use purchase	5	US$500 millions	IBM purchases	Lenovo will be the preferred supplier for all PCs required by IBM for its internal use

Source: Cazenove Asia, 31 December 2004.

buying the qualities in IBM that it does not possess now, including Western management know-how, brand equity, and an international presence. Lenovo wants to develop strategic assets, access to brands, and its distribution channel. These desires follow Deng's classification of Chinese MNCs' foreign investments motivations' (Deng, 2004).

Some specific advantages have been added to strengthen Lenovo's position, thanks to the IBM PC division purchase. For 18 months after the closing of the deal, Lenovo kept the right to use the IBM brand and logo. After 18 months, the possibility of co-branding was opened for the next 40 months. In the five years after the deal, Lenovo is supposed to rely only on "Think" brands and its own brand building efforts (See Box 9.2).

The link with IBM shows some features of a provisional alliance, since organizational learning within Lenovo seemed insufficient at the start to assert its ambition of global leadership. To avoid commercial disruptions IBM is supposed to continue providing operational support during the transition period by using its global sales infrastructure and its extensive corporate sales team. Lenovo's decision to allow IBM to take a stake in the group is likely to enable Lenovo to gain IBM's assistance in various areas in the future, even after the transition period of five years. IBM may

Box 9.2: Lenovo-IBM Trademark Agreement.

"For 18 months after the Initial Closing, the Business will be permitted to use the IBM trademark and logo on all Products existing as of the Initial Closing, and on other successor products that have substantially the same functions and attributes. During this period, the Business will also be permitted to use the IBM trademark and logo in marketing and advertising materials, but only as they appear on the Products or successors to the Products. The Business will not be required to add any qualifying wording in connection with its use of the mark during this period. For 40 months after the Initial Closing, the Business will be permitted to use the IBM trademark and logo together with a trademark of the licensee or guarantor as the licensee or guarantor selects, on all Products existing as of the Initial Closing, and on successor products that have substantially the same functions and attributes.

Until the expiry of five years after the Initial Closing, the Business will be permitted to use the IBM trademark and logo together with a trademark of the licensee or guarantor as the licensee or guarantor selects, on all Products existing as of the Initial Closing, and on other products that have substantially the same functions and attributes, provided that on those products, after the first 40 months following the Initial Closing, the Company may only use the IBM logo and trademark on a product together with an endorsement text, which must be approved by IBM. The Business will be permitted to use the common mark during the term of the license, and may seek registration on its own for newly created marks embodying the common term."

Source: Company internal sources, 7 December 2004.

be able to help in areas including research and development, management experience, and expertise. They will also gain a renewed R&D capacity with the R&D center in Raleigh, USA, the R&D center in Yamato, Japan for notebook development, and a Chinese R&D center for desktops development, application development, peripheral product development, and product engineering and testing.

Implementation issues are closely linked to branding issues for Lenovo, since building and maintaining a reputation for reliable products and services will be particularly crucial to keep and enhance IBM's corporate customer base. Lenovo managers now expect a stronger presence in all major markets globally for the sale of personal computers to enterprise customers. They also expect increased penetration of the consumer segment in markets other than China. They will try to further build the Lenovo brand globally, and push the "Think" brands ("ThinkPad", "ThinkCentre", "ThinkVision" and "ThinkVantage") for laptops. IBM's name or logo will disappear quite rapidly, taking into account the fact that IBM is putting its overall reputation at risk with the agreement. Lenovo is also certainly willing to speed up the process to further develop its own brand recognition.

4. Implications of Foreign Acquisitions for the Chinese Firms

The Chinese firms eager to follow the acquisition route tend to acquire primarily ailing divisions of foreign firms. The question remains an open one: why and how would such companies succeed where their Western or Japanese counterparts have failed? The time has come to assess more closely the viability of the acquisition of IBM's PC division, as analysts started questioning the strategic fit of the deal.

Growing through acquisitions remains a difficult task. The rate of failure in foreign M&As remains high in many countries (Garette and Dussauge, 2000). Acquisitions do not have a very good record of success in the PC industry either. In 1995, Korea's Samsung Electronics Co. bought AST Research Inc., once the fifth-largest PC maker world-wide, to enter into the US market. It spent around $377 million on AST before selling it four years later, in 1999, for $200 million to Beny Alagem. AT&T also lost billions after its 1991 union with NCR, before closing the venture in 1996. The HP-Compaq merger was highly criticized due to commercial break-ups.

Lenovo managers argue that it will be a different story this time. As Steve Ward, Lenovo's CEO in 2005 said, "We expect to capture synergies starting today through leveraging the complementary nature of Lenovo and IBM PC Division customer bases, product offerings, and geographic coverage while utilizing Lenovo's highly sophisticated operating platforms." (Company website). Economies in procurement for components would amount to US$35 million in 2006, and US$125 million in 2007 (an estimated 1.8 percent of Lenovo's cost of goods sold), according to Credit Suisse First Boston.

Entry into mature industries at a stage of the experience curve where achieving cost reductions at a faster pace than competitors is a difficult exercise. Cost savings are limited to purchasing synergies because IBM already manufactures in China and other low wage countries and Lenovo seems unlikely to improve the efficiency of IBM's operations. However, though Lenovo presents cost savings as one of the main benefits of the acquisition, such cost savings are not likely to constitute a significant source of competitive advantage for them.

The PC industry, globally, relies on a network of Taiwanese component producers and assemblers. "No one knows for sure how much of China's exports in information and communication hardware are made in Taiwanese-owned factories, but the estimates run from 40 percent to 80 percent" (*Business Week*, 16 May 2005). Lenovo also collaborates actively with Taiwanese specialists in PC design, worldwide qualification processes, "ThinkPad" co-development and manufacturing, and WiFi technology. These specialists include USI, Wistron Corp., Compal Group, First International Computer and Mitac. IBM's Taiwanese contractors such as Hon Hai Precision Industries, Asustek, and Quanta Computer may also start to sell to Lenovo in the near future, as will Sanmina SCI in the United States.[5] Lenovo profited from cost savings obtained through buying components from producers in China, especially Taiwanese ones. This way they could use components of the same quality as those of their foreign competitors (Xie and White, 2004). According to *Taiwan Economic News* (9 December 2004), the ratio of outsourced notebook computers from Lenovo would rise to 70 percent following year after the deal is completed.

In addition to low expectations in saving costs, support from IBM will be short-lived. Since this support is only temporary, Lenovo will have to learn how to manage the different services involved to make things work, even though they may be able to contract with IBM after the transition period.

Complementarities hardly make synergies. Product ranges between IBM and Lenovo have few overlaps. IBM is strong in portables and large corporate clients, whereas Lenovo is rather strong in desktops, small and medium-sized companies,

---

[5]On January 7, 2003, Sanmina-SCI signed a three-year supply agreement to provide IBM specific manufacturing services. Sanmina-SCI's revenues over the three-year term of the agreement are expected to be in excess of $3.6 billion. IBM will outsource manufacturing of a significant portion of its low and mid-range eServer xSeries products and IntelliStation workstations and custom configuration of some "ThinkPad" notebooks for customers in the Americas, Europe, the Middle East, and Africa to Sanmina-SCI. Sanmina-SCI will acquire the IBM manufacturing operations that support these products in Mexico and Scotland. In addition, Sanmina-SCI will distribute and fulfill customer orders for computing options for IBM. The agreement also includes the transfer of approximately 650 IBM employees in Greenock, Scotland, 400 IBM employees in Guadalajara, Mexico and 10 IBM employees in the Raleigh, North Carolina area (*Source*: Sanmina Press Release).

and individual clients. The lack of product overlap, if it limits the synergies to be attained, may be a chance to ensure easier transition and avoid customer defection to other brands. In fact, Lenovo's laptop business is small compared to IBM's. Lenovo will try to develop a single worldwide product portfolio, and, by increasing the number of common platforms, consolidate component sourcing and suppliers to maximize sourcing synergies. Lenovo and IBM having few overlaps, the risk of brand confusion is limited so far. As Lenovo's CEO says: "The only place we have any brand conflict whatsoever is in China. Lenovo is not sold in the United States, etc., so we're going to continue with IBM. We're going to continue with "ThinkPad" with no change whatsoever in the United States. In China, we will continue with IBM and "ThinkPad" and with Lenovo brands. IBM and "ThinkPad" will be positioned at the high-end corporate market and Lenovo is positioned for small and medium businesses. We do have an overlap in part of the corporate market that we'll have to resolve, and we'll do that before we get to the closing."

Brand image and implementation of the acquisition are closely linked. China's marketing expertise means little in the wider world, and Lenovo's corporate culture could hardly be more different from IBM's. The problem is that IBM customers are particularly sensitive; they tend to buy the connection to IBM. Therefore, a potential loss of sales may be expected. Lenovo will have to rely on IBM's existing teams to ensure the operational continuity of the business. Retaining key customers during the transition period will be crucial if Lenovo is to have some chance of success in the near future. Lenovo has transferred its headquarters from Beijing to New York. Ten thousand persons are supposed to move to Lenovo, in addition to Lenovo's 9,000-strong workforce. After the acquisition Lenovo was run by Steve Ward, a previous IBM executive, who was then replaced by William Amelio, the former manager of Asia for Dell.

The identity of the company was changing.

When asked by a journalist: "Is it wrong to think of Lenovo as a Chinese company?"

William Amelio, the President and CEO answered: "Yes. We have roots both in China and in the West. We have a Chinese chairman and an American CEO. In every country our country leader is a local. We do our R&D on notebooks in Yamato, Japan. How much more global do you want?" (*Fortune*, 2006).

On the Chinese side, Yang Yuanqing has been the chairman of the board of Lenovo Group Limited. Before assuming his current position, he was the president and CEO of Lenovo and under his leadership, Lenovo had been China's best-selling PC brand since 1997.

When asked by PWC: "How you have integrated these eastern and western corporate cultures?"

Yang Yuanqing answered: "This was one of the greatest challenges…But a company cannot transcend the cultures of nations …American companies doing business in China must learn about and understand Chinese culture. The same applies to Chinese companies when they do business overseas" (Pricewaterhouse-Coopers, 2007).

5. Conclusion

Chinese firms' internationalization through acquisitions works with the evolution of firms in more advanced economies. Value chain reconfigurations happen on a worldwide basis, changing the structure of whole industries and offering great opportunities for Chinese firms to assert their new power abroad. Still, some industries may escape potential Chinese acquirers. Only those industries that are truly global will be affected. Furthermore, certain global industries in which companies have already concentrated are locked-in by huge barriers to entry, such as the micro-processor industry.

Lenovo's example shows that Chinese companies may now be able to seize opportunities derived from Western Companies' refocusing efforts. It also illustrates the fact that the new Chinese MNCs will have to avoid positioning their products in the lower range, since they would face the competition of other Chinese subcontractors. Lenovo appears in some ways as a typical "stuck in the middle" company because it faces competition on the higher end from Dell and HP, and on the lower end from China's other low cost producers.

For Chinese MNCs, export market diversification is important to reach economies of scale and scope, but also get scarce foreign currency (Deng, 2004). However, these companies should beware not to over extend their international ventures. Because of growing transaction and coordination costs, the costs of investing into multiple markets would outweigh the benefits derived from internationalization.

Low margins are to be expected in the medium-term. It still remains to be seen how Lenovo can turn around a profit where IBM was losing money, all the more so as they will rely on a substantial part of IBM's staff, at least for the coming five years. Lenovo might still be in position to propose relatively sophisticated PCs, while being a price leader for each category. Given their resources and recent acquisition, and the fact that it does not stand as a low cost provider, Lenovo should use a strategy based on differentiation to compete. This would differ from the norm, which is firms from emerging economies trying to leverage their cost advantages to follow a cost-leadership strategy. To do so, they will have to rapidly leverage IBM's image to build their own brand. Chinese companies may be able to overcome those difficulties through a learning process that would improve their marketing skills in developed markets, and by using their own strategic advantages, mainly a strong domestic market position and distribution schemes in less mature markets. Lenovo may create partner networks to develop sophisticated yet affordable machines for the advanced economies, and, even more importantly, to new emerging markets, such as India, Russia, and even China itself, from the bigger urban areas to the less exploited smaller cities.

References

Aulakh, P.S., Kotabe, M. and Teegen, H. (2000). Export Strategies and Performance of Firms from Emerging Economies: Evidence from Brazil, Chile and Mexico. *Academy of Management Journal*, 43(3), 342–361.

Belen, V. and Mc Gahan, A. (2005). The Choice among Acquisitions, Alliances, and Divestitures. *Strategic Management Journal*, 26(13), 1183–1208.

Business Week. How Legend Lives Up to Its Name, 15 February 1999.

Cho, D.S., Kim, D.J. and Rhee, D.K. (1998). Latecomer Strategies: Evidence from the Semiconductor Industry in Japan and Korea. *Organization Science*, 9(4), 489–505.

Curry, J. and Kenney, M. (1999). Beating the Clock: Corporate Responses to Rapid Change in the PC Industry. *California Management Review*, 42(1), 8–36.

Deng, P. (2004). Outward Investment by Chinese MNCs: Motivations and Implications. *Business Horizons*, 47(3), 8–16.

Fortune Magazine. This American wants you to buy Chinese, 153(10) 29 May 2006.

Gao, P., Woetzel, J.R. and Wu, Y. (2003). Can Chinese brands make it abroad?. *The McKinsey Quarterly*, 4, 54–65.

Garrette, B. and Dussauge, P. (2000). Alliances versus acquisitions: Choosing the right option. *European Management Journal*, 18(1), 63–69.

Gereffi, G., Humphrey, J. and Sturgeon, T. (2005). The governance of global value chains. *Review of International Political Economy*, 12, 78–104.

Gold, A.R., Leibowitz, G. and Perkins, A. (2001). A Computer Legend in the Making. *McKinsey Quarterly*, 3, 73–83.

PricewaterhouseCoopers (2007). In-depth CEO interview: Yang Yuanqing Chairman, Lenovo Group.

Xie, W. and White, S. (2004). Sequential learning in a Chinese Spin-off: The Case of Lenovo Group Limited. *R&D Management*, 34(4), 407–422.

Zeng, M. and Williamson, P. J. (2003). The Hidden Dragons. *Harvard Business Review*, October, 81(10), 92–97.

Zweig, D. (2002). *Internationalizing China: Domestic Interests and Global,* Ithaca, NY: Cornell University Press.

Chapter 10

ALLIANCES, JOINT-VENTURES AND CHINESE MULTINATIONALS

Pierre Dussauge

HEC Paris

While foreign firms seeking to operate in China have long chosen — or been forced — to form joint-ventures in order to enter the Chinese market, Chinese firms in the process of expanding abroad are also resorting to alliances and joint-ventures to promote their foreign operations. Indeed, Chinese firms often leverage on the very same joint-ventures that had initially been set up as mechanisms for foreign firms to enter China, to help them access the international market. Wanxiang, China's largest producer of automobile parts for example, started out by forming a partnership with General Motors to supply GM with locally produced auto parts and thus assist them in complying with the government's requirement that automobiles sold on the Chinese market incorporate a certain level of local content. Later, Wanxiang used the relationship with GM to expand abroad by supplying Chinese-made parts to GM plants in the USA and around the world; finally, this partnership provided Wanxiang with the credibility and references to start supplying other automobile manufacturers in various parts of the world.

Joint-ventures and alliances set up by Chinese firms in their process of international expansion seem to exhibit certain specific features when compared to cooperative agreements as they have been formed over the last three decades by Western corporations. First, these alliances involving Chinese partners seem to combine competition and cooperation to an even greater extent than other alliances. Indeed, it is not unusual for Chinese firms to form multiple joint-ventures with various partners which are direct competitors. In a matter of months, Dongfeng, one of China's largest auto manufacturers, signed agreements to produce cars in the same broad product category for the Chinese market with Peugeot, Nissan and Renault. In a similar fashion, Bird, the largest producer of cell phone handsets in China, has joint-ventures with both Siemens from Germany and Sagem from France. Second, alliances and joint-ventures involving Chinese firms seem to be unusually unstable. While instability is an inherent feature of most joint-ventures anywhere in the world, it is notable that joint-ventures with Chinese firms seem to be, on average, particularly short-lived. For example, TCL's joint operation with Thomson was taken over by the Chinese party after only a few months of existence; similarly, the alliance between IBM and Lenovo to jointly manage IBM's PC business before handing it over entirely to Lenovo was broken up much earlier than had originally been announced. Third, alliances and joint-ventures with Chinese partners seem to often result in a takeover of the joint operations by the Chinese party. While it is not unusual for such an outcome to also happen in other contexts, large Chinese firms in the process of expanding overseas seem to use joint-ventures with foreign partners that they eventually take over in a more systematic way to acquire a permanent and independent international presence. TCL eventually took over its joint operations with Thomson and thus acquired both manufacturing facilities and a commercial presence in North America and in Europe in the process. In the same way, Lenovo became a global player in PCs when it took over its joint-venture with IBM.

In this chapter we will examine how Chinese firms have used alliances and joint-ventures with foreign companies to boost their international presence. We will first analyze how joint-ventures in China have initially helped Chinese firms enhance their technical capabilities, making it possible for them to compete, both in their own domestic market which is attracting more and more foreign rivals, and also in more open international markets. Second, we will examine how joint-ventures have become a device through which Chinese firms are able to rapidly develop a market presence in foreign countries. Third, we will discuss what appears to be a somewhat specific feature of the use by Chinese firms of international joint-ventures: securing a supply of raw materials. Finally, we will examine how many of these alliances and joint-ventures formed by Chinese firms create exacerbated rivalry with their partners; how, as a result, they are often terminated prematurely and how this has led several prominent Chinese firms to acquire entire business units from their former partners.

1. Joint-Ventures for Technology Acquisition

Chinese firms have extensively used alliances and joint-ventures to gain access to technology. In a very classic way, like Korean and other emerging country firms before them, Chinese companies have traded market access for technological know-how. Government regulations compelling foreign firms to form joint-ventures with Chinese counterparts in order to be allowed to operate locally have been instrumental in making this possible. In numerous industries, Chinese firms have thus built up their technical capabilities by working with foreign partners. Chinese automobile companies have progressively acquired first, manufacturing and second, product development skills by collaborating with the likes of Volkswagen, General Motors or Peugeot–Citroën, among others. As a result, they are now in a position to start exporting locally designed automobiles. Though, by most accounts, these Chinese automobiles–such as the Shuanghuan CEO Sport Utility Vehicle, or the Chery QQ — are still significantly less advanced than their Western or Japanese equivalents, they are priced very competitively and are starting to encroach on markets that, until recently, were totally controlled by American, European or Japanese auto makers. And there is little doubt that this first foothold in the business will rapidly lead to better products incorporating more sophisticated technologies and, eventually, to the emergence of world class automobile producers in China. In a similar way, the Chinese government is conditioning the purchase of commercial aircraft from Boeing and Airbus to the transfer of sensitive technologies to China via the formation of joint-ventures with Chinese aerospace firms. The official purpose of these joint-ventures is to carry out the assembly of aircraft destined for the Chinese market and to manufacture parts and components, not only for those aircraft sold in China, but for the entire output of the considered models. It seems unquestionable that these joint-ventures are also created to help the Chinese party acquire essential know-how. In a similar fashion, Huawei, one of the Chinese leaders in telecom equipment, has R&D agreements with such worldwide industry leaders as Motorola, Intel, IBM and Microsoft and also set up two jointly owned research laboratories with Texas Instruments and Infineon. As the management of the company very candidly puts it: "We are still behind in basic R&D capabilities. By cooperating with industry leaders, we expect to enhance our know-how and develop proprietary technology."

Indeed, experience has shown that for knowledge to be transferred through alliances, it is essential that activities in which the considered knowledge is embodied be carried out jointly (Dussauge and Garrette, 1999; Dussauge, Garrette and Mitchell, 2000; Inkpen, 2000; Child, Faulkner and Tallman, 2005). This is particularly critical when the knowledge in question is tacit, in other words when it cannot easily be described and codified. In such cases, it is only by working together and observing the partner accomplish tasks in which the sought knowledge is implemented that the transfer can take place. It is interesting to observe that most alliances involving technology in China take on the form of a joint-venture, i.e. a separate legal entity in which employees from both partner firms work together. Such joint activities are particularly conducive to inter-partner learning. In the case of the Bird/Sagem alliance described in Box 10.1, this alliance led to the formation of a manufacturing joint-venture in which managers from Sagem collaborated and

Box 10.1: Technology Development through Joint-Ventures at Ningbo–Bird.

By 2005, Bird had become China's largest producer of cellular telephone handsets as well as the No. 1 brand in the Chinese market, which by then was the world's largest market for such devices. In order to achieve such spectacular results, Bird extensively used joint-ventures with foreign companies.

Bird was originally created in 1992 to produce pagers that would display messages written in Chinese characters, a feature most foreign products did not offer at the time. Though this venture eventually became reasonably successful, the company faced many challenges along the way: developing both product and manufacturing technology proved much longer than expected and achieving the levels of quality and reliability that the consumers expected was much more difficult than anticipated. As a result, Bird's first products were very disappointing, leading to a lot of customer dissatisfaction; it wasn't until 1996 that Bird's first adequate products hit the market, thus making them miss the market boom in 1993–1995. By the end of the 90s, pagers were increasingly being displaced by mobile phones and, in 1999, the company decided to enter this new business. Having learnt from its prior mistakes, Bird's management realized the firm could not afford to enter this segment on its own. It did not possess the required technology to develop up-to-date products, nor was it capable of implementing an efficient and reliable manufacturing process. And if it did not move fast to take advantage of the phenomenal growth the market for mobile phones was expected to experience between 2000 and 2005, it would again miss a major opportunity to establish itself as one of the leading producers in China.

In light of this, Bird set out to find a foreign partner that possessed leading edge technology but had a limited market presence in China. In its quest for a suitable ally, Bird was helped by government regulations that, at the time, restricted entry of foreign firms into the Chinese market. By then, Motorola, Nokia, Philips, Siemens and Ericsson had all entered the Chinese market and the government was no longer granting new operating licenses to foreign firms. Sagem — which was later merged into the Safran Group — had not yet entered China and knew they would not be allowed to do so on their own. As a consequence, they agreed to sign a partnership agreement with Bird which resulted in the introduction of Bird's first cell phones to the market at the end of 1999. Through the partnership, Bird acquired production equipment and technology from Sagem and produced Sagem designed phones (for which they paid a royalty of US$1 to US$2 for each unit produced) that they sold under their own Bird brand in China. In 2002, the partnership was taken to new heights with the formation of a 50/50 joint-venture, "Bird Sagem Electronics Corporation Ltd." (NBBSE) which manufactured mobile phones in a plant set up alongside Bird's headquarters in the city of Ningbo. In 2005, NBBSE employed over 2000 people and had a total production capacity of 20 million units. The output of NBBSE was shared between the two partner firms that then marketed the jointly produced phones under their respective brand names.

(Continued)

Box 10.1: (*Continued*)

In 2005, the Bird/Sagem partnership was further extended when the two companies signed a Memorandum of Understanding (MoU) in order to coordinate their global strategy and jointly manage their sales worldwide: Bird was to take the lead in China while Sagem would be in charge in all other markets. Purchasing would also be conducted jointly. Finally, it was also decided to create a new 50/50 joint-venture dedicated to R&D; the purpose of this joint-venture was to optimise development costs for both companies by developing a common range of products for the Sagem and Bird brands. This new R&D joint-venture was expected to eventually employ up to 1000 engineers and technical staff.

Interestingly enough, Bird's increasingly tight collaboration with Sagem did not prevent the Chinese company from forming another significant alliance with one of Sagem's European rivals! In 2004, Bird signed an agreement with Siemens to set up a 50/50 manufacturing joint-venture, very similar to the NBBSE arrangement it had with Sagem, and to open up its retail network of over 30 000 distributors to Siemens products, thus giving the German firm access to the country's smaller cities as well as to its rural regions, which were posting the strongest mobile phone user growth in China. The rumour is that Sagem management was not exactly pleased with this Bird / Siemens agreement. To make matters worse, Bird was thought to be a candidate for the takeover of Siemens' mobile phone division when the German conglomerate decided to get out of the business in 2005. No doubt Sagem was delighted when it was ultimately announced that the Taiwanese company BenQ would take over the Siemens mobile phone division!

Finally, it must be noted that, despite having relied very heavily on Sagem technology to enter the mobile phone business, Bird made significant technology investments of its own as early as 1999 in order to develop its own capabilities in the business and reduce its dependence on its foreign partners, including in the more advanced and sophisticated segments of the business. This strategy of "walking on two feet" as Xu Lihua, the CEO of the company put it, allowed the company to produce phones of its own design as early as 2002, with 1 million of the total 7 million handsets it produced that year having been internally developed.

In 2005, Bird was exporting mobile phone handsets under its own brand to about 40 different foreign countries and was also an OEM supplier to Sagem and Siemens/BenQ. This made it the largest Chinese exporter of mobile phones, accounting for 60 percent of China's total mobile phone exports. In the fall of 2006, Safran was rumoured to be searching for an acquirer for its loss making Sagem mobile phone division and industry experts were speculating the prime candidate for such a takeover was Bird. As things turned out, however, Bird ran into major trouble in 2006 and, in the face of considerable financial losses, chose to pull out of the R&D joint-venture with Sagem in 2007, less than two years after the JV had been set up.

interacted with Bird employees; more specifically, all important jobs within the joint-venture were staffed by a pair of managers, one from Sagem, the other from Bird. Such an arrangement provided the Chinese partner with an ideal observation point on the way in which Sagem organized and carried out the manufacturing process. More recently, Bird and Sagem decided to set up a joint R&D facility which will further allow the Chinese company to participate in research and product development activities with its partner and gain access to more technologically advanced knowledge.

Finally, like Bird, many Chinese firms involved in technology sourcing joint-ventures with foreign companies have realized that joint-ventures alone would not provide them with technical independence. Instead, they need to carry out internal R&D to fully assimilate the skills of their partners and gain technical independence; through these internal R&D efforts, they can verify that they have indeed mastered all the essential capabilities that were being implemented jointly within the alliance and are capable of using them alone. More importantly, internal R&D efforts allow the Chinese firm to extend the technical base acquired from their foreign partner and thus start developing proprietary technologies on which they can build a sustainable competitive advantage. In aerospace, whatever technologies have been acquired through partnerships with foreign companies are being implemented by AVIC I Commercial Aircraft Co., Ltd. (ACAC) in the development of an indigenous aircraft, the ARJ21 commuter jet targeted at China's expanding regional air transportation market.

The lack of strictly enforced rules and regulations on patenting and intellectual property has obviously made the task of incorporating technology acquired through alliances and joint-ventures much easier. Many Chinese designed products in fairly advanced industries still closely resemble their foreign models. Even in a business like flower breeding, licensing out patented flower varieties to Chinese firms has proved problematic: Meilland, one of the leading developers of rose hybrids in the world found that one of its former Chinese licensees was growing and marketing one of its patented varieties on a very large scale without paying any royalties! The irony of this, in fact, is that it has sometimes made international expansion more difficult whenever the foreign firm from which the technology was sourced has sued for patent or copyright infringement. For example, GM Daewoo Auto & Technology Company, a unit of General Motors, filed a lawsuit against Chery in May 2005 on the grounds that its QQ model too closely resembled one of its own designs. GM Daewoo alleged Chery copied its Spark sedans and demanded 80 million yuans (about US$10 million) as compensation for patent infringement. If the courts ruled in favor of GM, it would make it much more difficult for Chery to sell the QQ in international markets. Similarly, BMW is suing China Automobile Deutschland, the importer of Shuanghuan's CEO SUV, on the grounds that the Chinese-made vehicle is a blatant copy of the German automaker's own X5 model; this will no doubt make foreign sales of that car problematic.

Through a combination of collaboration and internal R&D efforts, many Chinese firms are managing to enhance their level of technology. This becomes particularly apparent when it makes it possible for them to develop products that are adapted to local conditions. Very early on, Bird proved capable of developing pagers specifically tailored for the Chinese market and displaying messages written with Chinese characters. Later, Bird leveraged on the technology acquired from its alliances with Sagem and Siemens to introduce mobile phones with strong reception capabilities that were particularly suited to China's Western provinces where population density is low and very loose relay networks produce only weak signals. Further down the line, Bird introduced handsets with Chinese character SMS (Short Messaging Service) capabilities.

This ability to adapt the technology acquired from foreign partners through joint-venturing and licensing to local conditions, notably the particular conditions of emerging markets, has proved particularly useful when expanding abroad. Many of the countries where Chinese firms initiate their international expansion are developing countries in Southeast Asia, Africa or Eastern Europe. Like Chinese consumers, customers in such countries are price-sensitive and face somewhat rugged environments. Therefore, products adapted to the Chinese market are often well suited to market conditions in other emerging markets. As a consequence, it is no surprise that Chinese multinationals are making very significant inroads into such markets, in both consumer products and capital goods. In Algeria for example, French firms which used to dominate in many sectors of the economy have recently lost very significant contracts to Chinese competition: renovation of the Algiers airport, road construction, telecom infrastructure, power generation, etc. have gone to Chinese companies in the last few years.

2. Joint-Ventures for Foreign Market Entry

Chinese firms have used joint-ventures with local players to enter foreign markets, much in the same way that foreign firms have been forming JVs with Chinese partners to enter the Chinese market (Buckley and Glaister, 2002). These joint-ventures provide Chinese firms with access to sales and distribution networks, a better understanding of buyers and customers in the target market, local connections, and even a well-established brand in some cases. In emerging markets, joint venturing with domestic firms has been a way to establish the right connections with local decision makers and develop sales there. When Huawei entered the Russian telecom equipment market it chose to do so by forming a joint-venture (in which they own slightly less than 50 percent of the equity) with Beto, a Russian telecom equipment manufacturer. This Beto–Huawei joint-venture carries out both manufacturing and sales activities. For Huawei, it primarily provides them access to the local Russian market which would be extremely difficult for them to penetrate on their own. Beto's relationships with government officials, their sales force and their knowledge of the local environment are essential to Huawei's sales in that country. On the other hand, it appears Beto has chosen to cooperate with Huawei in order to gain access to some of their technology. According to Huawei officials, Beto entered into the partnership with them because they are more open to technology transfers than most other industry leaders such as Alcatel with whom Beto had formed an alliance in the past before choosing to switch their partnership activities over to Huawei. In much the same way, Huawei has grown in Thailand by forming a joint-venture with AIS, who was initially a small telecom operator and a customer of Huawei hardware.

Interestingly enough, in some cases, Chinese firms seeking to expand overseas have used partnerships with the very same foreign partners with whom they had previously formed joint-ventures when these partners were trying to enter the Chinese market. Wahaha's first major foray into foreign markets has been a direct consequence of their broad alliance with Danone (see Box 10.2). When Danone decided to set up manufacturing operations in Indonesia to locally produce dairy products and milk-based drinks, they invited Wahaha to join them. As a consequence, the operation in Indonesia was set up as a joint-venture in which Danone is the majority shareholder with a 70 percent stake, while Wahaha owns the remaining 30 percent. It appears that if Danone chose to bring Wahaha along in this project, it is because Wahaha had something valuable to contribute. Indeed, engineering teams from Wahaha carried out most of the work to set up the production lines and have since been in charge of managing the production process. Along with their experience in an environment which in many respects is somewhat similar to that of Indonesia in terms of labor qualifications, sanitary conditions, technical context, etc., Wahaha engineers and technicians had the added advantage of being much less expensive than expatriates from Europe.

A more radical use of joint-ventures by Chinese firms to enter foreign markets is when the Chinese company buys a stake in an entire business unit previously owned by a foreign multinational. The most prominent operations carried out along these lines are the acquisition by TCL, one of China's — and the world's — largest TV producers of 49 percent of Thomson's television activity (see Box 10.3), and the acquisition by Lenovo of a significant stake in IBM's PC business.

Forming outgoing alliances with established Western corporations has allowed Chinese firms to compensate for their very limited prior international exposure and more generally for their lack of sophisticated marketing skills, at least those marketing skills that are critical to success in open and competitive markets. Indeed, because China's economy had remained isolated from international markets from 1949 to the mid to late-eighties, Chinese firms had no established distribution networks that they could rely on in markets such as Europe or the USA. Also, most Chinese firms initially developed in a context where markets were not won and lost only on the basis of the relative merits of the products or services offered, but were,

Box 10.2: Wahaha–Danone.

The Wahaha Group started out in 1987 as the sales department of the Hangzhou school district. Less than 20 years later, it had become China's largest non-alcoholic beverages producer, accounting for over 15 percent of all packaged beverages sold in the country. Under the leadership of a charismatic manager, Zong Qinghou, and through the takeover of several ailing state-owned companies, Wahaha grew very rapidly, introducing over 30 varieties of milk and yogurt based products, bottled water, soft drinks, fruit and vegetable juices, tea-based drinks, soups, etc., soon expanding its reach to the entire country, through some two million distributors. In more recent years, Wahaha further diversified its activities to children's clothing, health products, vitamins, and was considering the introduction of a line of personal care products such as shampoo or toothpaste. With its Future Cola brand, Wahaha was considered to be Coca Cola's and Pepsi Cola's most serious local competitor in the booming Chinese soft drink market. Instrumental in Wahaha's growth and success was its alliance with the France-based packaged foods multinational Danone.

As early as 1996, Wahaha entered into a series of joint-venture agreements with Danone. That year, the multinational invested US$43 million in five Wahaha plants across China. In these jointly owned plants, Danone owned a 51 percent stake and Wahaha the remaining 49 percent, but the management responsibility for these plants remained with the Chinese partner. Such Danone investments in Wahaha plants continued over the years and by 2005, Danone owned a stake in over 30 of Wahaha's 80 or so manufacturing subsidiaries. Though it did not control the parent company, it was estimated that in 2005 Danone owned about 40 percent of the Wahaha Group's assets. Based on this, the Danone group claimed that the Wahaha brand was one of the top four brands it owned along with Evian, Danone and LU, these four brands accounting for 60 percent of the group's worldwide revenue. Interestingly enough, Danone public relations often suggested that Wahaha was a Danone subsidiary, while Wahaha's management made it a point to stress that Danone had jointly invested with Wahaha in a number of plants but by no means had a controlling stake in the Hangzhou-based company.

Its alliance with Danone was instrumental in Wahaha's first significant operation overseas. In 2004, the two partners jointly invested in a plant in Indonesia, with Danone owning 70 percent and Wahaha 30 percent. This factory produced Danone dairy products and biscuits, as well as Wahaha milk-based drinks for children; it was also rumoured it might start bottling Wahaha's "Future Cola" at some point. Though this joint-venture in Indonesia is primarily managed by Danone, Wahaha played a significant role in starting the operation and in running the production process. The production lines were set up by engineering teams sent over from Wahaha and the Chinese partner is in charge of supervising production.

Following this first foray into overseas markets, Wahaha has increased its export activities by entering Thailand in a significant way and has even managed to penetrate the US market on the West Coast, by appealing to the large Chinese community established there. Future projects include boosting sales in Europe by setting up manufacturing operations in Poland.

(Continued)

Box 10.2: (*Continued*)

Despite its deep involvement with Wahaha, Danone has established a number of other joint-ventures or acquired stakes in other companies in order to expand its business in the Chinese market. Danone acquired a 20 percent stake in the Shanghai Bright Dairy company, one of the largest producer of milk-based products in China and owns a controlling share in Robust, one of the Chinese market leaders in both bottled water and milk-based beverages. It was rumoured at one point that Danone was attempting to merge the Robust and Wahaha operations. This did not occur and seems to have been met with strong resistance from Wahaha's management.

A major dispute erupted between Danone and Wahaha in 2007. Danone has sued Wahaha's founder for using the Wahaha brand on products manufactured and sold outside the scope of the joint-venture activities, while Wahaha countered by claiming that exclusive ownership of the Wahaha brand was never handed over to the joint-ventures with Danone. In addition, Wahaha sued senior Danone-appointed board members claiming that their simultaneous membership on Wahaha's board and on the boards of other Danone subsidiaries in the beverage and dairy products businesses created a conflict of interest and was detrimental to Wahaha.

to some extent at least, allocated to one firm or the other by government authorities at the central, provincial and local levels, based on the individual connections of the management and on how favorably they were perceived by these authorities.

This was instrumental in their initial successes and subsequent growth as a provider of telecom equipment in China but is of little help when venturing abroad. Therefore, despite their low costs, aggressive pricing and, in many cases, adequate products, Chinese firms found it difficult to crack mature, developed and highly structured markets abroad without "assistance" from a partner with the necessary skills and assets. When TCL formed a worldwide alliance with Thomson in the TV business, it had very little commercial experience outside of China and most of its export sales were through the large purchasing departments of a few mass retailers such as Wal-Mart, Target or Best Buy. These retailers in fact came to TCL (as well as to other manufacturers in China) to purchase and, as a result, were in a position to impose very low prices. In a sense, the Chinese suppliers were not really expanding their commercial reach overseas and building up a durable international presence; instead, these large customers were shopping around in China for the best possible bargain and importing back to their home country. In this respect, the joint-venture with Thomson was instrumental in helping TCL build up a real commercial presence in both Europe and North America. Although the initial agreement stipulated that each partner firm should retain full control of its commercial assets (including brands, sales forces and after-sales service), this rapidly proved ineffective. Instead, Thomson contributed their sales forces in both those regions (400 people in Europe, close to 100 in the USA) to the joint operation.

Box 10.3: The TCL–Thomson and TCL–Alcatel joint-ventures.

TCL, originally a joint-venture formed in the mid–1980s between a Hong Kong investor and a municipally-owned Chinese company headquartered in Huizhou (Guangdong Province), in Southern China, that specialized in the production of magnetic tapes, grew very rapidly by entering the market for fixed line telephones in China. By 1990, TCL was one of the top telephone brands in the country. TCL entered the television business in 1992 and, through both internal growth and the acquisition of local competitors, rapidly became one of the largest TV producers in China. TCL also entered the PC and mobile phone businesses in 1998 and 1999 respectively. By having shares of the holding company or of the operating divisions listed on the Shenzhen and Hong Kong stock exchanges, TCL was able to raise funds in order to finance its expansion both in China and in foreign markets. By the late 1990s, TCL was exporting televisions under its own brand name to several emerging markets in Asia and the Middle East. In 2001, it began manufacturing TV sets for Philips and Toshiba who both acquired a small stake in the equity of TCL. By 2002, TCL was producing 8 million television sets and exporting 15 percent of its production.

Despite these successes, TCL's attempts to increase its presence in the USA and in Europe were made difficult by the high import duties and quotas imposed on Chinese manufacturers who were accused of dumping their products at below cost prices on both these markets. In 2002, in order to overcome this hurdle, TCL acquired Schneider Electronics AG, a bankrupt German manufacturer of TV sets. With this acquisition, TCL was hoping to get up-to-date technology, manufacturing assets as well as a strong sales network and brand that would enable them to become a significant player in the European market. Unfortunately, the acquired firm's assets proved to be much less valuable and effective than expected and ownership of Schneider did not dramatically improve TCL's position in Europe.

So in 2003, Li Dongsheng, the CEO of TCL, met with Charles Dehelly, the CEO of Thomson, to discuss a possible alliance between the two television giants. Thomson, headquartered in France, was one of the world leaders in consumer electronics, with a strong presence in both Europe and the United States. It owned such famous brands as RCA, General Electric, SABA or Thomson but, for a number of years, it had been losing ground to competition and incurring significant losses. Moreover, Thomson was initiating a major shift in its strategy and had chosen to focus primarily on the professional side of multimedia (production and broadcasting equipment) and to de-emphasize its involvement in consumer electronics.

An agreement to combine TCL's and Thomson's television businesses was soon pieced together and the deal was officially finalized in January 2004, during a visit to France by China's President Hu Jintao. Under the agreement, the two partner firms formed a joint-venture called TTE (TCL–Thomson Electronics Corporation) in which TCL had a 67 percent stake while Thomson owned the remaining 33 percent of the equity. All television manufacturing assets owned by the two partners were allocated to the joint-venture, except one plant in Angers (France) which was kept by Thomson

(Continued)

Box 10.3: (*Continued*)

for political and social reasons. TV-related research centers were also handed over
to TTE which, in addition, was granted licenses for the use of existing patents and
technologies. Each partner, however, retained ownership of those technologies that
had been developed and those patents that had been granted before the alliance was
established. Ownership of the brands was also retained by the parent companies, but
TTE was given a 20-year license to use the Thomson brand in Europe, the RCA brand
in North America and the TCL and Rowa brands in Asia. It had originally been decided
that sales forces would remain separate and controlled by the parent companies, but
that rapidly proved unmanageable so all TV-related sales forces were soon handed over
to TTE. In 2004, its first year in operation, TTE produced and sold almost 17 million
television sets, overtaking Sony and establishing itself as the world leader in the field.
The 2004 sales of the new entity, however, represented almost a 10 percent decline
when compared with the combined sales of the two groups in the prior year. Thirty-
four percent of TTE's sales were in China, 31 percent in Europe and 25 percent in
North America, while emerging markets and OEM production accounted for the rest.

Despite its market leadership position in the world, TTE was unable to turn a profit.
In 2005, its first whole year in operation, TTE lost US$77 million. During the first
nine months of 2006, it lost close to 200 million US$. Interestingly enough, while
operations in China and in the US were performing more or less to plan, it was in
Europe — on Thomson's home turf — that losses were staggering, amounting to about
50 percent of revenue in 2006. Indeed, TTE's main product line was cathode-ray tube
TVs at a time when the European market was massively switching to flat panel display
TVs. As a consequence, Thomson pulled out of TTE in August 2005 by exercising the
option it had to convert its 33 percent stake in the joint-venture into direct ownership
in TCL Multimedia, the parent company of TTL. Management of TTE was then taken
over entirely by TCL.

By the end of 2006, however, losses in Europe were becoming so huge that TCL
announced it would discontinue any direct presence in the European market, cutting
support to its own brands there and dismantling its sales networks, only selling
in Europe through OEM contracts with established competitors. TTE as a separate
entity was dismantled and its activities taken over directly by TCL Multimedia. TCL
announced it would no longer purchase services and fully assembled TV sets from
Thomson's Angers plant as had been decided in the alliance agreement. Thomson
immediately announced it would sell off part of its stake in TCL Multimedia, bringing
down its ownership from about 30 percent to less than 20 percent. Most analysts
expected Thomson to pull out entirely over the subsequent months.

Less than three years into the alliance, the Thomson–TCL alliance has de facto
fallen apart. TCL has become the largest television set manufacturer in the world with
a significant presence in all major markets. This position, however, was extremely
shaky because the assets and businesses taken over from Thomson were extremely
vulnerable, because the new company was too busy integrating the activities coming

(*Continued*)

Box 10.3: (*Continued*)

from the two parents to focus its efforts on successfully entering the flat panel display segment that, in the meanwhile, has become the fastest growing sector in the TV business. Between 2004, when it was formed, and late 2006, TTE saw its market value divided in half. Its corporate parent, TCL, had gone from being seen as the best example of the new breed of Chinese corporations on their way to conquer the world, to being perceived as a staggering giant, even in its home country.

As the TCL–Thomson alliance was crumbling, Thomson announced it was acquiring an 8 percent stake in Konka, another Chinese TV manufacturer, and one of TCL's major competitors. Almost simultaneously, Philips announced it would increase its ownership in TCL to close to 10 percent, thus becoming the third largest shareholder of the company.

Ironically, TCL entered into a very similar joint-venture deal with Alcatel, the French telecom equipment giant, in the mobile phone handset business more or less at the same time it was creating TTE with Thomson. In the fall of 2004, the Chinese company agreed to form the TAMP (TCL & Alcatel Mobile Phones) joint-venture in which it held 55 percent of the equity, with Alcatel owning the remaining 45 percent. Alcatel handed over all its R&D and manufacturing assets in the cell phone handset business to the joint-venture and granted TAMP a worldwide license to use the Alcatel brand name on its products. The deal was generally seen as an attempt by Alcatel to get rid of a cash-bleeding division but still retain a say in a business that they needed in order to offer integrated solutions to customers, notably mobile phone network operators. As for TCL, the deal provided them with a brand, a distribution network as well as technology to support their global ambitions. The formation of this alliance made TCL the second largest producers of mobile phone handsets in China, right after Bird. In May 2005, less than a year after it was established, in an attempt to increase the integration of operations, the partners announced that the TAMP joint-venture would be taken over entirely by TCL. This was seen by analysts as a confirmation of the widespread rumours according to which the cooperation was not working very well.

Thomson's brands (Thomson and Saba in Europe, RCA in North America) were licensed out to the joint-venture for a 20-year period. In much the same way, the IBM–Lenovo agreement immediately allowed for IBM's sales network in PCs to carry former Lenovo products while these products were re-badged with the IBM and Thinkpad brands. In early 2005, when Rover was entering into a joint-venture with Shanghai Automotive Industry Corporation (SAIC), the CEO of the British company had no delusions about what the Chinese partner was looking for in the alliance: "What they are interested in is our brand, our retail network in Europe and our automobile design know-how."

Unlike technology, however, brands and distribution networks cannot be progressively internalized by jointly working with partner-firms that possess them.

If a Chinese company wants to gain full control of a brand and distribution network in Europe, North America or elsewhere in the world it must eventually either build these assets from scratch or acquire them from a local firm. It is therefore no surprise to observe that several of the outward looking joint-ventures formed by Chinese companies with foreign partners have sooner or later resulted in a full buyout by the Chinese party. For TCL to become a major player in the European and US television markets, it could not rely forever on Thomson's brands and sales forces.

3. Joint-Ventures and Natural Resources

A somewhat more unusual use of joint-ventures by Chinese firms seems to be an attempt to secure access to raw materials. For a number of years now, Chinese officials have been concerned that the country's fast paced economic growth might eventually be abruptly halted by a shortage in essential raw materials such as iron, copper, oil, etc. By forming partnerships with local companies and thus achieving joint ownership of mines and oil fields in countries rich in natural resources, Chinese managers appear confident that their firms will be given priority in the event that demand were to far outstrip supply.

For the last 50 years or so, all major oil companies around the world have been forming joint-ventures with local players in order to be awarded concessions to conduct exploration or exploit identified oil fields. In this sector, joint-venturing is often a pre-requisite to be able to operate in most oil producing countries. And in this context, Chinese oil companies have joined the party and entered into partnerships in order to conduct both exploration and exploitation activities. CNPC (China National Petroleum Corporation) has acquired a large stake in Aktubinsk Oil & Gas Company, which operates the third largest oil field in Kazakhstan while CNOOC (China National Offshore Oil Corporation) owns numerous participations in exploration or exploitation consortia in Indonesia. That Chinese companies form such joint-ventures for the exploitation of raw materials when they are forced to do so by local authorities and regulations is not surprising. What is somewhat more unusual is when they form partnerships in countries that do not require this, in the hope that such arrangements will guarantee their access to the output of the jointly owned source of raw material.

In iron and steel for example, Baosteel, the largest producer of automobile grade steel plate in China, has entered into a joint-venture with CVRD (Companhia Vale do Rio Doce) from Brazil to secure a supply of iron ore. This Baovale Mineração joint-venture, formed in 2002, produced 8 million tons of high grade iron ore annually during the three subsequent years, with 75 percent of the output being acquired by Boasteel. Similarly, Baosteel formed the BaoHI Ranges joint-venture with Hamersley Iron, a subsidiary of the Rio Tinto group, to operate the Eastern Range mine in Western Australia. Through this joint-venture agreement,

Baosteel — who owns 46 percent of the JV — is awarded about half the production, i.e. 10 million tons, of ore per year. The joint-venture agreement is for 20 years and will thus provide Baosteel with a secure supply of some 200 million tons of iron ore until 2025. In non-ferrous metals, NFC (China Non Ferrous Metal Industry's Foreign Engineering and Construction Company) has formed similar joint-ventures with local companies to mine zinc in Mongolia and copper in Zambia.

In addition to forming joint-ventures to secure the supply of raw materials, Chinese firms have also made wholly owned investments when local conditions permitted. CNPC acquired PetroKazakhstan, the largest oil company in the country, in 2005, while Shougang acquired Hierro Peru, a local company operating the largest open air iron ore mine in that country.

The real question is whether such investments, especially those that are made through joint-ventures, are likely to secure, as is their objective, a steady and low cost supply of the needed raw materials. In contexts where free markets dominate, it is doubtful that such partnerships will produce the expected benefits. Indeed, in the event of price increases, the joint-venture partners will expect to take advantage from such rising prices and will want all shipments — including those made to the other JV partner, i.e. the Chinese company — to reflect market prices. Thus, adjusting to market prices would guarantee supply equally well, without any need to partake in the ownership or management of the source of raw material. And to gain protection from the potential price volatility of a particular raw material, any buyer can enter into a long-term fixed price contract, again with no need to own a share of the company producing the considered raw material; of course, such a protection against price fluctuations comes at a cost, but being a JV partner will in no way eliminate this cost. In fact, the investment by Chinese firms in mining and raw material extraction joint-ventures can be analyzed as the price to pay for hedging against a potential increase in raw material prices.

In the event that free markets no longer operate; for example, if a shortage of a particular raw material leads the governments of the producing countries to consider it of "strategic importance" and to declare an embargo on exports, then again, being a joint-venture partner in the facility producing the considered raw material is unlikely to provide any advantage. Political pressure from the Chinese government (or any other government for that matter) becomes the name of the game.

Overall, it is somewhat unclear what are the benefits of entering into such joint-venture agreements when local authorities do not require it. One possible explanation for this behavior may have to do with the context in which many large Chinese firms originally developed: a Communist system and a planned economy. In such a context, each economic unit was highly dependent on other players in the economy, notably suppliers, without the safety provided by an efficient market. Indeed, in a market economy, changes in the availability of any good, among them raw materials, are dealt with through price fluctuations. Provided they are willing to pay the market price, firms will not, in principle at least, be left without the inputs they require to carry out their activity. In a planned economy, firms are dependent on other economic actors and on the way in which the central planning administration allocates scarce goods to the various users. As history has shown, such a centrally planned organization of the economy does not always function efficiently and production units are often left without the basic inputs they need to operate. In response to this, Chinese firms have historically favored what would normally be considered abnormally high levels of backward vertical integration, thus becoming their own suppliers for as many of the inputs they routinely require as they can, and in this way isolating their own operations as much as possible from upstream activities in the economy. Despite the change toward a market economy, old habits run deep and many large Chinese firms remain much more vertically integrated than their western counterparts. Joint-venturing, as well as full ownership when it is possible, in mining and raw materials may well be a carry-over from times when the only way to secure procurement of a critical input was to own the source of that input. It remains to be seen if, over the years, Chinese firms increase or decrease their investments in such sources of vital raw materials.

4. Internal Rivalry within Alliances

As discussed earlier in this chapter, many of the motivations that drive Chinese firms to enter into joint-ventures and alliances to assist in their internationalization process are very similar to those of firms originating in other regions of the world. Concerning the way in which they manage their joint-ventures, however, Chinese firms seem to exhibit a number of somewhat particular characteristics that may have to do with the political context in which they developed or to certain particular features specific to the Chinese environment. First, Chinese firms appear to combine competition with cooperation to a greater extent than most other firms participating in alliances. Second, many joint-ventures involving Chinese firms appear to be more unstable and short-lived than alliances in other regions of the world. Third, what is traditionally considered to be a somewhat unusual, or even exceptional, outcome of alliances, i.e. full acquisition of the business by one of the firms participating in the alliance, seems to occur quite frequently when one partner is a large Chinese multinational; and when alliances with Chinese firms result in one partner acquiring the joint-venture, the acquiring party is overwhelmingly the Chinese partner firm.

Many inter-firm alliances, notably those that are formed with partners operating in the same industry or seeking to enter the same industry, create a potential for inter-partner rivalry. An essential feature of successful alliances is thus that the partner firms must be able to cooperate effectively despite the fact that they may be competing at the same time on other businesses or other markets, or that they expect to compete directly with one another some time in the future (Hamel, Doz and Prahalad, 1989; Hamel, 1991). In Europe, Peugeot and Fiat cooperate tightly in making engines but also compete head to head in the end automobile market; Volkswagen and Ford even went so far as to jointly produce a minivan that was sold under both brand names, which in no way prevented them from competing on all other models in their product range. In the US, General Motors and Toyota jointly produced the Toyota Corolla and Geo Prism twin models in the sub-compact category but competed directly in all other automobile segments. In this respect, alliances involving Chinese firms are not particularly different from others. However, Chinese firms do seem to know how to juggle cooperation and competition to a greater extent than others. For example, it is quite common for Chinese partner firms to simultaneously establish alliances with different partners to develop the same technologies, address the same business segment, or enter the same market. Dongfeng Motors, for example, has joint-ventures with Renault, Nissan, Peugeot and Honda, among others, and produces models of all four manufacturers in the same broad product categories. TCL formed a major joint-venture with Thomson (see Box 10.3) in 2004 despite the fact that it had a prior association with one of Thomson's fiercest competitors, the Dutch electronics giant Philips, and that the two firms had been collaborating to jointly manufacture and sell consumer electronics for several years. In addition, Philips owned a minority stake in TCL's equity. As one of Philips' senior managers put it: "We buy from them, we sell to them, we have shares in them and . . . we compete with them!" To add to the confusion, another consumer electronics giant, Toshiba from Japan, also owned a stake in TCL at the time when the deal with Thomson was signed. In the mobile phone handset business, Bird signed a technology, manufacturing and marketing joint-venture agreement with Siemens despite the fact it was cooperating extensively with Sagem (see Box 10.1). Amusingly, the two rival joint-ventures owned manufacturing facilities located side by side on Bird premises, right next to the company headquarters.

Why Chinese firms would want to simultaneously enter into such directly competing agreements is fairly plain to see: they can thus reduce their dependence on any one partner and be in a better position to bargain by pitting their various allies one against the other. They expect, as a result, to be able to wrest greater technology transfers from their partners, receive a larger share of the jointly achieved profits or acquire more valuable know-how from their joint operations. Why foreign partners would agree to such adulterous partnerships is undoubtedly related to the size of the Chinese market; foreign firms seeking to access the domestic market of a large Chinese company are willing to put up with the conditions imposed on them by their partner because there is too much to loose in being shut out of such a huge market.

This unusually intense inter-partner rivalry may account, at least in part, for the fact that many alliances with Chinese firms seem to be fairly short-lived when compared to others. The Thomson–TCL joint-venture was created in early 2004 and was terminated less than two years later, in mid-2005. Another joint-venture

TCL had entered into with Alcatel to jointly produce mobile telephone handsets was also terminated only about one year after it was formed. When they are not terminated altogether, many alliances with Chinese firms seem to be rapidly and frequently renegotiated and restructured. The Lenovo–IBM agreement whereby Lenovo would take over IBM's PC business and continue using the IBM brand for several years was downscaled after only one year in existence, with IBM continuing to provide sales and service support to Lenovo in the USA, but with the IBM brand entirely replaced by the Lenovo brand on the PC line worldwide. The unusually dynamic nature of the Chinese market may account for the high mortality rate of alliances with Chinese firms. Rapid changes in market circumstances require frequent adaptations and thus renegotiations of the initial agreement. Such renegotiations are a critical stage in the life of an alliance or joint-venture because when the partner firms cannot reach an agreement, renegotiations inevitably result in termination. With demand for most goods and services growing at incredible rates in the Chinese market, renegotiations often lead to escalating demands from the Chinese party who feel they "own" the market. When the foreign party feels unfairly treated during these repeated renegotiations, this can result in a breakdown of the agreement.

A third interesting feature of joint-ventures and alliances with Chinese firms is that they often result in the takeover of the joint operations or even of the entire business by the Chinese partner firm. Examples such as TCL and Thomson, TCL and Alcatel or even, to some extent, Lenovo and IBM are particularly striking. All these alliances were short-lived and ended with the Chinese acquisition of the JV. In the case of Thomson and TCL, the agreement was formally signed in January 2004. By August 2005, however, Thomson pulled out by swapping its shares in the joint-venture for 29 percent of the equity of TMTHL (TCL Multimedia Technology Holding Limited), the consumer electronics business of TCL, leaving TCL entirely in charge. In the fall of 2006, Thomson reduced its stake in TMTHL to 19 percent and announced it would sell off the rest of its ownership over the next few months. In a very similar way, Alcatel formed the TAMP joint-venture with TCL in the fall of 2004, only to pull out a few months later, in May 2005, leaving TCL alone at the helm. In the case of IBM and Lenovo, the eventual takeover of IBM's PC division by Lenovo had been agreed upon right from the start, but full control of the PC business as well as the substitution of the IBM brand by the Lenovo brand came much sooner than initially planned; here again, Lenovo was rapidly left to manage the integration of the two businesses and fend for itself in the global PC industry, IBM only assisting its partner in the role of an agent and distributor. Another potentially similar case that was still unresolved at the time this chapter was written is that of the Bird and Sagem alliance: at the beginning of 2007, rumors had it that Sagem was trying to exit the mobile phone handset business in which it was incurring significant losses and was negotiating the total sale of its cell phone division to Bird.

What these cases suggest is that the ultimate takeover of many of these joint-ventures by the Chinese partner firm may be the consequence of a somewhat particular pattern of alliance activity. The formation of many of these joint-ventures is initially motivated by the fact that the Western partner is unable to manage one of its businesses profitably, often because its costs are too high in the face of increasing competition from emerging market firms. It thus sees an alliance with a low cost Chinese partner as a last resort attempt to restore the troubled business to profitability. When that fails, exit from the business — and the joint-venture — becomes the only way out. On the Chinese side, these joint-ventures are seen as a way to rapidly access all the resources needed to expand into major foreign markets such as North America and Europe. When it becomes clear the joint-venture is unable to operate profitably, the Chinese partner has too much to loose in pulling out: it would durably cut itself off from foreign markets that are essential to its future development in what is one of its core businesses. It thus has no other choice than to take over the JV and try its best to cut the losses. When Thomson formed its TTE joint-venture with TCL, its strategy vis-à-vis the consumer electronics business in general and televisions in particular was very opportunistic. It had decided to focus on the professional side of the media industry and was willing to quit consumer electronics if it could not make money there. When it became obvious TTE would not be profitable before a long time, Thomson pulled out. In parallel, Thomson sold off other businesses in the same sector: its TV tube division to Videocon from India and its small electronic devices and accessories to Oristano from Switzerland. TCL on the other hand was much more committed to the consumer electronics business and particularly to television, one of its core activities, and could not pull out of TTE without dire consequences. In a very similar move, Alcatel formed the TAMP joint-venture with TCL to offload its loss-making cell phone handset business it no longer thought it could restore to profitability and which it no longer perceived as having any long-term strategic value. In the case of IBM, things are even clearer: it saw PCs as an unattractive business and chose to sell it off to Lenovo who had focused on that business and was eager to globalize rapidly.

What has made the break-up of all these joint-ventures difficult for the Chinese partner is not so much the fact that they are left with an unprofitable business to manage, but rather that the handover has come too fast, leaving them largely unprepared. Indeed, while alliances and joint-ventures are a mechanism through which to acquire new knowledge and capabilities, this can only take place by working with the firm who controls that knowledge for an extended period of time. If collaboration falls apart too soon, the Chinese firm has to start making decisions in areas it has too little understanding of. For example, TCL has had to make decisions relative to the US or European markets without having any in-depth understanding of those two markets other than through former Thomson employees, whose trustworthiness it was not in a position to assess: no one at TCL's headquarters had enough experience of the markets of North America and Europe to be able to judge whether the strategies suggested by the local management were reasonable.

Several large Chinese corporations thus seem to have been caught in a "race to learn", which is quite typical of complementary alliances (Hamel, 1991; Hennart and Zietlow, 1999). In such alliances, when the partner firms have diverging goals, it is critical for any one partner to reach its goals before the other does, or it will become extremely vulnerable to the other quitting the alliance. When partner firms want to learn from each other — for example one partner wants to acquire technology while the other wants to enhance its knowledge of a local market — whichever partner learns first no longer needs the alliance and is then in a position to either exit the joint-venture or force its partner out. Several large Chinese firms seem to have fallen victim to this syndrome. They are at the loosing end of a deal in which they want to eventually acquire their partner's business but need time to learn about foreign markets, while their foreign partners want to either turn around a bleeding business or get out as soon as possible if that objective cannot be met very rapidly. These diverging goals make it difficult to agree on a strategy for the joint-venture: the foreign partners are unwilling to invest resources and commit long-term to the success of the joint-venture while it is critical for the Chinese party that the business be turned around successfully, even if it entails further investments. Disagreements on these policy issues rapidly result in a premature takeover by the Chinese partner. It is therefore not really surprising that several Chinese firms who first entered into JVs with Western counterparts, and then rapidly bought out their partner, have faced serious problems later on.

References

Buckley, P.J. and Glaister, K.W. (2002). What Do We Know About International Joint Ventures? In Contractor, F. and Lorange, P. (eds.), *Cooperative Strategies and Alliances*. Oxford: Pergamon Press.

Child, J., Faulkner, D. and Tallman, S. (2005). *Cooperative Strategy: Managing Alliances, Networks and Joint Ventures*. Oxford: Oxford University Press.

Dussauge, P. and Garrette, B. (1999). *Cooperative Strategy: Competing Successfully through Strategic Alliances*. Chichester: J. Wiley & Sons.

Dussauge, P., Garrette, B. and Mitchell, W. (2000). Learning from Competing Partners: Outcomes and Durations of Scale and Link Alliances in Europe, North America and Asia. *Strategic Management Journal*, 21, 99–126.

Hamel, G., Doz, Y. L. and Prahalad, C. K. (1989). Collaborate with your Competitors – and Win! *Harvard Business Review*, January–February, pp. 133–139.

Hamel, G. (1991). Competition for Competence and Inter Partner Learning within International Strategic Alliances. *Strategic Management Journal*, Vol. 12 (special issue), pp. 83–103.

Hennart, J. F., Roehl, T. and Zietlow, D. S. (1999). Trojan Horse or Work Horse? The Evolution of US-Japanese Joint Ventures in the United States. *Strategic Management Journal*, 20, 15–29.

Inkpen, A.C. (2000). Learning through Joint Ventures: A Framework of Knowledge Acquisition. *Journal of Management Studies*, 37, 1019–1043.
Inkpen, A.C. (2000). Learning through Joint Ventures: A Framework of Knowledge Acquisition. *Journal of Management Studies*, 37, 1019–1043.
Ming, Z. and Hennart, J.F. (2002). From Learning Races to Cooperative Specialization: Towards a New Framework for Alliance Management. In Contractor, F. and
Lorange, P. (eds.), *Cooperative Strategies and Alliances*. Oxford: Pergamon Press.

CONCLUSION
CHINA'S UNIQUE ADVANTAGE

Jean-Paul Larçon

HEC Paris

The development of China's outward international investment and the internationalization of Chinese companies are direct consequences of the Chinese government's "reform and opening up" policy and the rapid growth of the Chinese economy and international trade.

The search for energy and natural resources, as well as Chinese companies' need to overcome new trade barriers and protectionist measures typically generated by the success of Chinese exports, has accelerated the internationalization phenomenon and led Chinese companies to invest more abroad.

These investments abroad — which have always been controlled, closely monitored and supported by Chinese government — have accelerated since 2001, when a phase of large cross-border M&A began.

The Lenovo–IBM deal, the Thomson–TCL partnership, Haier's successful investments in the US and European market, and the attempt of CNOOC to buy Unocal Oil Company are good examples of the ambitions and mobilization capacity of Chinese companies on the international scene.

In most cases Chinese companies have carefully selected their country targets, generally giving priority to emerging markets because of the ease of entry. They have also carefully selected their potential partners so as to build on complementary resources or skills.

The difficulties, however, usually came at the implementation level. These radical moves mean that Chinese companies face conditions which they have not experienced before. Compared to their prior experiences of growth, acquisition, and restructuring within the domestic market, they have had to face new dilemmas such as managing joint-ventures abroad with partners who have potentially diverging long-term goals, or integrating companies with a totally different organization or culture.

The quest for knowledge and technology is an important element of Chinese companies' internationalization process. Another important element is the ambition not only to compete on price, but to be on par with the best of the class in terms of technology. The Chinese government makes immense efforts to increase the R&D central budget, develop international standards, and create incentives to develop proprietary technology. The combination of three factors creates the opportunity for Chinese companies to challenge their western competitors both in emerging and developed markets: big volumes generated on the domestic market, lower cost for good quality product and services, and proprietary technology. Huawei Technology is an example of this combination in the telecommunications infrastructure business.

Chinese companies face several challenges. They have to acquire technology, develop international marketing skills, cultivate relationships with distribution networks, and create global brands. Haier has demonstrated its capacity to build a business model with strong local responsiveness and the ability to serve the differentiated needs of its consumers in China, in emerging markets, and in large segments of developed economies such as the EU and the US.

In some cases, Chinese companies might have been overconfident and taken risks that they would not have taken if they had received less generous support and encouragement from the government and financial institutions.

The step by step transformation of state-owned enterprises and the planned reduction of the number of SOEs affiliated with the central government will contribute strongly to the development of more focused international strategies.

If a majority of Chinese multinationals are still SOEs or minority SOEs, one could expect the rapid development in the next decade of successful, purely private Chinese multinationals. They will build on assets that they may have already developed such as volume, low cost, speed, and flexibility.

However, they will also have to nurture key sources of competitive advantage such as an autonomous capacity for innovation and cross-cultural skills within their organization.

ANNEX 1

List of companies most frequently quoted in the book

Usual name	Legal name of Parent company	Major activity
Baosteel Group 宝钢集团	Shanghai Baosteel Group Corporation 上海宝钢集团公司 (Shanghai baogang jituan gongsi)	Steel
BAIEC 北京汽车工业进出口公司	Beijing Automotive Import & Export Corporation 北京汽车工业进出口公司 (Beijing qiche gongye jinchukou gongsi)	Automobiles
Bird 波导	Ningbo Bird Co., Ltd. 宁波波导股份有限公司 (Ningbo bodao gufen)	Mobile phones youxian gongsi
BOE Technology Group 京东方科技集团	BOE Technolody Group Co., Ltd. 京东方科技集团股份有限公司 (Jingdongfang keji jituan gufen youxian gongsi)	Display technology
China Worldbest Group 中国华源集团	China Worldbest Group Co., Ltd. 中国华源集团有限公司 (Zhongguo huayuan jituan youxian gongsi)	Textile & Pharmaceutical

(Continued)

231

(Continued)

Usual name	Legal name of Parent company	Major activity
CNOOC 中海油	China National Offshore Oil Corporation 中国海洋石油总公司 (*Zhongguo haiyang shiyou zong gongsi*)	Oil & Gas
CNPC 中国石油集团	China National Petroleum Corporation 中国石油天然气集团公司 (*Zhongguo shiyou tianranqi jituan gongsi*)	Oil & Gas
Haier Group 海尔集团	Haier Group Corporation 海尔集团公司 (*Haier jituan gongsi*)	Home appliances
Hisense Group 海信集团	Hisense Company Limited 海信集团有限公司 (*Haixin jituan youxian gongsi*)	Household appliance and telecommunication
Holley Group 华立集团	Holley Holding, Ltd. 华立集团股份有限公司 (*Huali jituan gufen youxian gongsi*)	Electricity meters
Huawei Technologies 华为技术	Huawei Technologies Co., Ltd. 华为技术有限公司 (*Huawei jishu youxian gongsi*)	Telecom equipment

(Continued)

(*Continued*)

Usual name	Legal name of Parent company	Major activity
Jincheng Group 金城集团	Jincheng Corporation Co., Ltd. 金城集团有限公司 (*Jincheng jituan youxian gongsi*)	Airborne equipment & Motorcycles
Lenovo Group 联想集团	Lenovo Group Limited 联想集团有限公司 (*Lianxiang jituan youxian gongsi*)	Personal computers
NFC 中色股份	China Nonferrous Metal Industry's Foreign Engineering and Construction Co., Ltd. 中国有色金属建设股份有限公司 (*Zhongguo youse jinshu jianshe gufen youxian gongsi*)	Nonferrous metal
Nuctech 威视股份	Nuctech Company Limited (originally Tsinghua Tongfang Nuclear Technology Co.) 威视技术股份有限公司 (*Weishi jishu gufen youxian gongsi*)	Container inspection Technology
Shanghai Electric 上海电器	Shanghai Electric Group Co., Ltd. 上海电器集团股份有限公司 (*Shanghai dianqi jituan gufen youxian gongsi*)	Power generation equipment

(*Continued*)

(*Continued*)

Usual name	Legal name of Parent company	Major activity
Shougang Group 首钢集团	Beijing Capital Iron and Steel Group Co. Beijing Shougang Co., Ltd. 北京首钢股份有限公司 (*Beijing shougang gufen youxian gongsi*)	Steel
TCL Corporation TCL 集团	TCL Corporation TCL集团股份有限公司 (*TCL jituan gufen youxian gongsi*) TCL Multimedia TCL Technology TCL 多媒体科技 (*TCL duomeiti keji*) TCL Communication Technology TCL 通讯科技 (*TCL tongxun keji*) TTE Corporation (TCL–Thomson Electronics) TCL 汤姆逊电子有限公司 (*TCL tangmu xun dianzi youxian gongsi*)	Consumer electronics

(*Continued*)

(*Continued*)

Usual name	Legal name of Parent company	Major activity
Tsingtao Beer 青岛啤酒	Tsingtao Brewery Group 青岛啤酒股份有限公司 (*Qingdao pijiu gufen youxian gongsi*)	Beer
Wahaha 娃哈哈	Hangzhou Wahaha Group Co., Ltd. 杭州娃哈哈集团有限公司 (*Hangzhou wahaha jituan youxian gongsi*)	Beverages
Wanxiang Group 万向集团	Wanxiang Group Corporation 万向集团公司(*Wanxiang jituan gongsi*)	Automotive parts
Youngor 雅戈尔	Ningbo Youngor Group Co., Ltd. 雅戈尔集团股份有限公司 (*Yage'er jituan gufen youxian gongsi*)	Garment

ANNEX 2

Major International Moves of Selected Chinese Companies

BAOSTEEL GROUP, BOE TECHNOLOGY GROUP, CNPC, CNOOC, HAIER GROUP, HISENSE GROUP, HOLLEY GROUP, HUAWEI TECHNOLOGIES, JINCHENG GROUP, LENOVO GROUP, NFC, SHANGHAI ELECTRIC, SHOUGANG GROUP, TCL CORPORATION, AND WANXIANG GROUP.

Source: HEC Paris Strategy Department and the Institute of World Economics and Politics — CASS (2007).

A.1: Shanghai Baosteel Group Corporation (Baosteel Group) — 上海宝钢集团公司.

Shanghai Baosteel Group Corporation is a large, diversified iron and steel group created in 1998 after absorbing different steel companies. Baosteel, a central government-controlled SOE is the largest steel producer in China, with a crude steel production capacity of about 20 million tons. China's total steel production for 2006 was 381.5 million tons. Baosteel has been listed on Shanghai's Stock Exchange since 2000.

1996   USA — creation of Baosteel America Inc. a wholly-owned trade company to market Baosteel iron and steel products in all American countries.

2001   Brazil — creation and co-management of a company in Brazil, Baovale Mineracao S.A. and long-term iron ore supply contract between Baosteel and Companhia Vale do Rio Doce (CVRD), the world's largest iron ore producer.

(Continued)

A.1: (*Continued*)

2002 Australia — creation of a joint-venture (Baosteel 46 percent) with Hammersley Iron (RioTinto 100 percent) to develop the Paraburdoo mine in Western Australia.
It will supply 10 million tons of finished ores per year to Baosteel.

2003 Brazil — new contract with CVRD. Total iron ore shipments to be made to Baosteel will reach 20 million tons per year by 2010.

2004 Brazil — Baosteel and CVRD agree on the feasibility study of a joint project to build and operate an integrated steel plant in São Luís, state of Maranhão, Brazil, to produce about 3.7 million tons per year of steel slabs.

2006 Brazil — CVRD and Baosteel, representing all Chinese steel makers, settle benchmark iron ore prices for 2007. CVRD became in 2006 the largest individual iron ore supplier to China.

2006 Brazil — Baosteel and CVRD sign a letter of intention with the state government of Espirito Santo, Brazil to build a steel slab plant with an initial production capacity of 5 million tons per year. The joint-venture, Baosteel Victoria Iron & Steel Co., Ltd. is located in Anchieta, Esprito Santo: Baosteel 80 percent — CVRD 20 percent.

2007 Australia — creation of a Joint-Venture with Fortescue Metals Group Ltd. to explore and develop magnetite, another iron ore product, in Western Australia. Baosteel signed a 10-year purchase agreement to supply up to 20 million tons of iron ore a year.

A.2: BOE Technology Group Co., Ltd. — (BOE) 京东方科技集团股份有限公司.

BOE Technology Group Co., Ltd., founded in 1993 is a non-governmental enterprise.

It was listed in 1997 on the Shenzhen B Share Stock exchange. Based in Beijing technological cluster and a member of the "Zhongguancun Next Generation Internet Industry Alliance," BOE is a high-tech firm specialized in display technologies, products and services. It is number one in China and number nine worldwide in the thin-film transistor liquid-crystal display (TFT-LCD) industry.

2001 Korea — acquisition of 45 percent of Hydis — flat-panel-display technologies for US$380 million.

2003 Korea — acquisition of the TFT-LCD business of Hydis from Hynix Semiconductors for US$380 million. Creation of BOE-Hydis Technology Co., Ltd.

(*Continued*)

A.2: (*Continued*)

2003   Hong Kong — acquisition of 26.36 percent of TPV Technology Ltd. (listed in Hong Kong and Singapore) for US$1.345 billion. TPV is one of the largest manufacturers of Cathode Ray Tube (CRT) and LCD computer monitors.

2007   Korea — BOE Hydis, in deep financial trouble, is to be sold to a Taiwan and Hong Kong-based syndicate.

2007   Hong Kong — BOE Technology Group Co., Ltd. is obliged to sell its stake in TPV Technology Ltd. in order to improve its financial structure.

A.3: China National Petroleum Corporation (CNPC) —
中国石油天然气集团公司.

CNPC is a central government-controlled SOE, founded in 1988. It is China's largest integrated oil and gas company and it ranks 10th among the world's top 50 petroleum companies. Including the activities of its subsidiary, PetroChina, it was the second largest company in the world in terms of number of employees in 2006. CNPC has oil and gas exploration, development and production projects in 30 countries, including Azerbaijan, Canada, Indonesia, Myanmar, North Africa, Oman, Peru, Russia, Sudan, Thailand, Turkmenistan, and Venezuela.

PetroChina has been listed on the New York Stock Exchange (NYSE) and Hong Kong Stock Exchange since 2000 and has acquired the overseas assets from its parent company in 2005.

1995   Sudan — JV with the government of Sudan and other partners — acquisition of 40 percent of the Great Nile Petroleum Operation Company (GNPOC) and the operational rights in zones 1, 2, and 4 in Sudan's oil fields. The largest production base for CNPC in a foreign country.

1997   Kazakhstan — acquisition of a 60.3 percent stake in Aktubinsk Oil & Gas Company.

2002   Indonesia — acquisition of the oil and gas assets of Devon Energy — 100 percent stake for US$262 million.

2003   Kazakhstan — acquisition of 100 percent of the equity of Texaco North Buzachi oilfield.

(*Continued*)

A.3: (*Continued*)

2005	Kazakstan — acquisition by PetroChina of PetroKazakhstan for US$4.18 billion.
2005	Ecuador — purchase of EnCana's Ecuador assets for US$1.4 billion.
2006	Russia — cooperation with Rostneft: purchase of shares of Rosneft for US$500 million, agreements on oil and gas exploration and development and sales of refined products; creation of the Oriental Energy Company Ltd. for oil and gas exploration bidding in Russia.
2007	Chad — a joint-venture refinery company between CNPC Int'l. and the government of the republic of Chad.

A.4: China National Offshore Oil Corporation (CNOOC) — 中国海洋石油总公司.

CNOOC is a central government-controlled SOE and China's largest producer of offshore crude oil and natural gas. Established in 1982 to explore China's offshore petroleum resources, CNOOC is listed on the New York and Hong Kong Stock Exchange.

1995	Indonesia — acquisition of a 39.51 percent interest in the Malacca Strait production sharing contract (PSC).
2002	Indonesia — acquisition of Indonesian assets of Spanish oil major Repsol–YP for US$585 million in cash. This made CNOOC the largest offshore oil producer in Indonesia and increased its production by around 17 percent.
2002	Indonesia — acquisition of BP interests in Tangguh Liquefied Natural Gas Project.
2002	Indonesia — CNOOC Muturi Limited, a wholly owned subsidiary of CNOOC acquires a 12.5 percent stake of the PSC in the Tangguh Liquefied Natural Gas Project for US$275 million.
2003	Australia — acquisition of 25 percent stake in the China LNG Joint-Venture, a new joint-venture established within the Northwest Continental Shelf Natural Gas Project for US$348 million.
2003	Kazakhstan — acquisition of 8.33 percent interest in the North Caspian Sea Project for US$615 million.

(*Continued*)

A.4: (*Continued*)

2005 USA — CNOOC is forced to withdraw a US$18.5 billion takeover bid for energy firm Unocal Corp., due to opposition from the US Congress.

2006 Nigeria — investment of $2.28 billion cash to acquire a 45 percent interest in an offshore oil drilling license from South Atlantic Petroleum of Nigeria.

2007 Australia — CNOOC wins a new permit to explore for oil and gas in an area offshore of Western Australia. A potential investment of A$162.1 million (HK$1.08 billion) over six years.

A.5: Haier Group Corporation (Haier Group) — 海尔集团公司.

Founded as Qingdao Refrigerator Co. in 1984, the Haier Group is still under partial public ownership. It is the third largest household appliances manufacturer in the world. It produces refrigerators, freezers, air-conditioners, microwave ovens, washing machines, dishwashers, televisions, mobile phones, and computers.
  Qingdao Haier Refrigerator Co. has been listed since 1993 on the Shanghai Stock Exchange. Haier Electronics Group Co., Ltd. has been listed on the Hong Kong Stock Exchange since 2005. Haier's 2006 global revenue was RMB107.5 billion. The company had 50,000 employees.

1996 Indonesia — creation of a joint-venture, PT. Haier Sapporo, in Jakarta (Haier 51 percent) to manufacture refrigerators.

1997 Philippines — creation of a joint-venture Haier LKG Electrical Appliances Ltd. to manufacture household electrical appliances.

1997 Malaysia — creation of a joint-venture with a Malaysian company to manufacture household electrical appliances.

1997 Serbia — creation of a joint-venture in Belgrade to manufacture air conditioners.

1999 USA — Haier builds its first US home appliances factory in Hamilton, South Carolina and creates Haier America Refrigerator Corp., Ltd.

2001 Italy — acquisition of a refrigerator factory in Padova belonging to Meneghetti.

2002 Japan — creation of a joint-venture Sanyo-Haier Company, with Sanyo. Sanyo's products would be sold in

(*Continued*)

A.5: (*Continued*)

China through Haier's sales network under Sanyo and Haier brand names, while sales of Haier's products in Japan would be promoted by a joint-venture, Sanyo-Haier Co. The agreement was terminated in 2007.

2004   Jordan — opening of Haier (Middle East) Industrial complex. An annual production capacity of 1 million appliances.

2005   USA — Haier fails to buy the appliance maker Maytag, which is acquired by Whirlpoool.

2006   Pakistan — creation of a joint-venture with Ruba General Trading Company Ltd. to develop near Lahore a home appliances manufacturing base. Haier has a 55 percent stake in the joint-venture. The two partners are expected to invest around US$250 million in the construction of the zone over the next five years.

2007   India — acquisition of the appliance division of Anchor Daewoo and its refrigerator plant in Pune.

A.6: Hisense Group Co., Ltd. (Hisense Group) — 海信集团有限公司.

Founded as "Qingdao No. 2 Radio Factory" in 1969 to produce transistor radios, Hisense specializes in consumer electronics, household appliances and information technology.

The company's main products are televisions, air conditioners, refrigerators, computers, mobile phones, software, and network devices. Hisense ranks among China's top ten electronic manufacturers and plays a key role in the industry, thanks to its R&D capabilities. Hisense exports its products to over 50 countries and regions and has production sites in Algeria, Hungary, Iran, Pakistan and South Africa. Ownership structure of Hisense remains complex with a strong influence of the Qingdao Municipal Government.

1996   South Africa — creation of a joint-venture Hisense South Africa Development Enterprise (Hisense controlling stake 60 percent) to assemble air conditioning units and TV sets.

1999   Brazil — creation of Brazil-Hisense Company (Sao Paulo): air conditioning manufacturing and sales.

2000   Indonesia — creation of a TV manufacturing joint-venture — investment of US$1 million.

(*Continued*)

A.6: (*Continued*)

2001	South Africa — acquisition of Daewoo television factory near Johannesburg. An investment of US$4 miliion.
2004	Pakistan — partnership with Pakistan company to assemble air conditioners.
2004	Hungary — creation of Hisense Hungary Kft. (HKK) for assembling and marketing of color TV in the EU market. The plant which is located in Sarvar is managed in cooperation with Flextronics.

A.7: Holley Group Co., Ltd. (Holley Group) — 华立集团有限公司.

Holley Group is a diversified company specialized in metrological instruments, power equipment, information technology, biopharmaceuticals and real estate. Holley is the world's largest electricity meters manufacturer. Holley Holding Ltd. is the parent company of the group that includes three listed companies in China.

2000	Thailand — first overseas plant in Bangkok to manufacture and sell electricity meters.
2001	USA — acquisition of 58 percent of a small Nasdaq-listed company "American Champion Entertainment." The company was restructured and transformed by Holley Holdings (USA) Ltd. in Pacific Systems Control Technology, specialized in developing technology solutions for power automation and metering systems.
2001	USA & Canada — acquisition of research and development teams of Philips Semiconductors specialized in mobile phone communication, based in Dallas and Vancouver.
2003	Argentina — creation of a joint-venture with TTES to develop an electricity meter assembly factory. Meters are to be sold in Argentina, Brazil, Uruguay and Paraguay. A total investment of US$800,000.

A.8: Huawei Technologies Co., Ltd. (Huawei Technologies) — 华为技术有限公司.

Established in 1988, Huawei Technologies, based in Shenzhen, is one of the world's leading networking and telecommunications equipment suppliers. Huawei is a private company, 100 percent owned by its employees.

In 2006 Huawei had 62,000 employees worldwide and served 31 of the top 50 telecom operators. Close to 70 percent of its revenues comes from markets outside China.

Huawei's main R&D centers are located in China and abroad in Sweden (Stockholm), the US (Dallas and Silicon Valley), India (Bangalore), and Russia (Moscow).

1993	USA — creation of a research center in the Silicon Valley.
1996	Hong Kong — joint project with Hutchinson Whampoa Group in providing fixed-line network products.
1997	Russia — creation of a joint-venture Beto-Huawei, in Ufa to manufacture telecom equipment.
1999	USA — opening of a research institute in Dallas.
2001	USA — creation of FutureWei Technologies Inc. the North American subsidiary of Huawei Technologies Co., Ltd.
2003	USA — creation of a joint-venture named Huawei-3Com (H3C) with 3Com for Internet Protocol-based routers and switches.
2007	USA — Huawei participates in Bain Capital bid to acquire 3Com the communications networking company, for US$2.2 billion in cash. As part of the transaction, Huawei would acquire a minority interest in the company and become a commercial and strategic partner of 3Com.

**A.9: Jincheng Corporation Co., Ltd. (Jincheng Group) —
金城集团有限公司.**

Founded in 1949, Nanjing-based Jincheng Motors Group, a state-owned enterprise, is specialized in the development, manufacturing, and distribution of aviation products, motorcycles and gasoline engines. The group is involved as well as in international trade and urban real estate.

Jincheng Corporation is among top three leading motorcycle manufacturers in China and a leading exporter. In 2006 it exported more than 500,000 bikes to 51 countries. It has established JVs in Columbia, Argentina, and Nigeria and set up offices and maintenance centers in Iran, Nigeria, Vietnam, and Indonesia.

1996   Colombia — creation of Jincheng de Colombia (Jincol), a 50–50 joint-venture with Colombia Easter Auto Trading Company to manufacture motorcycles. Parts imported from China represented 15.5 percent of the Group's total annual export turnover. Jincol targets markets of the Andean Pact countries, Central America, and the Caribbean region.

2000   Argentina — creation of a 50-50 joint-venture with Daltac Company, to set up a motorcycle assembly plant with an annual production capacity of 30,000 units. Jincheng provides technology, equipment and motorcycle CKD kits, while the Argentinean side will contribute marketing skills, sales networks and capital for the new JV. The JV will sell its products in Argentina, Brazil and Paraguay.

2002   Nigeria — creation of a Chinese-funded company by Jincheng 85 percent and trading company China National Aero-Technology Import & Export Xiamen Corporation (CATICXM) (15 percent) to assemble motorcycles. The company has a designed annual capacity of 10,000 units.

Jincheng's International Manufacturing and Distribution Partnership

• Jincheng has an exclusive agent Devon Motorcycles to distribute its motorcycles in the United States.

• In Europe Jincheng signed in 2006 a partnership with Aprilia (a subsidiary of the Piaggio Group); Jincheng will manufacture a new line of Aprilia motorcycles and engines for the European market.

A.10: Lenovo Group Ltd. (Lenovo Group) — 联想集团有限公司.

Legend Holdings Ltd. (**联想集团有限公司.**— *Lianxiang konggu youxian gongsi*)
Originally known as New Technology Developer Incorporated and Legend Group
Ltd., Legend Holdings was incorporated in Hong Kong in 1988 and was listed on
the Hong Kong's Stock Exchange in 1994. It issued Level I American Depositary
Receipts (ADRs) in 1995.

Lenovo Group
Lenovo Group Ltd. is the international technology company formed by the former
Lenovo Group and IBM's Personal Computing Division. Lenovo Group Ltd. has
its headquarters in New York and primary operational hubs in Beijing, Paris,
Research Triangle Park (North Carolina), and Singapore. Major research centers
are in Japan (Yamato), China (Beijing, Shanghai and Shenzhen), and the U.S.
(Raleigh, North Carolina).
   PC manufacturing and assembly facilities are in China (Shenzhen, Huiyang,
Beijing and Shanghai), as well as OEM s worldwide.
   The company employs more than 25,000 people worldwide and is ranked third
globally in the PC business.

Lenovo Group Ltd's ownership structure (2007).
The listed holding company was incorporated in 1988 in Hong Kong

*   Public shareholders 39.6 percent.
*   Legend Holdings Limited 42.4 percent (*).
*   IBM 7.9 percent
*   TPG Capital, General Atlantic LLC and Newbridge Capital
    LLC 10.1 percent

(*)Legend Holdings Limited is controlled by the Chinese Academy of Sciences
(CAS) 65 percent and the Employees' Shareholding Society of Legend Holdings
35 percent.

1998	Hong Kong — creation of Hong Kong Legend Technology Company by Lenovo's predecessor, the Beijing Computer Research Institute, and acquisition of Quantum, a company specialized in PC mother boards.
2004	USA — Lenovo and IBM announce their agreement by which Lenovo will acquire IBM's Personal Computing Division, its global PC (desktop and notebook computer) business.
2005	USA — Lenovo completes the acquisition of IBM's Personal Computing Division, making it a new international IT competitor and the third-largest personal computer company in the world.
2007	Europe — Gateway Inc. binding offer prevents Lenovo's potential opportunity to buy Packard Bell B.V.

A.11: China Non ferrous Metal Industry's Foreign Engineering and Construction Co., Ltd. (NFC) — 中国有色金属建设股份有限公司.

NFC is specialized in project contracting and non-ferrous metal resources exploitation in the global market. NFC was listed on Shenzhen Stock Exchange in 1997 after asset restructuring.

1995	Thailand — creation of a joint-venture to recycle non-ferrous metals. The JV sells the lead alloy extracted from recycled used batteries to battery manufacturers.
1998	Zambia — development of Zambia Chambishi copper mine project. Creation of NFC Africa Mining Plc a joint-venture between NFC (85 percent) and ZCCM Investment Holdings PLC. The largest Chinese overseas investment in a non-ferrous metal mining company.
2000	Mongolia — creation of Sino-Mongolian JV Tsairt Mineral Co., Ltd. A zinc mining engineering and construction project worth US$42.8 million.
2000	Iran — construction of Iran zinc smelter — development of the Jajarm Alumina Plant — development of the Iran Khatoon Abad Copper Plant.
2003	Australia — cooperation agreement to develop Australia's electrolytic aluminum plant and alumina mine.

A.12: Shanghai Electric Group Co., Ltd. (Shanghai Electric) — 上海电器集团股份有限公司.

Shanghai Electric (SEC) is one of the largest electromechanical equipment industrial groups in China. SEC is a state-owned enterprise, that controls three listed companies. Shanghai Electric Co., Ltd., Shanghai Electric Apparatus Co., Ltd. and Shanghai Diesel Engine Co., Ltd.

2002	Japan — acquisition, along with the Morningside Group (Hong Kong), of Akiyama Machinery Manufacturing Corporation, the leading Japanese manufacturer of multi-color printing presses.
2004	Germany — acquisition of a 53.5 percent stake of Wohlenberg GmbH, a leading machine tool manufacturer based in Hanover.
2004	Japan — acquisition of a 75 percent interest in Ikegai Corp., a machine tool manufacturer, for $4.5 million.
2007	Vietnam — SEC start building a Vietnamese-invested thermoelectricity power plant with a capacity of 600 MW in northern Quang Ninh province. The investor is Quang Ninh thermoelectricity joint stock company.

A.13: TCL Corporation (TCL) — TCL 集团股份有限公司.

Founded in 1981, TCL Group is a consumer electronics manufacturer headquartered in Huizhou, Guangdong Province. TCL products include televisions, mobile phones, personal computers, home appliances, electric lighting, and digital media sold to domestic and overseas markets.

TCL Group, formally a state-owned enterprise includes three listed companies.

TCL Corporation, listed in Shenzhen, has a diversified ownership structure, with local government controlling 29.89 percent, top managers 25 percent, and foreign investors 25 percent.

TCL Multimedia Technology Holdings Limited, listed in Hong Kong, is specialized in television. It controls 100 percent of TTE.

TCL Communication Technology Holdings Ltd., listed in Hong Kong, is specialized in mobile phones.

1999	Vietnam — creation of TCL (Vietnam) Company — a 100 percent subsidiary of TCL Corp. — to assemble color TV sets for the local and South Asian market.
2000	India — creation of a joint-venture (TCL 51 percent) — TCL Baron Electronic Co., Ltd. with the Baron International Ltd. — an investment of US$28 million.
2000	Singapore — creating of a regional marketing and sales office for Indonesia, Malaysia, Brunei, and Myanmar.
2002	Germany — acquisition of bankrupted TV manufacturer Schneider Electric for 8.2 million euros.
2003	USA — acquisition of GoVideo, a DVD producer, its trademarks, and patents for US$10 million.
2003	France — creation of a joint-venture, TCL — Thomson Electronics (TTE), with Thomson Electronics. TCL has 67 percent of the shares. TTE has a production capacity of 22 million color TV sets and sells 18 million sets per annum, accounting for about 11 percent of the global color TV market and leading the industry.

(Continued)

A.13: (*Continued*)

2004   India — creation of a whole-owned subsidiary TCL India Holdings Pvt Ltd. and a joint-venture with Sri Nahusha Electronics Private Limited (holding 76 percent equity in the JV) to manufacture consumer electronics and consumer durable goods at Visakhapatnam (Andhra Pradesh)

2004   France — creation of a joint-venture with Alcatel, TCL & Alcatel Mobile Phones Limited (TAMP) taking over Alcatel mobile phone global business.
      TCL acquired 55 percent of the shares in 2004 and 100 percent in 2005.

2005   France — TAMP becomes a wholly-owned subsidiary of TCL Communication.

2007   Hong-Kong — TCL is to sell 82 percent of its computer company's stakes to solve the company's debt problems accumulated over last years.

A.14: Wanxiang Group Corporation (Wanxiang Group) — 万向集团公司.

Founded as a township enterprise in 1969 in the Zhejiang province, Wanxiang is specialized in automobile spare parts and related mechanical and electrical products such as universal joints, bearings, and CV joints. Wanxiang is also diversified in unrelated sectors such as large-scale agriculture, aquaculture, real estate development, and infrastructure development projects. In 2006 Wanxiang had 40,000 employees and US$4.2 billion in revenue.

1994   USA — foundation of Wanxiang America Corporation in Chicago with a registered capital of US$500,000.

1997   UK — acquisition of 60 percent stake in AS Company, a sales company selling all kinds of bearings in the European market. Foundation of Wanxiang European Bearing Company.

1997   USA — acquisition of 75 percent stake in a golf course in Michigan — foundation of Wanxiang Grassland & River Co.

2000   USA — acquisition of Zeller, among top three auto part suppliers in America and a client of Wanxiang.

2000   USA — acquisition of 35 percent stake of LT, the largest American supplier of hub units.

(*Continued*)

A.14: (*Continued*)

2001   USA — acquisition of 21 percent stake of Universal Automotive Industries Inc., the largest American brake component supplier.

2001   USA — purchase of a 12.95 percent stake in oil and gas exploration project in Texas, USA — creation of a joint-venture, Wanxiang Horton Insurance Brokerage, with the Horton Insurance Group. Wanxiang controls 51 percent.

2003   USA — acquisition of 33.5 percent of Rockford Powertrain Inc. the largest American supplier of wing-type drive shafts.

2006   USA — negotiations between Wanxiang and Delphi.

2007   USA — Wanxiang is to buy the Monroe pro-shaft business from Ford Motor Co.

ABBREVIATIONS

ADR	American Depositary Receipt
BOO	Build, Operate and Own
BOOT	Build, Operate, Own, Transfer
BOT	Build, Operate and Transfer
CAS	Chinese Academy of Sciences
CASS	Chinese Academy of Social Sciences
CBRC	China Banking Regulatory Commission
CCPIT	China Council for the Promotion of International Trade
CEO	Chief Executive Officer
China Eximbank	The Export-Import Bank of China
CIC	China Investment Cooperation
CIRC	China Insurance Regulatory Commission
CSRC	China Securities Regulatory Commission
CKD	Completely Knocked Down
DRC	Development Research Center
EPC	Engineering, Procurement and Construction
FDI	Foreign Direct Investment
FTC	Foreign Trade Corporations
GAC	General Administration of Customs
GDP	Gross Domestic Product
GPA	Government Procurement Agreement

HK$	Hong Kong Dollar
IMF	International Monetary Fund
INR	Indian Rupees
IPO	Initial Public Offering
IPR	Intellectual Property Rights
IT	Information Technology
JV	Joint Venture
M&A	Merger and Acquisition
MII	Ministry of Information Industry
MES	Modern Enterprise System
MNCs	Multinational Companies
MOC	Ministry of Construction
MOF	Ministry of Finance
MOFCOM	Ministry of Commerce
MOFTEC	Ministry of Foreign Trade and Economic Cooperation
MOST	Ministry of Science and Technology
MoU	Memorendum of Understanding
NDRC	National Development and Reform Commission
NSFC	National Natural Science Foundation of China
ODM	Original Design Manufacturer
OECD	Organization for Economic Co-operation and Development
OEM	Original Equipment Manufacturer
PBOC	People's Bank of China
PRC	People's Republic of China
R&D	Research and Development
RMB	Renminbi
SAIC	State Administration for Industry and Commerce
SASAC	State-owned Assets Supervision and Administration Commission

SC	State Council
SETC	State Economic and Trade Commission
SINOSURE	China Export & Credit Insurance Corporation
SMEs	Small and Medium-sized Enterprises
SOEs	State-owned Enterprises
TNCs	Transnational Corporations
UNCTAD	United Nations Conference on Trade and Development
UNIDO	United Nations Industrial Development Organization
US$	US Dollar
VC	Venture Capital
WTO	World Trade Organization

TABLES, FIGURES AND BOXES

Tables

Figures

Boxes

BIBLIOGRAPHY

Asia Pacific Foundation of Canada and China Council for the Promotion of International Trade (2005). *China Goes Global: A Survey of Chinese Companies Outward Direct Investment Intentions.* Vancouver: Asia Pacific Foundation of Canada.

Boston Consulting Group (2006). *The Strategic Implications of Chinese Outbound M&A.* Boston, MA: Boston Consulting Group.

Buckley, P.J., Clegg J., Cross A., Lui X., Voss H. and Ping Z. (2007). Host Country Determinants of Chinese Outward Foreign Direct Investment. *Journal of International Business Studies*, 38(4), 499–518.

Chen, Q. and Chen, X. (2006). Guowuyan an fazhan yanjiuzhongxin qiye yanjiusuo (Development Research Center of the State Council Enterprise Resrarch Institute DRC). *The Internationalization Strategies for Chinese Enterprises.* China: Remin Chubanshe.

Cheng, S. (2001). *Studies on Economic Reforms and Development in China.* Hong Kong: Oxford University Press.

Child, J. and Rodrigues S.B. (2005). The Internationalization of Chinese Firms: A Case for Theoretical Extension? *Management & Organization Review*, 1(3), 381–410.

Du, Y. (2003). Haier's Survival Strategy to Compete with World Giants. *Journal of Chinese Economics and Business Studies*, 1(2), 259–266.

Dussauge, P. and Garrette B. (1999). *Cooperative Strategy.* New York: J. Wiley & Sons.

Fernandez, J.A. (2006). *China's State-Owned Enterprise Reforms: An Industrial and CEO Approach.* UK: Routledge.

Foreign Investment Advisory Service (FIAS) (2005). *Survey of Chinese MNCs.* Washington, DC: International Finance Corporation.

Hirt, M. and Orr, G. (2006). Helping China's Companies Master Global M&A. *The Mckinsey Quarterly August Issue.*

Huchet, J.F., Richet, X. and Ruet, J. (2007). *Globalization in China, India and Russia Emergence of National Groups and Global Strategies of Firms.* New Delhi: Academic Foundation.

Inkpen, A.C. and Pien W. (2006). An Examination of Collaboration and Knowledge Transfer: China-Singapore Suzhou Industrial Park. *Journal of Management Studies*, 43(4), 779–811.

Izraelewicz, E. (2005). *Quand la Chine chaage la Monde.* Paris, Grasset.

Lin, J.Y., Cai, F. and Li, Z. (1996, 2003). *The China Miracle: Development Strategy and Economic Reform.* Hong Kong: The Chinese University of Hong Kong.

Mathews, J.A. (2002). *Dragon Multinationals: A New Model for Global Growth.* Oxford: Oxford University Press.

Mathews, J.A. (2006). Dragon Multinationals: New Players in 21st Century Globalization. *Asia Pacific Journal of Management*, 23(1), 5–27.

MOFCOM (2005). *Foreign Market Access Report.*

MOFCOM (2005). *Guidelines for Overseas Investment Industries.*

Narula, R. and Dunning J.H. (2000). Industrial Development, Globalization and Multinational Enterprises: New Realities for Developing Countries. *Oxford Development Studies*, 28(2), 141–167.

Nolan, P. (2001). *China and the Global Economy.* Basingstoke, UK: Palgrave.

Nolan, P. and Zhang J. (2003). Globalization Challenge for Large Firms from Developing Countries: China's Oil and Aerospace Industries. *European Management Journal*, 21(3), 285–299.

OECD (2007). *OECD Review of Innovation Policy: China.* Paris: OECD Synthesis Report.

Panitchpakdi, S. and Clifford, M. L. (2002). *China and the WTO: Changing China, Changing World Trade.* Singapore: John Wiley & Sons.

Ping, D. (2007). Investing for Strategic Resources and Its Rationale: The Case of Outward FDI from Chinese Companies. *Business Horizons*, 50(1), 71–81.

PricewaterhouseCoopers (2007). *Greater China IPO Watch* 2006.

Rugman, A.M. and Li J. (2007). Will China's Multinationals Succeed Globally or Regionally. *European Management Journal*, 25(5), 333–343.

Sigurdson, J. (2005). *Technological Superpower China.* Cheltenham and Northampton, MA: Edward Elgar.

UNCTAD (2000). *World Investment Report 2000: Cross-border Mergers and Acquisitions and Development.* New York and Geneva: United Nations.

UNCTAD (2003a). *World Investment Report 2003: FDI Policies for Development: National and International Perspectives.* New York and Geneva: United Nations.

UNCTAD (2005). *China in a Globalizing World.* New York and Geneva: United Nations.

UNCTAD (2005). *World Investment Report 2005: Transnational Corporations and the Internationalization of R&D.* New York and Geneva: United Nations.

UNCTAD (2006). *World Investment Report 2006. FDI from Developing and Transition Economies: Implications for Development.* New York and Geneva: United Nations.

Wang, Z. (2004). Zhongguo guojia ziran kexue jijin xiangmu (National Natural Science Foundation of China's Project). *Zouxiang Shijie de Zhongguo Kuaguo Gongsi* (Overseas Expansion of Chinese Multinational Companies). Beijing: Zhongguo Shangye Chubanshe.

Wells, L.T. (1983). *Third World Multinationals: The Rise of Foreign Investment from Developing Countries.* Cambridge, MA: MIT Press.

Williamson, P.J. and Zeng M. (2007). *Dragons at Your Door: How Chinese Cost Innovation is Disrupting Global Competition.* Boston: Harvard Business School Press Books.

Wu, F. (2005). Corporate China Goes Global. *World Economics*, 6(4), 171–181.

Xu, B. (2007). Trade, Foreign Direct Investment, and Productivity of China's Private Enterprises. In *Private Enterprises and China's Economic Development.* UK: Routledge.

Index